**W9-DJA-830**

The Lifetime Network

# The Lifetime Network

*Essays on "Television for Women" in the 21st Century*

Edited by
EMILY L. NEWMAN *and*
EMILY WITSELL

McFarland & Company, Inc., Publishers
*Jefferson, North Carolina*

ISBN (print) 978-0-7864-9830-7
ISBN (ebook) 978-1-4766-2459-4

LIBRARY OF CONGRESS CATALOGUING DATA ARE AVAILABLE

British Library cataloguing data are available

Front cover images © 2016 iStock

Printed in the United States of America

*McFarland & Company, Inc., Publishers
Box 611, Jefferson, North Carolina 28640
www.mcfarlandpub.com*

To Charlie, Dean, and Fred, for the countless hours you have kept us company watching Lifetime, thank you for being the best companions.

—ELN and EW

To the woman who shared her love of all things Lifetime with me, Laurie Newman, and to Allison Newman for always listening to me talk about it, thank you both for your support and guidance. All my love. To my Papa, Thornton Wright, thank you for your wisdom. For my Mema, June Wright, who will always be my cheerleader and always have a big piece of my heart.

—ELN

To my mother and father, Mary and Ed Witsell, who have always supported my strange and wonderful interests, and who gave me a love of books that led me to create one myself.

—EW

Special thank you to all of our contributors.

# Table of Contents

# Introduction

Emily L. Newman *and* Emily Witsell

Lifetime has forged its own path in the cable television industry. Founded in 1984, the network took aim at an under-tapped audience: women. As Jonathan David Tankel and Jane Banks described, "The programmers then wanted to establish a female identity by offering a 'place' for women that valued their selves with appeals to their unique interests and perspectives" (260). It worked. By 1987, Lifetime was making a profit through successfully articulating its audience and wisely courting sponsors. In 1990, Lifetime made its first television movie, *Memories of Murder*. While it met with moderate ratings, it was not a success with critics. Arturo Interian, Vice President of Original Movies at the network starting in 2001, has perceptively described Lifetime movies by noting "there was always a relatable character in it and then the most extreme stuff would happen. Your husband was a serial killer or you were addicted to gambling. If you were going through a rough patch in life, I guarantee you—your life wasn't as bad as what was happening to some characters in Lifetime movies" (Yahr). In its increasingly prolific creation of original films, Lifetime has created a recognizable, successful, and prevalent brand. People tune into the network to see what everyone is talking about, regardless of whether the films are award-winning.

In dedicating its programming to women, Lifetime strategically set itself apart, and as Heather Hundley has astutely articulated, "Lifetime symbolically reveals that women are important as both consumers and citizens. Gendercasting's success implies the widespread integration of feminist-inspired attitudes and concerns into a television industrial context that simply wouldn't have seemed possible a generation ago" (180). In just a few years, Lifetime has established itself as a powerful cable network and a wise investment. Ten years after it began, Lifetime was in 59 million households and was the eighth-most-watched basic cable network in prime time, but most importantly, it was first in one of its key demographics: 18- to 49-year-old women watching

1

basic cable during the daytime (Hundley 178). Therefore it is not surprising that a crop of other networks rose up in response. In 1997, the television channel Romance Classics began, though in 2000, it switched to its new name, WE: Women's Entertainment. Oxygen, part of NBCUniversal, began in 2000 and has targeted young, multi-cultural women with its programming. In 2011, Oprah Winfrey shifted her focus from running her talk show to heading a television network, the Oprah Winfrey Network (OWN). It was rather clear that Lifetime's model was the most successful network of its type, though, as in 2006 Lifetime was getting more views than its competitors Oxygen and WE combined (Lieberman).

Even then, Lifetime expanded its brand into other channels. Lifetime Movie Network (LMN) began airing a range of movies including both made-for-television movies and those released cinematically in 1998. The network now also airs a number of reality programs including a variety of true-life murder or stalking stories, tales of run-ins with ghosts, and A&E's popular *Intervention*, about people dealing with addiction. Further, Lifetime added Lifetime Real Women (LRW) to its lineup in 2001, which focuses on talk shows and the ever-growing and increasingly popular reality programming line-up. In 2001, the network expanded to Canada (taking over the channel known as Showcase Diva), as well as branching out to the UK and Ireland in 2013. The network has also actively worked to expand its brand, developing a strong Internet presence, beginning with a website and multi-part online drama *The House of Dreams*, an early web series in 1996 (Hundley 178).

The brand shows no signs of slowing down, which is particularly significant as some of its main competitors are reconfiguring their own audiences. Geared towards fashion and women, the Style Network, which began airing in 1998, was completely retooled as the Esquire Network in 2013, and now features programming geared towards both genders, focusing on those programs that might skew more traditionally masculine. WE: Women's Entertainment has changed its name to WE TV and no longer uses women in its name, in a push to draw more people to their audience, particularly as it expands its focus on original reality programming.

As competition both increases and changes, how can Lifetime maintain its relevance? On one hand, Lifetime stays true to its most famous slogan, "Television for Women." Simply put, the programs focus on subjects about and for women. The films' protagonists are women who drive the plot forward and are often engaging, spirited subjects. The television shows, whether syndicated, scripted, or reality, are centered on women's lives and stories. Lifetime continues to develop a large number of its own films on a wide variety of female-centered subjects, even as many of them are derided as poor quality or over-the-top. Despite criticisms about melodramatic tendencies and mockery about subject matter, Lifetime pushes forward. Trevor Walton, a Lifetime executive, has seen the network work to move beyond the idea of a woman in trouble, incorporating more light-hearted films as well as expanding its true story film series. Walton explains:

> "When I got to Lifetime, it was the little engine that could—a concept, a network, that everyone thought was a great idea. Over the years of being there, we were able to bring women in and make it their destination. What's unique is we got to change people's lives, politically and domestically. Lifetime is one of the rare networks where advocacy and programming go hand in hand, so that was incredibly gratifying. Over and over we would hear we had changed someone's life or inspired them in some way, and that made working at Lifetime a very special experience for so many of us" [qtd. in Elias].

Tackling tough subjects like domestic abuse, sexual assault, eating disorders, and addiction, Lifetime has worked to tell often-silenced stories of women. Each film is often accompanied by information that can provide access to help, be it 24-hour access hotlines or therapeutic resources.

Moreover, Lifetime has also made a concerted effort to hire female directors, estimating that about half of its films are directed by women, in comparison to the industry standard of just six percent (Yahr). Even more than that, Lifetime is actually putting its money where its mouth is, announcing an initiative called Broad Focus in May of 2015. Designed to help female creative talent (writers, developers, producers, and directors), the movement will work to encourage content dedicated to women's experiences. In a shrewd plan, Lifetime will partner Broad Focus with Geena Davis' Bentonville Film Festival, which prioritizes women and diversity (Petski).

It is useful to focus on 2014 in depth here, as it not only represents Lifetime's thirtieth year, but also allows us to examine the wide range of programming the network is currently undertaking. Lifetime's willingness to address topical concerns and popular culture phenomena appears in the range of television movies that the network released in that year which can be tied directly to significant cultural moments. For example, *The Red Tent*, a miniseries based on Anita Diament's 1997 novel that creates a life and narrative for Dinah, Jacob's only daughter, was made in response to History Channel's *The Bible*, a blockbuster mini-series (and later a cinematic release) that was produced by Mark Burnett and Roma Downey. While *The Bible* focuses on the male-dominated narrative of the Old and New Testament, Diament takes her leads from a biblical story told in Genesis. Creating a place for women in the more traditional story, she emphasizes sisterhood and community. In the film's focus on how the women passed on traditions and created safe, sacred spaces for one another, a not-so-subtle symbolism of what Lifetime and its sister channels and Internet presence work to create for contemporary women is apparent.

Book clubs are another important space for women to gather and bond over time, as the massive widespread success of Oprah Winfrey's Book Club exemplifies. It should not come as a surprise, then, that taking inspiration from popular fiction has been an important touchstone for Lifetime for years. The novels of Jodi Picoult, Mary Higgins Clark, Danielle Steel, and Nora Roberts have frequently served as the basis for Lifetime films. Not only has Lifetime showcased the stories of women, it has actively created an audience for the adaption of novels written by women. In 2014, Lifetime took on some of the most popular authors living today—men and women. For instance, the network adapted Stephen King's 2010 novella *Big Driver* into a film of the same name. Telling the story of the violent rape and attempted murder of a novelist, played by Golden Globe–nominated actress Maria Bello, the film showcases her elaborate plan for revenge. Additionally, in the same year Lifetime chose to adapt the work of Terry McMillan, whose novels focus on personable female characters, often of color. Produced by and starring the acclaimed Whoopi Goldberg, *A Day Late and a Dollar Short* focuses on a matriarch who has just received a terminal diagnosis and sets off on a journey to make amends and reconnect with her family members. Lifetime also produced a new version of *The Trip to Bountiful*, an Academy Award–, Pulitzer Prize–, and Emmy Award–winning play written by Horton Foote in 1953. This was a film version of a 2013 Broadway revival which starred Cicely Tyson, who won a Tony Award for that performance. Tyson reprised her role from the revival, starring as an elderly woman who journeys to her hometown one last time, against the wishes of her family members. Each of these television movies brought a very different audience to the table with its selection of authors and yet managed to tie into Lifetime's core audience of women by focusing the stories on the lives and journeys of strong, independent women.

During the same time period, Lifetime produced a new version of *Flowers in the Attic*, based on the infamous 1979 novel by V.C. Andrews which sold three million copies its first year in print and spawned a number of sequels and one previous film release (Aurthur). The book, with its tantalizing tales of incest, sex, and torture, embedded itself in the minds of many young women and men. The fascination with the book proved to still be strong, as the movie debuted to 6.1 million viewers (Marechal). Relying on both the power of nostalgia and society's fascination with the taboo, Lifetime successfully courted viewers with its campy, poorly-acted version of the novel that subsequently led to the production of three more films (*Petals on the Wind,* 2014; *If There Be Thorns,* 2015; *Seeds of Yesterday,* 2015).

Not content to just revamp past works or novels, Lifetime also worked with Nicholas Sparks, one of the leading romance writers today who has seen many of his novels adapted on both big and small screens. Sparks executive produced the film *Deliverance Creek*, a western focused on single mom, played by Lauren Ambrose, who must take care of her children while dealing with the effects of the Civil War, including runaway slaves and Confederate outlaws (one of whom happens be her former lover). The film was unusual in that it was made to air as a backdoor pilot—that is, it was a test run for a potential television series—but unfortunately, the low viewership and problematic, convoluted plot did not result in the show being picked up to series. Regardless, the sweeping film with its high production quality and impressive cast represented an ambitious undertaking, one set in an uncommon historical period for the network and affiliated with reliable and consistently bankable producers and was thus a remarkable accomplishment for the network.

In the midst of these innovative moves, Lifetime did not entirely stray from its expected programming. There were still the over-the-top dramas with strong female leads and heavy doses of morality with which the network is traditionally associated In *Run for Your Life*, Amy Smart plays a woman in an abusive relationship who struggles with the decision to disappear and hide from her ex or to kill him. Based in part on a true story, the film draws from Katherine Kotaw's memoir *Quicksand: One Woman's Escape from the Husband Who Stalked Her*, which was published under the pen name Ellen Singer in 2001. The author uses a pseudonym, and filmmakers took more liberties to further obscure her identity (Konstantinides). The film was premiered in October, in honor of National Domestic Violence Awareness Month, with the support of the domestic violence prevention organizations NO MORE and the Joyful Heart Foundation (founded by Mariska Hargitay of *Law and Order: SVU*). Amid the National Football League's very public scandals regarding domestic violence perpetrated by its players, particularly the video of Ray Rice of the Baltimore Ravens abusing his then-fiancée in an elevator, Lifetime contributed to the conversation presenting one woman's options when faced with domestic abuse.

Similarly, *The Assault* modeled itself on the notorious Stubenville, Ohio, rape case, wherein a number of young men filmed the repeated rapes of an underage woman. Taking on the rise of eating disorder online communities, *Starving in Suburbia* focuses on a young dancer caught up in a vicious cycle of anorexia and bulimia. Each of these films features lesser-known actors and extreme plotlines that test the viewer's limits of believability, but in the end, the women persevere and inevitably come out of the scenarios stronger and better people; these themes have been repeated since Lifetime began making movies and serve as a familiar touchstone for viewers.

Sometimes, however, Lifetime seizes a cultural moment and acts on it. Late night talk show host Jimmy Fallon's repeated calls for a *Saved by the Bell* reunion epitomized a fondness for the show felt by many 20- and 30-year-olds. Lifetime took the opportunity to produce *The Unauthorized Saved by the Bell Story*, which was very loosely based on the one-sided account of the show's history, *Behind the Bell* (2009), written by Dustin Diamond, who played Screech on the show. The success and notoriety of the film, regardless of its poor reviews, led Lifetime to pursue similar docudramas based on the casts and history of *Melrose Place, Beverly Hills, 90210*, and *Full House* in 2015.

Additionally, Lifetime has capitalized on the spectacle of young celebrity women dying too soon. *The Brittany Murphy Story* begins with the young actress' rise to fame and mysterious death at home. Two months later, *Aaliyah: The Princess of R&B* told the story of the beloved pop star who died in 2001 at the age of 22, though it was met with substantially more criticism and controversy than the film on Murphy. Originally, Disney star Zendaya Coleman was cast as Aaliyah, however, after backlash about the inappropriateness of her biracial background, she stepped away from the role and was replaced with Alexandra Shipp. The film aired November 15. Based on an unauthorized biography (Christopher John Farley's 2001 *Aaliyah: More Than a Woman*), the movie did not get full rights to her music catalog and could not recreate the songs for which the artist was best known; the film also handled her marriage (and subsequent annulment) problematically (Weber). While critics and Aaliyah's family may not have been pleased with the film, it had a surprising and powerful impact on social media. Twitter came alive with hashtags and mentions, topping Nielsen's TV ratings for the week, generating just under one million posts from 258,000 different authors, to a unique audience of 3.4 million Twitter followers (Maglio). Again, while the quality of the film and the acting itself may have been lacking, the press and attention for the network and the film itself show the power and impact of the network brand.

Lifetime capitalized on the social media attention during the 2014 Christmas season. The network has always devoted much of its programming in late November and December to the holiday, but in this year, its choices epitomized the direction the network has been going in the past few years. The climax of its programming was a film featuring Grumpy Cat, an Internet phenomenon. The cat, whose real name is Tardar Sauce, garnered attention and fame after appearing on Reddit in 2012. Born with feline dwarfism, the cat has an underbite that causes her to look perpetually cantankerous. In 2014 (and right around the time the Lifetime film aired) reports surfaced that the cat's owner, Tabatha Bundesen, had earned almost $100 million from endorsements and appearances (Thompson). While Bundesen has denied this amount, it is obvious that Grumpy Cat has secured a comfortable life for her owners, and *Grumpy Cat's Worst Christmas Ever* undoubtedly contributed to the total. The film features Grumpy Cat, voiced by Audrey Plaza, an actress known for her role on NBC's *Parks and Recreation* as well as her droll and sarcastic delivery. The plot revolved around a girl who could hear and communicate with Grumpy Cat and an over-the-top sabotage of the kidnapping of one of Grumpy Cat's dog counterparts at the pet shop where she lived. Unexpectedly, and against typical Lifetime conventions, the film repeatedly broke the fourth wall, with Grumpy Cat looking and speaking into the camera numerous times, one time even mocking the idea of being in a Lifetime film itself.

This campy, fun film contrasted with the rest of the new programming in the holiday season. Lifetime mined the work of famed novelist Wally Lamb, producing a film based on his short novel *Wishin' and Hopin'*. Focusing on a fifth grade boy attending Catholic school in the 1960s, the movie starred Molly Ringwald, Annabella Sciorra, Meat Loaf, and Cheri Oteri. The film is narrated by Chevy Chase as the adult version of the main character, in a device remarkably similar to both the TV show *The Wonder Years* (1988–1993) and the seminal film *A Christmas Story* (1983). This maudlin film was paired with a more contemporary holiday film, *Seasons of Love,* which focused on two people struggling to find love and dealing with family issues. Besides the difference in eras, the casts of the two films varied significantly: *Wishin' and Hopin'* featured well-known white actors, while *Seasons of Love* featured lesser-known African American actors, with the exception of Cliff "Method Man" Smith and a cameo by Taraji P. Henson. Both films relied on sentimentality and nostalgia to attract audiences. Additionally, Lifetime released two more new films in the 2014 holiday season: *Santa Con*, a humorous story of a con-man forced to work as a Santa at a department store, and *An En Vogue Christmas*, starring the R&B group who rose to popularity in the 1990s. The singers must reunite in order to perform at a charity function to save a failing opera house. The 2014 holiday season alone shows the range of programming that Lifetime was undertaking, all in an effort to create a slate of films that could appeal to the broadest audience possible.

*An En Vogue Christmas, Seasons of Love*, and even *A Day Late and a Dollar Short* illustrate that an important part of Lifetime's plan to attract newer audiences was to attract people of color, especially by making quality programming. These films, among others, garnered the network an impressive sixteen National Association for the Advancement of Color People (NAACP) Image Award nominations in 2014, the most of any cable network that year. In its continued desire to reach new audiences, Lifetime added four new reality programs in 2014. *Raising Asia,* a spinoff of the immensely popular *Dance Moms* (2011–present), focused on dancer Asia who had already appeared on *Dance Moms*. Her spitfire personality and performance ability earned her a 14-episode run of her own program. Of black and Chinese descent, Asia broadened the depictions of the predominantly white dancers and parents on *Dance Moms*. Further, the network added *Bring It!*, which featured the Dancing Dolls of Jackson, Mississippi. Coached by Dianna "Miss D" Williams, the group, composed of girls aged ten to seventeen, competes in hip-hop majorette competitions. While the style of dance may be different, both *Dance Moms* and *Bring It!* focus on the relationships of the moms, dancers, and coaches/teachers. The types of competitions differ, as do the race of the cast members. The shows illustrate Lifetime's attempt for a broader appeal while integrating a tried and true formula for success. *Girlfriend Intervention* also complicatedly and often problematically dealt with race, as it was a makeover show where the "experts" were all black women and the women being made over were white. Lastly, *BAPs* focused on rich "Black American Princesses and Princes" living and working in St. Louis. While *Bring It!* has proven successful and aired a second season, the three other shows did not make it past their first season (though *Raising Asia* has aired in repeats), with *BAPs* fairing the worst, airing only four of six planned episodes.

This attempt to expand Lifetime's programming has resulted in a number of misses, so these cancellations are perhaps not caused by the network's attempts to develop its audiences but its willingness to push the envelope. In the light of that, Lifetime has made great efforts to enlarge its reality programming, trying a wide variety of shows. *Project Runway* and its spinoffs have been one of the grounding programs of the network ever since the show moved from Bravo to Lifetime in 2009. In 2014, the network added another spinoff, *Project Runway: Threads*, a fashion design competition for preteens and teens, with each competition lasting just one episode. Another new show that year, *Little Women: LA*, follows six little people, all women, living their lives in Los Angeles in what logically seems Lifetime's answer to Bravo's *Real Housewives* juggernaut line up mixed with TLC's programming on people with genetic or medical conditions that result in short stature (*Little People, Big World*, 2006–present; *The Little Couple*, 2009–present; *Our Little Family*, 2015–present). The show aired to success, and now has two of its own spinoffs (*Little Women: NY*, 2015–present, *Little Women: Terra's Little Family*, 2015–present). Lastly, *True Tori* was an attempt to document Tori Spelling's tumultuous relationship with her husband Dean McDermott as she tries to come to terms with his affair. The show was aired as quickly as it could be edited and felt incredibly immediate and timely and yet simultaneously staged with Spelling's own scripted confessional scenes. Websites like *Jezebel*, *Perez Hilton*, *Radar Online*, and *Hollywood Life* all went to great lengths to question the sincerity and truth of the show. While the first season regularly garnered one million viewers per episode, the second season saw a 25 percent drop in its audience, and the show has not returned for a third season (Schaefer). The firestorm surrounding the cheating scandal was able to achieve immediate but not longstanding ratings success.

Lifetime has traditionally struggled with its original scripted programming, and 2014 was no different. Few shows have lasted more than two seasons on the network, with the exceptions being *Any Day Now* (1998–2002, four seasons), *Strong Medicine* (2000–2006, six seasons), *The Division* (2001–2004, four seasons), *Army Wives* (2007–2013, seven seasons), and *Drop Dead Diva* (2009–

2014, six seasons).[1] The year 2014 saw the end of *Drop Dead Diva* (which had been granted a surprise resurrection of one last season after it had been cancelled in 2013), as well as the end of *Witches of East End* (2013–2014) and *The Lottery* (2014). *Devious Maids*, which began in 2013, was the only original scripted show to survive 2014, and it is still airing at the time of this writing. Created and produced by Marc Cherry, the show centers on five Latina maids working in Beverly Hills. Bearing the same basic structure and soap opera feel of Cherry's *Desperate Housewives* (2004–2012, ABC), the success of this show mirrors other long-running Lifetime scripted shows, which have each prominently featured people of color in lead roles.

What is clear, thinking about 2014 retrospectively, is that diversity works for Lifetime. Shows with casts that feature a broad spectrum of people and races succeed much more frequently than those without that diversity. Additionally, looking at the scripted shows that have succeeded on Lifetime, it is clear that shows tackling real and often fraught relationships and topics have longer runs. *Army Wives* connected to its audiences and had a broad impact because of its seriousness and its diverse cast, whereas *The Lottery* and *Witches of East End* failed quickly as they were both too convoluted and unable to find their audiences.

Over the past thirty years, as Lifetime has diversified its casts and its topics, the network continues to find relevance. Its films become discussion fodder on talk shows and Twitter, just as the programs continue to rack up award nominations. Yet the serious scholarship produced on the network since its inception is remarkably modest. In the early 1980s, one only finds mentions of Lifetime in trade journals and magazines that discuss the network's goals and logistics, as in the article "Lifetime: Cable Service Aims for Power through Partnership," published in the journal *Broadcasting* in 1984. By the late 1980s, Lifetime was frequently the focus of articles about the rise and successes of cable narrowcasting (see, for example, Walley, "Female Audience Lifeblood of Lifetime," 1988, and Lipman, "Lifetime Television Will Court Women," 1989). A distinct group of articles from this era detail Lifetime's beginnings as a medical network, such as the article Bruce B. Dan wrote mourning the loss of Lifetime's medical programming in the medical journal *Lancet* in 1995.

The most significant contribution to the scholarly study of the Lifetime network to date is a 1995 special issue of the journal *Camera Obscura: A Journal of Feminism, Culture, and Media Studies* entitled *Lifetime: A Cable Network "For Women."* Edited by scholar Julie d'Acci, the issue contains ten articles about Lifetime's history and programming, ranging from audience theory to marketing to studies of specific shows. D'Acci's introduction posits that Lifetime in the mid–1990s was a network of paradoxes that claimed to be a television network for all women while ignoring minorities in its programming outside of special events and catering to men in prime time (7).

Carolyn Bronstein ("Mission Accomplished? Profits and Programming at the Network for Women") asserts that in 1995, Lifetime was performing a delicate balancing act between serving the needs of women and airing programming that would bring in advertising dollars. In the 1980s and 1990s, Lifetime experimented with infomercials, direct sales shows, advertiser-created specials, and product placement on its network-produced programming. Bronstein argues that this financially-lucrative programming combined with a primetime schedule composed primarily of "mainstream, formulaic" shows created less room in the network's schedule for alternative, innovative programming aimed at women (230). In fact, Lifetime in this era had a fractured identity in which its daytime schedule was targeted to women, but the evenings were designed to reach as many people as possible (231).

Eithne Johnson ("Lifetime's Feminine Psychographic Space and the 'Mystery Loves Company' Series") explores Lifetime's use of psychographics, the study of consumer feelings and motivations, to identify its typical viewers as professional, working women who are concerned with women's issues and women who spend time at home during the day and use the television as a companion and information source (44). She details how Lifetime came to the conclusion that all women, no matter their current employment status, could relate to the working woman's struggle to balance work and family, and thus privileged this figure as the emblematic Lifetime woman (49). In examining Lifetime's packaging of three mystery and suspense programs (mystery series *Veronica Clare*, series *The Hidden Room*, and reality series *Confessions of Crime*), Johnson connects the cancellation of these programs with the network's "ambivalence about its 'feminine identity'" during prime time" (65).

In "Once in a Lifetime: Constructing the 'Working Woman' through Cable Narrowcasting," Jackie Byars and Eileen R. Meehan trace the development of women's television from the days of soap operas on the radio to the present cable television environment. They describe the changing environment of the 1970s—feminism, economic recessions, and changes in women's working lives, the television industry, and technology—that gave rise to cable's narrowcasting networks, including Lifetime (18). While the authors conclude that Lifetime's daytime schedule fulfills its promise of reaching out to women, Lifetime's original nighttime movies and television series are "male-friendly women's television" that envisions a strong career woman sharing the television with a male figure (26), and that Lifetime's portrayals of women who work outside the home, have a family, and care for the home "addresses lived experience in its frustrations and rewards" (36).

The remaining articles in the special issue of *Camera Obscura* address varying issues facing Lifetime in the mid–1990s. A number of articles describe specific programs, including film noir as portrayed in *Veronica Clare* (White), narrative and memory in *China Beach* (Torres), and the acquisition and reimagining of the sitcom *The Days and Nights of Molly Dodd* (Wilson). Two essays take up the popular program *thirtysomething*, with Stempel Mumford describing issues of syndication and Wlodarz discussing queer sexuality on the show. The remaining two articles take a more theoretical approach: Feuer addresses the rewriting of 1980s yuppie culture for a 1990s audience, while Streeter and Wahl take up the interaction of audience theory and feminism. The issue offers readers a vivid image of how Lifetime strategized and targeted its programming in its first decade of existence.

In the 1997 book essay "Lifetime Television and Women: Narrowcasting as Electronic Space," Jonathan David Tankel and Jane Banks identified Lifetime as a narrowcaster that "offered a broad range of program genres and forms and used more broadcast-style, daypart, sensitive scheduling and promotional strategies to accomplish its goal" (258). They argue that Lifetime was conceived not as a passive experience of watching content, but rather that the audience is "asked to identify with each other as well as to attend to the program offerings, offering a sense of community from which viewers may derive social pleasures" (259). They note that while Lifetime targeted a diverse audience of women, one unifying factor was socioeconomic status: the Lifetime woman was "upscale" and easy to market to advertisers (262). Lifetime also reimagined what television for women could be by embracing women's issues but also by reframing existing shows, such as *L.A. Law* and *China Beach* (two shows purchased in syndication by Lifetime), to women's interests through marketing (264). Tankel and Banks find Lifetime's use of narrowcasting to sell women's interests to broadcasters problematic, stating that "Lifetime has co-opted liberal feminism by claiming the rhetoric and organizing women into audiences to be exploited by advertising," while allowing that Lifetime also addresses issues that are important to women (267).

Byars and Meehan reunited in 2000 for the essay "Telefeminism: How Lifetime Got Its Groove, 1984–1997," which posits that Lifetime has co-opted liberal feminism in its movies and through its relationships with liberal women's organizations, such as the National Organization for Women (34). The authors explore how this co-opting developed through five stages of Lifetime's development, from the prehistory period (1982–1984) to what they call the "absorbed" period ending in 1997 (35).

In 2001, Jonathan Nichols-Pethick explored Lifetime's acquisition of the syndication rights to the crime procedural *Homicide: Life on the Street* in the article "Lifetime on the Street: Textual Strategies of Syndication." Nichols-Pethick argues that when Lifetime cut scenes and repositioned commercials in certain episodes of the show, the network communicated who its ideal viewer was and gendered the television text to respond to the desires of women (64). With these edits, Lifetime was able to emphasize certain relationships and themes that may not have been at the forefront of NBC's original broadcast of the material (68).

Heather Hundley's 2002 article "The Evolution of Gendercasting: The Lifetime Television Network—Television for Women" describes Lifetime's history and choice of programming throughout the network's history. Hundley identifies three keys to Lifetime's early success: the targeting of women through its tagline "Television for Women" while refusing to limit its audience by defining a specific type of woman, creating original movies that garnered higher ratings than movies purchased from other studios, and the commitment to producing original content rather than relying exclusively on costlier syndicated content (176–77). Carefully targeted syndicated purchases also increased Lifetime's viewership (179). She also notes that the decision to drop its Sunday medical shows, which brought in 25 percent of the network's advertising money in the early years, allowed Lifetime to counterprogram Sunday sporting events and make Sunday the largest viewing day of the week (176–177). Hundley points to the previous success print media and radio have had in narrowcasting, but notes that before cable, television had targeted a mass audience; narrowcasting allowed Lifetime and other similarly targeted cable networks to attract advertisers while building a carefully curated audience that finds sympathetic and engaging programming on its network (180). Hundley concludes that although advertisers are clearly profiting from the creation of Lifetime, "narrowcasting is mutually beneficial" because "gendercasting's success implies the widespread integration of feminist-inspired attitudes and concerns into a television industrial context that simply wouldn't have seemed possible a generation ago" (180).

A recent study has placed Lifetime in the context of other women's television networks, such as Oxygen or WE: Women's Entertainment. In her monograph *Redesigning Women: Television After the Network Era*, Amanda D. Lotz argues that narrowcasting has led to unprecedented representation for women and minorities on television programming, and that this programming offers viewers a depth and nuance in the portrayal of women's lives that was not present in the era of broadcast television (176). Lotz additionally proposes that feminist television scholarship must change to reflect the changing television landscape as exemplified by Lifetime, among other narrowcasters (179).

Finally, for a history of Lifetime's brand-making made-for-television movies, Emily Yahr's "From Guilty Pleasure to Emmy Awards: The Delightfully Weird History of Lifetime Movies," published in early 2015, offers a recap of how Lifetime chose to create melodramatic movies in its early years and how those movies have changed in recent years. Drawing from interviews with Lifetime executives, Yahr discusses how Lifetime movies fit into the careers of rising and established stars, the appeal of cheesy melodrama, and Lifetime's success with "issue" films.

While all of these studies are significant contributions to the study of Lifetime, it is important to also consider that Lifetime's programming has expanded and increased dramatically in the past fifteen years, and this has received very little if any scholarly treatment. While the network still shows syndicated programs during the daytime, in the evenings it has gone beyond original made-for-television movies into scripted and reality programming. Additionally, it continues to try to find a talk show format that works for the network, though with little success. Further, it has branched out online, creating different applications, games, and streaming services to perpetuate the success of the brand. Through three different parts, this book will address the network's path-breaking and often uncommon strategies to success.

In the first part, "Reality and Internet Programming," three essays explore the fraught development of the genre on Lifetime. In Shelby L. Crosby and Susannah Bartlow's "'What did we teach you?' Racialized Sisterhood in *Girlfriend Intervention*," the polarizing reality makeover show is given reconsideration. While the show may perpetuate extremely problematic stereotypes, Crosby and Bartlow wisely articulate that *Girlfriend Intervention* (aired 2014) can present both insight into the position of gender and race in the twenty-first century and raise questions regarding the lingering historical conflicts between white and black women. Exploring an internet space that could encourage interactions between women, Lindsay Giggey's "'You too can make your own Lifetime movie': Branded Labor via Lifetime's Movie Mash-Ups" addresses a short-lived internet tool found on Lifetime's website in 2008. A small number of original Lifetime movies were made available for limited editing through a digital program on the site, and from there, people were able to post their videos and discuss them with other participants. This unique project allowed women to experience the films in an entirely different way, all while potentially expanding their computer skills but reinforcing the network's ideas and brands. Shortly after the Mash-Up project was abandoned, Lifetime acquired *Project Runway* and re-evaluated and revamped the network's public presentation. In "'One day you're in and the next day you're out': Making *Project Runway* Work from Bravo to Lifetime," Emily Witsell examines the evolution of the show *Project Runway* from its inception on Bravo to its success on Lifetime. In the transition, the show expands its audience, figuring out new ways to expand fans' interaction with the programming while maintaining the show's core identity.

The second part, "Original Episodic Programming," includes two essays that evaluate recent scripted television shows that illustrate a willingness to tackle unconventional subjects for the network. Mary Douglas Vavrus discusses the willingness of Lifetime to work with the military and government in "Feminizing Militainment: Post/Post-Politics on *Army Wives*." While the army may unite the main characters and provide for plot points, Douglas

Vavrus argues that the heart of the show was dependent upon the prioritizing of crafting compelling personal narratives. By striving to emphasize post-feminist and postracial politics, *Army Wives* (2007–3013) manages to appease the Department of Defense and present carefully-crafted stories that remain uncritical of United States politics. Tackling two short-lived series, *The Lottery* (2014) and *Witches of East End* (2013–14), Lisa K. Perdigao addresses how these shows may feel technologically savvy and futuristic but actually present old-fashioned ideas about women in "'In Extremis': Unnatural Selection in Lifetime's Speculative Fictions." For all its attempts to reconsider its programming by airing science fiction and fantasy shows, Lifetime here relies on narratives that are unchanged throughout the years, including women in trouble, reproductive and surrogacy issues, and family traumas.

Those themes have figured prominently in the films that Lifetime has aired and are explored in more depth in the third part, "Original Movies." Emily L. Newman's essay, "'She needs some food': Eating Disorders, Lifetime and the Made-for-TV Movie," notes that eating disorder films are not only filled with a heavy dose of moralizing, they often are seen as providing instructions to young women who are trying to lose weight. By tracing the history of eating disorders on film, she shows that Lifetime emerges as a source for a documentation of popular culture's changing view of anorexia, bulimia, and eating disorders not otherwise specified (EDNOS). Staci Stutsman explores two films about kidnapped children from 2012 in "'Your Life. Your Time': Addressing a Fractured Audience through Docudrama." In *Taken Back: Finding Haley* and *Abducted: The Carlina White Story*, Stutsman argues that the prevalence of photographs, pictures, and television is used to help explore both sets of mothers and daughters as they confront and deal with their fractured identities due to the traumatic situations they experience. As Lifetime was going through its own identity crisis in the same year, as it changed its motto and went through some major rebranding, these films can be seen as emblematic of that change. Also looking at recent films, Jenny Platz reconsiders the way Lifetime is depicting rape in her essay "Subversion of the Final Girl in Rape Revenge Narratives and the Normalization of Violence Against Women in *The Tenth Circle* and *The Assault*." Looking at the way that Lifetime challenges more conventional rape revenge narratives, Platz notes that it also reinforces many realities of rape culture along the way. Simultaneously, the network rethinks how women can be rape and sexual assault victims, but solidifies their victimhood.

In this introduction, we have looked at Lifetime's groundbreaking programming in 2014 and how it pursued its brand by producing consistent types of programming while expanding its offerings. In 2015, the network pushed itself even further, introducing a new scripted drama and a bold original film agenda, which will be explored in the conclusion. Lifetime is not a network content to keep doing the same thing over and over, and it shows in its continued success. As other networks flounder and are trying to broaden their appeal beyond just women, Lifetime has only increased its risk-taking. After thirty years of creating challenging, exciting, and at times extremely sensational programming, Lifetime seems to be looking ahead to see how it can continue to create waves in the next thirty years.

NOTE

1. A unique exception to this list is *The Days and Nights of Molly Dodd*, which aired five seasons total; however, its first two seasons were run on NBC in 1987 and 1988, with those seasons re-airing on Lifetime, as well as the network producing three more seasons airing from 1989 to 1991.

WORKS CITED

Aurthur, Kate. "Ghost of V.C. Andrews: The Life, Death, and Afterlife of the Mysterious *Flowers in the Attic* Author." *BuzzFeed News*. Buzzfeed.com, 15 Jan. 2014. Web. 13 Sept. 2015.

Bronstein, Carolyn. "Mission Accomplished? Profits and Programming at the Network for Women." *Lifetime: A Cable Network "For Women."* Spec. issue of *Camera Obscura: A Journal of Feminism, Culture, and Media Studies* 33–34 (1994–1995): 213–242. Print.

Byars, Jackie, and Eileen R. Meehan. "Once in a Lifetime: Constructing the 'Working Woman' through Cable Narrowcasting." *Lifetime: A Cable Network "For Women."* Spec. issue of *Camera Obscura: A Journal of Feminism, Culture, and Media Studies* 33–34 (1994–1995): 13–41. Print.

D'Acci, Julie. "Introduction." *Lifetime: A Cable Network "For Women."* Spec. issue of *Camera Obscura: A Journal of Feminism, Culture, and Media Studies* 33–34 (1994–1995): 7–12. Print.

Dan, Bruce B. "Information Lives; Medical Television Dies." *Lancet* 11 Nov. 1995: 1280–1281. Print.

Elias, Justine. "Original Movies Evolve." *Television Week* 23.15 (2004): S20. Print.

Feuer, Jane. "Feminism on Lifetime: Yuppie TV for the Nineties." *Lifetime: A Cable Network "For Women."* Spec. issue of *Camera Obscura: A Journal of Feminism, Culture, and Media Studies* 33–34 (1994–1995): 133–146. Print.

Hundley, Heather. "The Evolution of Gendercasting: The Lifetime Television Network—'Television for Women.'" *Journal of Popular Film and Television* 29.4 (2002): 174–181. Print.

Johnson, Eithne. "Lifetime's Feminine Psychographic Space and the 'Mystery Loves Company' Series." *Lifetime: A Cable Network "For Women."* Spec. issue of *Camera Obscura: A Journal of Feminism, Culture, and Media Studies* 33–34 (1994–1995): 43–76. Print.

Konstantinides, Anneta. "Is Lifetime's *Run for Your Life* a True Story? The Real Woman Behind the Film Shares her Story." *Bustle*. Bustle.com, 4 Oct. 2014. Web. 13 Sept. 2015.

"Lifetime: Cable Service Aims for Power through Partnership." *Broadcasting* 13 Feb. 1984: 174. *Business Insights: Essentials*. Web. 5 Oct. 2015.

Lipman, Joanne. "Lifetime Television Will Court Women." *Wall Street Journal* 31 Mar. 1989: 1. Print.

Lotz, Amanda. *Redesigning Women: Television after the Network Era.* Urbana: University of Illinois Press, 2006. Print.

_____. "Textual (Im)Possibilities in the U.S. Post-Network Era: Negotiating Production and Promotion Processes on Lifetime's *Any Day Now.*" *Critical Studies in Media Communication* 21.1 (Mar. 2004): 22–43. *JSTOR.* Web. 15 Mar. 2015.

Maglio, Tony. "Aaliyah Lifetime Biopic Backlash Propels Movie to No.1 Nielsen Twitter TV Rating." *The Wrap.* TheWrap.com, 17 Nov. 2014. Web. 13 Sept. 2015.

Marechal, A.J. "*Flowers in the Attic* Blooms on Lifetime with 6.1 Million Viewers." *Variety.* Variety.com, 21 Jan. 2014. Web. 13 Sept. 2015.

Meehan, Eileen R., and Jackie Byars. "Telefeminism: How Lifetime Got Its Groove, 1984–1997." *The Television Studies Reader.* Ed. Robert C. Allen and Annette Hill. New York: Routledge, 2004. 92–104. Print.

Nichols-Pethick, Jonathan. "Lifetime on the Street: Textual Strategies of Syndication." *Velvet Light Trap* 47 (2001): 62–73. Print.

Petski, Denise. "Lifetime Launches Industry Initiative for Female Creatives." *Deadline.* Deadline.com, 6. May 2014. Web. 13 Sept. 2015.

Schaefer, Megan. "*True Tori* Canceled? Low Ratings Puts Tori Spelling Reality Series in Danger After *Mystery Girls* Cancellation." *International Business Times.* Ibtimes.com, 31 Oct. 2014. Web. 13 Sept. 2015.

Stempel Mumford, Laura. "Stripping on the Girl Channel: Lifetime, *thirtysomething,* and Television Form." *Lifetime: A Cable Network "For Women."* Spec. issue of *Camera Obscura: A Journal of Feminism, Culture, and Media Studies* 33–34 (1994–1995): 167–192. Print.

Streeter, Thomas, and Wendy Wahl. "Audience Theory and Feminism: Property, Gender, and the Tele-visual Audience." *Lifetime: A Cable Network "For Women."* Spec. issue of *Camera Obscura: A Journal of Feminism, Culture, and Media Studies* 33–34 (1994–1995): 243–261. Print.

Tankel, Jonathan David, and Jane Banks. "Lifetime Television and Women: Narrowcasting as Electronic Space." *Voices in the Street: Explorations in Gender, Media, and Public Space.* Ed. Susan J. Drucker and Gary Gumpert. Cresskill, NJ: Hampton Press, 1994. 255–270. Print.

Thompson, Derek. "The Wealth of Grumpy Cat." *The Atlantic.* TheAtlantic.com, 8 Dec. 2014. Web. 13 Sept. 2015.

Torres, Sasha. "War and Remembrance: Televisual Narrative, National Memory, and *China Beach.*" *Lifetime: A Cable Network "For Women."* Spec. issue of *Camera Obscura: A Journal of Feminism, Culture, and Media Studies* 33–34 (1994–1995): 147–166. Print.

Vavrus, Mary Douglas. "Lifetime's *Army Wives*, or I Married the Media-Military-Industrial Complex." *Women's Studies in Communication* 36 (2013): 92–112. Print.

Walley, Wayne. "Female Audience Lifeblood of Lifetime." *Advertising Age* 11 Apr. 1988, S22. Print.

Weber, Lindsey. "Where Lifetime Went Wrong with the Aaliyah Movie (and What It Could Learn Going Forward)." *Vulture.* Vulture.com, 17 Nov. 2014. Web. 13 Sept. 2015.

White, Susan. "*Veronica Clare* and the New *Film Noir* Heroine." *Lifetime: A Cable Network "For Women."* Spec. issue of *Camera Obscura: A Journal of Feminism, Culture, and Media Studies* 33–34 (1994–1995): 77–102. Print.

Wilson, Pamela. "Upscale Feminine Angst: *Molly Dodd,* the Lifetime Cable Network and Gender Marketing." *Lifetime: A Cable Network "For Women."* Spec. issue of

*Camera Obscura: A Journal of Feminism, Culture, and Media Studies* 103–132 (1994–1995): 103–130. Print.

Wlodarz, Joe. "Smokin' Tokens: *thirtysomething* and TV's Queer Dilemma." *Lifetime: A Cable Network "For Women."* Spec. issue of *Camera Obscura: A Journal of Feminism, Culture, and Media Studies* 33–34 (1994–1995): 193–212. Print.

Yahr, Emily. "From Guilty Pleasure to Emmy Awards: The Delightfully Weird History of Lifetime Movies." *Washington Post.* WashingtonPost.com, 15 Jan. 2015. Web. 13 Sept. 2015.

# PART I

# Reality and Internet Programming

# "What did we teach you?"
## *Racialized Sisterhood in* Girlfriend Intervention

SHELBY L. CROSBY *and*
SUSANNAH BARTLOW

In an era of violent anti-blackness, Lifetime's *Girlfriend Intervention* (2014) stages a celebration of the "strong black woman inside"—inside white women, that is. Yes, *Girlfriend Intervention*, as many critics have noted, is "insulting [to] white women and Black women" (Ajayi). And, yes, it is also "hard to know what's most irritating—the sweeping declarations about black women as if they were monolithic, or the forced remodeling of women who are perfectly comfortable with their looks and style after subjecting them to a 'catwalk of shame'" (Lowry). However, it is also true that the show "flips the script by allowing black women to say 'yes, we have curves and have had them before society said they were ok.' It's putting the power in the hands of women of color and giving them credit, letting them hold the reins" (Townes). Adding to the show's complexity, the hosts are also presented as content experts and skilled catalysts for meaningful transformation. In this way, *Girlfriend Intervention* attempts to place black women in a power position, much in the same way as *Queer Eye for the Straight Guy* (2003–07) attempted to credit gay men; curiously, *Queer Eye*, while criticized for a similar exploitation of gay stereotypes, ran for five seasons while *Girlfriend Intervention* barely made it through the initial eight episodes ordered. It is not possible or desirable to redeem what is fundamentally a caricature of reality television that parades a host of racist tropes in each segment. Yet it is a fascinating case study in early twenty-first century American racism. *Girlfriend Intervention*, by positioning itself explicitly at the intersection of race, gender, and class, sets up a cacophony of contradictions that have much to teach us about the social positions of black and white women at this racial moment. Even as the show centers the experiences and personal transformation of white women in its narrative, it depends upon harsh and routine critiques of white femininity that require white women to do and be *more* (not less, as is often the case with other representations of white femininity). While the show traffics in the worst, most degrading racist stereotypes, it is one of few televised representations that regularly highlights the skills and expertise of professional black women. The show's hosts routinely signify their complex understanding of race, class and gender hierarchies that they then simultaneously reproduce. In short, it is worth a closer look.

*Girlfriend Intervention* is a reality show in which four black women help a white woman, called the Basic Woman, remake her look and life. The show's hosts are Tanisha, the soul coach and primary host; Tiffiny, the stylist; Tracy, the beauty consultant; and Nikki, the interior designer. As with other makeover shows, clients are nominated by their families or friends and surprised by the hosts in their homes early in the episode in a segment called the Home Invasion. The ladies then escort the Basic Woman to Girlfriend Headquarters where they put her on the Catwalk of Shame, a display of regular outfits in the Basic Woman's wardrobe. Once on the Catwalk, the Basic Woman and her clothes are critiqued by the experts. After the Catwalk comes the Rack Attack, in which the Basic Woman tries on various outfits to find her style, fit and comfort levels; the hosts also provide feedback, usually in the form of challenges to the Basic Woman's self-critical body image. The next stage is the home redecorating segment Out with the Old, where Nikki, the interior designer, decides which room she going to redecorate, taking aesthetic cues from the Basic Woman's existing style and expressed desires. While her home is being redecorated, the Basic Woman is undergoing a body and soul makeover through a beauty consultation with Tracy and a Soul Patrol Activity with Tanisha (and the rest of the hosts). The Soul Patrol activity is usually dancing or some other physical activity (frequently coded Africana/black) designed to build the Basic Woman's confidence. And, finally, the show ends with the Catwalk of Fame where the "new" version of the Basic Woman is revealed to the delight of the hosts and her friends and family.

This formula corresponds with the larger structure of many reality television shows. Feminist media critic Jennifer Pozner has said of reality television that "we continue to watch because these shows frame their narratives in ways that both play to and reinforce deeply ingrained societal biases about women and men, love and beauty, race and class, consumption and happiness in America." Pozner's assertion is based on the explicit admission of reality television producer Mike Darnell, who Pozner quotes as saying that crafting reality television is "a delicate science" depending on three factors: a simple premise, schadenfreude, and a "social belief" (qtd. in Pozner). By this basic formula, the script of *Girlfriend Intervention* uses a traditional makeover show format (premise) to stage theatrical performances of black and white femininity (schadenfreude) on the stage of racial stereotypes (social beliefs about race and racism). (The strongest adherent to the formula is the show's "soul coach," Tanisha, previously infamous for her performances of volatile black femininity on *The Bad Girls Club*.) One of the basic assumptions of this article is that there is no such thing as unscripted reality television, particularly in 2014 (when the show was released); as Pozner and many other media critics have noted, all reality shows employ writers, casting directors, videographers, producers, editors, advertisers and more.[1] For the purposes of this article, we invest in the formulaic fiction that is *Girlfriend Intervention*, examining what it teaches us about our collective racial reality.

## Historical Roots

Within the formula, *Girlfriend Intervention*'s editors and writers make a spectacle of Tanisha, Tiffiny, Nikki, and Tracy as a troupe of aides for a rotating cast of mealy-mouthed Miss Annes,[2] forcing each Basic Woman to confess her failings and vulnerabilities in public while the hosts mimic complementary stereotypes of Mammy, Sapphire, and Sassy Best Friend. By following a familiar character stereotype, the magical Negress, the show provides audiences with what it thinks they want: black women who are "flashy-dressing, finger-waving, fast-talking fixers whose mission is making Cinderella presentable for the ball" (Holmes). Simultaneously, as the hosts perform this service labor for the Basic Woman's self-actualization, the show re-centers heteronormative black femininity as the ideal figure of womanhood, which is a direct reversal of the historical realities of black womanhood in America.

Black women are "taught that no matter what else is going on in your life, as long as you look fabulous, that's all that matters" (Tanisha, episode 1). It is untenable within America's racialized and gendered political structure for black women to attain and hold a position of power unless it is also a servile one, which is precisely the problem *Girlfriend Intervention* tries to intervene in by straddling the line between magical Negress and authority figure. Rather than present black women who are real, complex, and individual, the show presents black women as superwomen—a myth that Michele Wallace identifies in *Black Macho and the Myth of the Super Woman* (1979):

> From the intricate web of mythology which surrounds the black woman, a fundamental image emerges. It is of a woman of inordinate strength with an ability for tolerating an unusual amount of misery and heavy, distasteful work. This woman does not have the same fears, weaknesses, and insecurities as other

women, but believes herself to be and is, in fact, stronger emotionally than most men. Less of a woman in that she is less "feminine" and helpless, she is really more of a woman in that she is the embodiment of Mother Earth, the quintessential mother with infinite sexual, life-giving, and nurturing reserves. In other words, she is a superwoman [107].

The myth of the black superwoman began in 1619 when the first nineteen Africans were brought to what would become the United States of America. Within 55 years of her arrival the African woman's body was explicitly and implicitly claimed by slavery and she became a breeder. Like livestock, the black woman's body becomes a site of commerce and profit for white slaveholders. Virginia codified this in 1662 by passing a law stating that "the child shall follow the condition of the mother," meaning that the sexual violence of white male slaveholders would result in not only a satisfaction of their desire but also an increase in their pecuniary holdings (Hine). Moreover, black women's bodies would be simultaneously abhorred and overtly sexualized. While white womanhood was held up as the pinnacle of respectability and desirability through the cult of true womanhood, black women were denied access to womanhood or basic humanity. The cult of true womanhood expected that all women would be pious, pure, domestic, and submissive.[3] These tenets were nearly impossible for the most privileged woman to live by, let alone black women (slave or free). As Harriet Jacobs notes in *Incidents in the Life of a Slave Girl*, slave women "ought not to be judged by the same standards" as white women; black women would have been able to develop these characteristics if they had been protected by the laws and customs of the country: "But, O, ye happy women, whose purity has been sheltered from childhood, who have been free to choose the objects of your affection, whose homes are protected by law, do not judge the poor desolate slave girl too severely! If slavery had been abolished, I, also could have married the man of my choice; I could have had a home shielded by the laws" (Jacobs 79). Jacobs is critiquing the double standard that black women in America have had to navigate. Black women's bodies, literally, did not belong to them. Since 1619, black women have been placed in an impossible situation: remain pure, pious, domestic, and submissive, while also being sexualized and objectified.

With this historical backdrop, and the centuries of racist representation and institutional racism that have continued, it is little wonder that *Girlfriend Intervention* was universally rejected. The show itself and its critical reception also reflect our racist national moment, for they both falter in imagining new possibilities for relationships between black and white women that do not reproduce irreconcilable, unequal, and aggressively structured differences. We do not criticize the writers who have appropriately panned the show for its overtly offensive post-racist minstrelsy (in which black women are required to serve the humanity and interests of white women). The show equally mandates that white women perform white fragility in order to uncover their true humanity, constructing a post-racist fantasy of racial redemption that reduces us all. Yet in the show's recreation of this dynamic, we find the opportunity to look more closely at the failures and fissures of white supremacy, because we believe that (despite having been designed to be contradictory and to separate us), the historical relationship between black and white women is also a site of powerful resistance.

## Race and Audience

Notwithstanding the fact that the hosts' performance reflects how American culture views black women, *Girlfriend Intervention* still can't work even when it lives up to stereotypes, because our social narratives do not allow space for black womanhood unless it supports white or black masculinity. Ostensibly, the show advances white supremacy by helping white women; however, teaching white women to "embrace and celebrate their lives, speak their mind, lighten up and love themselves" (*GI* casting call) does not support the subservient role patriarchy demands of women of any color, especially if it is black women teaching even superficial empowerment. Many critics have assumed that *Girlfriend Intervention* was made for a black audience and that Lifetime was deliberately attempting to diversify its shows and appeal to wider viewing audience (meaning black women). However, as one critic notes, the show seems to be created by "white people who've never met any black people" (Ajayi).

While it is clear that *Girlfriend Intervention* is an effort to diversify Lifetime, we read the show as intended for white women with little to no connection with black women because it replicates stereotypes about black women and because it mimics the historically unequal service relationship between black and white women while trying to subvert it—an impossibility or master's tools problem if ever there was one. Part of what informs this analysis is that none of the Basic Women rescued by the show's hosts offer substantive challenges to the show's framing of a "helping" relationship. As well, the show's editing and narrative trajectory are clearly designed for audiences who are not race-conscious and/or African American—the show celebrates the "social belief[s]" about black women and white women as opportunities to attain agency within capitalist patriarchy, and the hosts frequently use language that positions themselves as interpreters of African American culture for a non-black or mixed race audience. Finally, the show's editing, narrative elements, and dialogue all set up adversarial (or at least potentially tense) relationships between the hosts and clients. From the Home Invasion and the Rack Attack to the Catwalk of Shame and the Soul Patrol, the black women hosts are positioned as hyper-vigilant, paramilitary soul sisters (reinforcing scripts about black aggression) and the coaching and/or active choice of how the Basic Women represent themselves is around their vulnerability and desperation (as a classic "angel in the house" who has lost her way).

This adversarial dynamic leads us to question: when *Girlfriend Intervention* seeks to represent white and black women, what definitions of race are being used on the show? Although the cast and hosts make endless remarks about "African American" and "Caucasian" or "black" and "white" culture, experience, narrative, emotional life, and history, they never define "black" or "white," leaving racial identity (and the show's makeover project) to become a floating signifier. It seems simply the *idea* of race that the show wishes to invoke—what race does for the participants and the viewers, or what the participants want the viewers to imagine as they perform gendered interactions on a racialized stage. Thus, who is "white" on the show has more to do with the notion of whiteness as advanced in critical race and whiteness studies; whiteness as social category and contract, rather than signaling any specific ethnic or cultural heritage. On the show, white women are always generalized, with each Basic Woman standing in for all white women—an unusual reversal of the common practice of individual women of color being required to represent or stand in for all women of color. Further shifting the gaze, the show consistently mocks the Basic Woman as a representation of what is wrong with the way that white women "do" femininity. The Basic Woman fails her white race and her female gender, and in so doing fails her social group category, sacrificing her standing and crying out for redemption in makeover form.

The hosts regularly comment both that white women don't know how to celebrate their bodies at any size and that each Basic Woman has a problem embracing her particular assets; it is an accepted feature of Basic Women that they do not do the required heterosexual labor of "keeping themselves up" and "embracing their curves." In the Rack Attack segment, when the white woman dresses in potential looks for critique by Tracy, Tanisha, and Nikki, the Basic Women frequently resist stylist Tiffiny's selections as too revealing of the midsection and booty. The generalizability of race, and the expectation that each Basic Woman stand in for an expected white femininity, becomes evident in episode six, when Ramela (whose background is Armenian) resists the gendered whiteness that the girlfriends attribute to her. When Ramela is dressed in tight-fitting jeans and a snug top, the women admire her butt, but she is patently uncomfortable, saying to them that she feels exposed and vulnerable; in her solo interview, Ramela says "maybe it's a cultural thing." When Tanisha confirms that Ramela's background is Armenian, presumably in response to a similar statement, Tanisha scoffs to Ramela "girl you better get your Kim K on!" Tanisha references Armenian celebrity Kim Kardashian, whose cooptation of racialized signifiers and immersion in hip-hop culture (through her marriage to Kanye West), make her what anthropologist Lorraine Delia Kenny calls an "insider-Other"—a white women whose refusal to adhere to expected norms reasserts her whiteness and reaffirms racial boundaries. Tanisha explicitly encourages Ramela to adopt another "white" woman's appropriation of the Jezebel/Sapphire[4] trope. In this case, although Ramela exhibits the same reservations about displaying her body that all the other Basic Women have, it's because of her strong ethnic Armenian identification, not the self-effacing, body-shaming modesty of white womanhood. Yet from the one-drop rule to the segregated school system, in the American racial caste system, if you're not black, you're white; so Ramela is encouraged to "get [her] Kim K on" and participate in white appropriation of black signifiers (temporarily erasing an ethnic identity that could give her a potentially empowering relationship with the American racial system).

In addition to this reinforcement of racial categorization, *Girlfriend Intervention* takes on the Sisyphean task of characterizing true womanhood. In one of its more interesting internal contradictions, the show makes the radical proposition that white women are doing something wrong with respect to their own femininity and places responsibility on black women for restoring the modern-day cult of true womanhood, because they are getting it right. The only white women on the show who have any voice are the clients/Basic Women, and occasionally the friends and/or family who have nominated them for transformation. As Tanisha explains in episode one, a Basic Woman is a woman who has "lost her way"—a woman who doesn't participate in heteronormative gender expression, lacks sexual and social confidence or "soul," and accepts second-best treatment. The girlfriends' impossible job is to redeem the white women from her abjection—like a female slaveowner whose power within institutional slavery relies upon exploiting a Mammy or other domestic laborer, the Basic Woman requires the redemptive labor of the Girlfriend to find her way. This historically exploitative labor relationship relies also upon race and gender so that white women can claim their patriarchal dividend (whether it is the ability to host extravagant fundraisers for Confederate soldiers, or to become a successful real estate agent, as is the case with episode two's Emily).

As mentioned above, the show has been compared with *Queer Eye for the Straight Guy*, in which another group whose standpoint permits "insider" knowledge into the workings of patriarchy passes along that knowledge to a group with more privilege through service labor. One of the unintended outcomes of the show's critical reception is that it cuts off the possibility that black women do have substantive knowledge to contribute, and that white women need to (in the words of black feminist critic Hazel Carby) listen. Although many academic and activist critiques over the years have identified white women's role in capitalist patriarchy (from Anna Julia Cooper to contemporary debates about white feminism), and although the whiteness of white women is always at the center of popular representation (from *Pretty Little Liars* to Jennifer Lawrence as Katniss Everdeen), it is rare for critique or even self-consciousness of white femininity to coexist with its performance. The realities of heterosexism additionally require white women to comply with the sexual double standard and to present normative femininity at all times. So *Girlfriend Intervention* is one of the few spaces where white women are required to face a mirror reflecting their own racialized and gendered failings. The show is highly critical of Basic Women's inability to stand up for themselves; one of its major themes is to parade women's white fragility (in the words of Robin D'Angelo). The show illuminates what many critical race and identity development scholars have named: white privilege leaves white women adopting an insincere vulnerability that is abusive of others and limits their own humanity. This emphasis on risk and vulnerability strikes deep for many of the clients, who begin with discomfort and progress to breakdowns or deep resistance as they are confronted with their own (perceived) limitations. The pathology becomes increasingly evident as the show progresses and puts a greater emphasis on the emotional transformation the Basic Women undergo.

For instance, episode five's Danelle, whose experiences provide the title of this essay, maintains a cheerful exterior masking a chronic inability to say no and focus on her own needs. Tanisha discloses that the Soul Patrol exercise she selected is intentionally beyond Basic Woman Danelle's capabilities: "I picked aerial dancing because she needs to stand up to us and say no." In each "Soul Patrol" segment, Tanisha takes the Basic Woman through a series of activities designed to push her out of whatever guardedness is keeping her back from a more "authentic" self. These activities are typically dancing (or, notoriously in episode two, rapping) and creative activities, intentionally "culturally African American," that connote sexuality and are promoted as a way for the Basic Woman to find her "soul" or become more genuinely vulnerable. As Soul Coach, Tanisha wants to push Danelle to her limits because Danelle needs to develop her sense of self and her ability to say no (not her sexuality or her athleticism, as with other clients). The heavily edited scene flips back and forth between Danelle's escalating physical exhaustion (in a solo interview, Danelle says, "I felt like crap. I couldn't focus…. Even though I'm gonna throw up I didn't wanna let the girls down") and her interactions with Tanisha, Tiffiny, Nikki, and Tracy. Having directly identified Danelle's boundary issues and people-pleasing tendencies as the primary barrier to her finding her True Black Woman inside, Tanisha and the other hosts observe from the sidelines as Danelle clings to the fabric swing and resists the hosts' encouragement, actually doubling down on her self-criticism: "I feel horrible that I'm feeling so sick."

This intense level of narcissism—a preoccupation with one's own limitations leading to a degree of self-punishment that recreates them—persists even through direct encouragement from the hosts to stop doing the activity they have instructed her to do. As Danelle flops in the aerial swing clearly nauseous and overwhelmed, they call out active encouragements for her to stop the activity that they are simultaneously instructing her to do, pushing so she will push back: "Don't do it" and "You can say no—we taught you how to say that earlier." Danelle replies in a high-pitched whine, "Here I am wanting to just do it because I am wanting to make everybody happy." The white womanhood being enacted here is a degree of active resistance and learned helplessness, a degrading of Danelle's literal physical limits in order to live up to the expectation that she should always live up to every external expectation. She then literally hides behind the fabric swing, as would a toddler avoiding bedtime. In a reiteration of the Mammy trope that is also a moment of deep catharsis, Tanisha responds by calling her out by name, slowly and deliberately: "Danelle. What did we teach you? Danelle. What did we teach you?" Danelle peeks her head out and says, "No." She then repeats herself, to hollers and cheers from the hosts and other spectators.

And, readers, we teared up and clapped; we felt the joy of Danelle's self-realization. We then realized that a part of the show's narrative offers a fantasy of empowerment, assertiveness, self-presentation, and integrity associated with black femininity (the myth of the black superwoman, with a dose of Mammy and Sapphire). The show attempts to sell a promise that there is somehow a trick, a way, to be authentically white and black women within capitalism—that it is possible for white women to have it all, including whiteness, and that having it all takes superhuman strength for white women that only black women know and can teach. Danelle admits to this transformation, saying, "Tanisha pushing me that hard did force me to be real." Tanisha closes the Soul Patrol segment with the assertion "empowering yourself never disappoints anyone." Whether true or false, for anyone caught in the trap of racialized and patriarchal negotiation, hearing an individualistic encouragement after an experience of transformative pressure would generate a sense of deep authenticity. This authenticity comes from being challenged at the boundary—not just of self-assertion, but of assertion against the fragile, white feminine self that always already limits one's self-expression. It also comes at the cost, yet again, of black women's service labor, and this exploitation must be linked with its historical roots.

The Mammy, Sapphire, and Jezebel myths that define popular representations of black womanhood to this day emerged as a way to rationalize white attitudes toward black women in antebellum and post–Civil War America. The Mammy was created to "challenge critics who argued that slavery was harsh and demeaning. After all, [mammies] were depicted as being happy and content with their duties as servants" (Jewell 38). Moreover, these women are portrayed as "docile and maternal," when in reality most domestic servants were young women, most probably teenagers. Physically, Mammy is remembered as "big, fat, soft, dark-skinned, and unfeminine" and grandmotherly. By contrast, the Jezebel, as a myth, attempted to excuse white male violence toward their female slaves. This myth claims that "black women are lascivious, seductive, and insatiable" (Harris-Perry 55); however, its real intention is to reconcile "the forced public exposure and commodization of black women's bodies with the Victorian ideals of women's modesty and fragility. The idea that black women were hypersexual beings created space for white moral superiority by justifying the brutality of Southern white men" (Harris-Perry 55). The Sapphire myth was first seen on the *Amos 'n' Andy* radio show during the 1930s; the character Sapphire is portrayed as "nagging, assertive, uniquely and irrationally angry, obnoxious, and controlling" (Harris-Perry 88). Sapphire has become synonymous with the angry black woman, as well as being part of the myth of the Black Superwoman.

A direct connection with these larger narratives becomes particularly clear in the show's treatment of body image. It is true that *Girlfriend Intervention* attempts to "flip the script" and be body positive, reminding the "Basic Woman" that "just like race, your dress size is not indicative of your self-worth" (Tiffiny). We applaud this body-positive message; however, it is essential to understand the historical relevance of black women's bodies, especially their booties. African women's curves brought them to global prominence in the early nineteenth century. The Anglo-European world is fascinated with African women's curves; this fascination led their bodies to be put on display like circus animals or freaks. One of the most famous of these women was the Hottentot Venus. She has become an iconic figure for the utter degradation of African women and their female descendants.

The Hottentot Venus, Sarah Baartman or Saartjie Baartman, first appeared in London in 1810. Praised and advertised as the Hottentot Venus, Baartman won "her fame as a sexual object, and her combination of supposed bestiality and lascivious fascination focused the attention of men who could thus obtain both vicarious pleasure and a smug reassurance of superiority" (Gould 296). Her career/enslavement consisted of being exhibited along a "stage two feet high, along which she was led by her keeper and exhibited like a wild beast, being obliged to walk stand or sit as he ordered" (Qureshi 235). London crowds paid one shilling to see and shout vulgarities regarding the South African woman's enlarged buttocks and unusually elongated labia, a genital anomaly common to Khoisan women. This genital anomaly was named the Hottentot Apron by nineteenth century scientists. The upper crust of London society would pay Baartman's handler for private viewings in which Baartman was forced to allow them to examine her naked body.

In 1814 Baartman was sold to an animal trainer in Paris and exhibited in a traveling circus until her death in 1816. Within 24 hours of her death Baartman was autopsied, dissected, her skeleton articulated, and her body cast in wax. Her genitalia and brain were pickled and displayed at the Musée de l'Homme (Museum of Mankind) in Paris. She remained on display until 1974 when she was relegated to a storeroom and forgotten. Her body remained a contested site when in 1995 the South African government requested that her remains be returned to her homeland and be laid to rest. The French government resisted for seven years, but eventually yielded, and she was returned and laid to rest in 2002. While Baartman did not receive the promised wealth or type of fame she anticipated in 1810, her image did indeed become one of the controlling images of black women throughout the nineteenth century. Thus, the black woman became an animal to exhibit or sell, not a human being, and like Baartman was "reduced to her sexual parts, and these parts came to represent a dominant icon applied to Black women throughout the nineteenth century.... In the creation of the icon applied to Black women, notions of gender, race, nation, and sexuality were linked in overarching structures of political domination and economic exploitation" (Hill-Collins 137). All of these myths (or stereotypes) are part of a larger social agenda designed to limit black women's involvement with the body politic. By presenting these myths as fact, black women in America have had little success in entering and participating in the political life of their nation because their authority, ethics, and morality are always in question. Consequently, the black woman is not able to control how her image is presented or received by audiences; she is at the mercy of a patriarchal culture that devalues being black and a woman. Tiffiny reinforces this message in episode six, asserting "those curves send a message to mankind everywhere."

As discussed above, body image issues arise in every episode and are discussed widely (particularly by Tiffiny and Tanisha) as a key problem for the Basic Woman. In episode five, Tanisha explicitly criticizes white women's proclivity for body image problems as politically naïve:

> "I think Caucasian women tend to have body issues because the pressure is put on them. It's a spotlight on Caucasian women to be perfect, every image of beauty is a woman no bigger than a size 3 or 4. But what they don't tell you is, this lil' thing sat in 6 hours of hair & makeup to look like that, and they airbrushed her and photoshopped her on top of that. Honey, nobody wakes up looking like that. *Don't let these people fool you*" [emphasis added].

In Ramela's episode, Tanisha declaims that being concerned about having a large booty "is a white girl problem if I ever heard one." This media analysis—of a kind with mainstream feminist campaigns like the film *Miss Repre-sentation* and the Dove Real Beauty campaign—explicitly links body image and capitalism with white femininity, inviting the Basic Women who are smart enough to get that none of the lies about body image are true. As women always already marginalized from meeting beauty standards who are also beauty experts, the Girlfriends hold up a mirror to the absurdity of white women's collusion with the beauty industry. Tanisha's intersectional analysis is in explicit, immediate tension with her own self-presentation and with the model of normative femininity on the show—as all the Girlfriends wear long, flowing hair and present in accordance with white beauty industry standards. Yet, it is clear that the hosts wish to transmit those beauty secrets as modes of power, not only of self-love. One of the things that *Girlfriend Intervention* sells is the promise of entering into a sisterhood that will awaken white women from the sleep of patriarchy, by embracing the norms of femme pres-entation.

*Girlfriend Intervention* both disrupts and reproduces white supremacist patriarchy—by staging the affective bonds between white and black women, the show signals the possibilities and forecloses them into stereotyped service relationships. With echoes of every cross-racial narrative from *Uncle Tom's Cabin* to *The Help*, the show requires its African American hosts to perform emotional labor in order to expose white women's vulnerability. The hosts are not just consultants, they are "girlfriends"—like Oprah before them, the hosts emulate a caregiver even as they subvert white women's foolishness. With this emphasis on relationship, *Girlfriend Intervention* evokes what Sharon Patricia Holland has termed "the erotic life of racism":

> A scene of everyday racist practice opens in two directions: one in which the scene focuses relentlessly upon the individual, seemingly to the exclusion of such leitmotifs of antiracist struggle as structure and caste; and the other in which the event unravels a series of dependencies and intimacies both unex-plored and unexplained [Holland].

The second dimension of this interaction on *Girlfriend Intervention* addi-tionally takes place on three levels. Firstly, heterosexism: on Lifetime, women need other women, preferably strong black women, to tell them the truth about their lives, and many of their needs are not able to be met by men. Sec-ondly, this relational dimension depends upon white women's privileged blindness to institutional racism: the white women on the show testify to the authentic impact the hosts have had on them—particularly Tanisha, whose exaggerated performance often reads as implausible, but who (as one Basic Woman testified in a tearful climax) "made me feel like you really care about me." And, most importantly, at the end of the experience, black women get paid. This labor exchange disguised as relationship, with echoes of 300 years of white and black women's racial history from enslaved wet nurses to *The*

*Help*, only deepens the show's ahistorical presentation of its twenty-first century subjects. These cultural narratives of racial identity were built to rationalize the development of capitalism. With neoliberal sass, the participants' and hosts' blustering racial performances erase the echoes of Mammy in a mythic invocation of authentic connection—just like Danelle's tearful proclamation in episode five, "I just wanna take each and every one of you home in my pocket and keep you forever." The transaction of the Basic Woman owning oneself, of being vulnerable, becomes also a non-mutual intimate ownership of the Girlfriend—"take each and everyone of you home … and keep you forever."

Despite—or perhaps in part through—the problematic racial politics, the hosts and the participants emphasize feeling affected by and connected with to one another. Joanie, the Basic Woman from episode one, even defends and celebrates the show and the impact her transformation had on her marriage, writing, "We've been married 18½ years and that was a beautiful moment for us and *I will defend its truthfulness.* Also my speech at the end was edited of course because of its length, but that was also 100% from my heart" (Ajayi, emphasis added). Joanie qualifies her statement with caveats about editing, and critiques the stereotypes on the show, but is clear to protect what was valuable in her experience: the positive impact on her partnership and her experience of genuine relationships with the hosts. In an interview with bustle.com, host and stylist Tiffiny Dixon expresses frustration at the show's reception, saying that *Girlfriend Intervention* is "no different than what we see in most reality shows, not to mention throughout most of pop culture." Moreover, she goes on to note that the strength of the show lies in its insistence on crossing racial boundaries: "I think that bringing the races together is kind of the antithesis to the problem we're having now with racism. Finally, we are coming together, we're embracing, the fact that, you know what, I'm proud of my race, my culture. You're proud of your culture. Let's come together and merge and learn from each other" (qtd. in Rosenfeld).

*Girlfriend Intervention* attempts to define black womanhood in positive, ahistorical, and overtly celebratory terms for a white audience, which creates a disconnect between their definition and the reality of black women's lives—not all black women are strong, independent, and fierce, just as not all white women are weak, passive, and lack confidence. In some sense, the show forwards the us/them relationship that white and black women have struggled with for years and presents its audience with "simplified representations of white and black people" (Townes). This is a dangerous endeavor that does not allow either black or white women to be individuals; in fact, critics have claimed that it is "conformity dressed up as individuality, and it's submission to the expectation of others dressed up as self-confidence. Only now, with obnoxious racial politics slathered all over the entire thing" (Holmes). Ironically, what is missing in this critique is what is missing in the show: an acknowledgment and examination of the historically fraught relationship between black and white women. That, while the show is attempting to develop cross-racial understanding and sisterhood, it is still working within a patriarchal world that benefit from the oppositional relationship between black and white women.

## Conclusion

When we began this essay, we both acknowledged how loaded the show was. We hoped we could contribute something a little more complex to the conversation, as we each experienced the show to be an incredibly complicated representation of racialized sisterhood. Yet what we found is that writing this paper, in addition to revealing how *Girlfriend Intervention* unmasks and recreates racial and gendered inequities, also recreated or made more visible our own racialized and class-marked divides. At several moments in the process we experienced radically differing interpretations of the hosts and clients' behavior, choices, and reactions. We also had different experiences of how much we could actually enjoy or get lost in the makeover construct/fictional reality of the show. We believe that these contradictory (yet equally truthful) reactions offer a microcosm of the contradictory yet equally truthful barriers to cross-racial sisterhood. Our gap in perspectives, informed by our intersectional experiences, was only possible to bridge because we have, at prior moments in our collaboration and friendship, worked through the unequal service dynamic the show simply reproduces. We could experience and call out these differences because of the existing trust in our relationship and the black feminist/womanist academic training we share.

As well, we noted differences not only in our reactions to the show, but in our approaches to writing about the paper—Shelby's historically grounded contextualization and Susannah's facility with theoretical language, while balancing one another for academic writing, are directly informed by our experiences growing up as black, woman, poor; white, queer woman, academic class. Part of what *Girlfriend Intervention* does is erase the history of representations of black women; it also erases the reality of the differences across which we were able to form a more profound understanding of each other's perspective. Most importantly, *Girlfriend Intervention* recreates an unequal, fundamentally racist, labor relationship that positions black women as a caricature of a superwoman rescuing white women from their own narcissistic failings. The show fell backwards (or perhaps forward, with eyes wide open) into this historically loaded relationship, but we believe that it is possible not only to name it, but to work together to undo it at the structural as well as the interpersonal level. So we choose to close the essay with our reflections on process.

*Susannah:* The process of writing this essay was also a process of unpacking the layers of white racial socialization that mask my humanity. Watching from episode to episode, identifying with the critiques of white femininity and with the Basic Women themselves, the gaze was flipped at a level that spun me. Although I am often aware of racialized interactions in daily life, in a classic example of white privilege, I am rarely challenged to shift my own performance of white femininity in order to negotiate racial realities (though it is my responsibility to seek out challenges or pose them to/with myself). Watching white femininity interrupted, week after week, while simultaneously having racist stereotypes reinforced by the hosts' performance, was a very serious exercise in mirroring the worst of my own internalized supremacy (and, as a femme woman, my complex relationship to cisgender privilege). This project was also, like Danelle's failed dance, an exercise in risk, accountability and care. I've written about racism in feminism before, and work on it every day, but the process of immersing myself in a critical gaze on white femininity and having to unpack both the show and our responses to it in a highly valued relationship left me disturbed, transformed, and inspired. This project has deepened my understanding about how toxic white femininity can be and my commitment to undoing its harms.

*Shelby:* As a woman of color, *Girlfriend Intervention* tries my patience and, at times, hurts my feelings. Repeatedly watching the season, writing about it, and discussing it with my collaborator helped me come to a richer understanding of race, gender, and sisterhood in America. My hurt feeling about how black women were represented transformed into a more focused anger at how circumscribed the relationship between black and white women still is in American culture. And, yet, here I was writing this piece with a white woman, who is not only my colleague but a trusted friend, a sister. I worried that we would not be able traverse the gulf that patriarchy continually strives to place between us. I worried that my sister and I would not be able to navigate the murky waters of race and patriarchy without losing our way and each other. But I knew that if we could, then, this essay would be richer and more nuanced than anything either of us could have done on our own.

## NOTES

1. Although we choose to focus here on a critical race analysis of *Girlfriend Intervention*, we can't pass mentioning its dizzying potential as a subject for racial narrative study. It is a scripted "reality" show about the complex fiction of race that ignores race's very real effects.

2. Carla Kaplan's *Miss Anne in Harlem* (Harper, 2013), in a frontispiece, notes four separate definitions of the term "Miss Anne." It is generally used in African American Vernacular English as "a derisive term for a white woman" (qtd. in Kaplan).

3. Historian Barbara Welter forwards this idea in her essay "The Cult of True Womanhood: 1820–1860," *American Quarterly* 18.2 (1966): 151–174.

4. As Patricia Hill Collins notes in *Black Sexual Politics* (83–84), the Jezebel/Sapphire trope is an image of a hypersexualized black woman.

## Works Cited

Ajayi, Luvvie. "Girlfriend Intervention's Attempt at Fixing Needs Fixing: Premiere (and Only) Recap." *Awesomely Luvvie.* N.p., 28 Aug. 2014. Web. 23 Feb. 2015.

Carby, Hazel. "White Woman, Listen! Black Feminism and the Boundaries of Sisterhood." *The Empire Strikes Back: Race and Racism in Seventies Britain.* London: Hutchinson, 1982. 212–235. Print.

Collins, Patricia Hill. *Black Feminist Thought.* New York: Routledge, 2000. Print.

_____. *Black Sexual Politics.* New York: Routledge, 2005. Print.

Gould, Stephen Jay. *The Flamingo's Smile: Reflections in Natural History.* New York: W.W. Norton, 1985. Print.

Harris-Perry, Melissa. *Sister Citizen: Shame, Stereotypes, and Black Women in America.* New Haven: Yale University Press, 2011. Print.

Hine, Darlene Clark. *A Shining Thread of Hope: The History of Black Women in America.* New York: Random House, 1998. Print.

Holmes, Linda. "Lifetime Promises to Bring Out the 'Strong Black Woman' in White Women." *NPR.org.* NPR, 27 Aug. 2014. Web. 23 Feb. 2015.

Jacobs, Harriet. *Incidents in the Life of a Slave Girl.* Ed. Jennifer Fleischner. New York: Bedford/St. Martins, 2010. Print.

Jewell, Sue K. *From Mammy to Miss America and Beyond: Cultural Images and the Shaping of U.S. Social Policy.* New York: Routledge, 1993. Print.

Kaplan, Carla. *Miss Anne in Harlem.* New York: Harper, 2013. Print.

Kenny, Lorraine Delia. *Daughters of Suburbia: Growing Up White, Middle Class and Female.* New Brunswick: Rutgers University Press, 2000. Print.

Lowry, Brian. "TV Review: *Girlfriend Intervention.*" *Variety* 25 Aug. 2014. Web. 23 Feb. 2015.

Mystic Art Pictures. "Now Casting: Girlfriend Intervention." Mysticartpictures.com, n.d. Web. 14 Aug. 2015.

Qureshi, Sadiah. "Displaying Sara Baartman, the 'Hottentot Venus.'" *History of Science* 42 (2004): 233–257. Print.

Rosenfeld, Laura. "*Girlfriend Intervention* Stars Tanisha Thomas and Tiffiny Dixon Address the Show's Racial Controversy." *Bustle.* Bustle.com, 27 Aug. 2014. Web. 2 Apr. 2015.

Townes, Cariman. "The One Bright Spot in the Racist Ridiculousness That Is *Girlfriend Intervention.*" *ThinkProgress.* Center for American Progress Action Fund, 11 Sept. 2014. Web. 23 Feb. 2015.

Wallace, Michele. *Black Macho and the Myth of the Superwoman.* New York: Verso, 1979. Print.

# "You too can make your own Lifetime movie"
## Branded Labor via Lifetime's Movie Mash-Ups

### Lindsay Giggey

Although Lifetime Television dropped its "Television for Women" moniker in 2006 in an attempt to broaden its audience, the concept lives on within its branded identity. Since the network's inception, programming and marketing have successfully convinced viewers that Lifetime is the destination for women's entertainment. From the immediate aftermath of dropping "Television for Women" until 2009, when the network acquired *Project Runway*, Lifetime underwent several transitional years in which it fine-tuned its branded identity and subtly redefined the network by moving away from a dependence on made-for-TV movies to a larger focus on reality programming. During these years, Lifetime was unclear about stating exactly who its ideal viewer was as the network broadened its program offerings and vastly expanded its Internet presence. As a result, Lifetime's brand fractured as it attempted to empower and inspire women across multiple platforms while upholding larger cultural structures preventing them from questioning their place in society, and more importantly, reinforcing their need for products to uphold their assigned role. This ideological dichotomy is reflected in Lifetime's expansion in the digital space, specifically in its Movie Mash-Up venture.

In 2008, Lifetime introduced a short-lived movie mash-up tool to its website as a reaction to the popularity of YouTube and industrial trends suggesting that viewers wanted more interactive experiences with their television programming (Schley). Mash-ups are digital videos integrating audiovisual materials from at least two different sources. The mash-up interface provided

37

access to part of Lifetime's made-for-television movie catalog along with instructions and software so users could deconstruct, re-edit, and exhibit them within Lifetime's website. By incorporating basic templates and user-friendly tools, Lifetime challenged the stereotype that women are somehow inherently technologically inept by empowering them to "Make [Their] Own Lifetime Movie!" and participate in a growing Internet community. At the same time, however, Lifetime imposed several restrictions on its mash-up tool that prevented users from critiquing and dismantling the source material, making the resulting mash-ups largely incomprehensible. More broadly, the network seized the opportunity to "provide national sponsors an unrivaled opportunity to reach women with targeted cross-platform experiences" as well as a branded space to teach digital skills (Lifetime Networks, "Lifetime Networks Expands Leadership Position").

Lifetime Movie Mash-Ups originally seemed to suggest the same kind of possibility for feminist reception and production practices that had long been associated with the feminist grassroots practice of "vidding." In vidding, users appropriate clips from movies and television shows and set them to "music in order to comment on or analyze a set of preexisting visuals, to stage a reading, or occasionally to use the footage to tell new stories" (Coppa, "Women" sec. 1.1). Since the mid–1970s, vidders have been reassembling existing film and television source material as an intellectual critique and expression of their devotion. The community is primarily female, and as a result, vids reinterpret material from a feminist perspective. Despite the similarities in production practices between vidders and Lifetime users, Lifetime Movie Mash-Ups co-opted and diminished the possibility for feminist critique as a means of maintaining control over Lifetime's larger branded image. Although vidders at large and through the Lifetime channel were producing new material, their content and meanings were vastly different due to network limitations. Rather than express critiques regarding Lifetime's brand and signature movies in the tradition of feminist vidding, the movie mash-ups instead reinforced dominant ideas disseminated by the network.

However, while the mash-ups seem to offer a space for creative reimagining or critique, Lifetime Movie Mash-Ups instead cultivated women's production as another means of exposing and reinforcing Lifetime's brand through women's interactions. Although the Lifetime Movie Mash-Up tool disappeared within a year of its 2008 launch, it provides a fascinating example of a network grappling with changing times, demographics, and its own sense of identity. There has been subsequent brand development and refinement since, but this essay only explores changes up until late 2009 when Lifetime Movie Mash-Ups suddenly vanished from its website. Moreover, the Lifetime Movie Mash-Ups tool's complete erasure from Lifetime's site by late 2009 exemplifies the difficulties in doing network brand research involving digital media when all traces of the original tool and its user-created contents have disappeared as the network further evolved its digital presence and branded identity.

## Fan-Made Videos: Women as Cultural Appropriators

Lifetime's software, catalog access, and instructions for viewers to create their own Lifetime movies via Lifetime Movie Mash-Ups connected its presumably female users with the larger history of feminized and eventually feminist editing work from the days of silent Hollywood film to the grassroots fan vidders of the 1970s to the present. In order to fully understand the potential and limitations of Lifetime Movie Mash-Ups, it is vital to first illustrate the historically gendered associations of fan video production and community.

Creating a tool for female fans to engage in pleasures related to their love of highly emotional, relationship-driven television movies is part of larger tradition of fandom. Mass media fandom itself is highly disparaged as feminized, and its fans have been popularly considered "emotionally unstable, socially maladjusted, and dangerously out of sync with reality" (Jenkins, *Textual Poachers* 13). Moreover, media fan culture is further gendered as female fans are often sexualized or thought to be unable to control themselves when in contact with the objects of their fandom (Jenkins, *Textual Poachers* 15). These stereotypes overlook how many fans use their fandom as a means to form communities of desire that both celebrate texts and use them as a means to tell stories that critique larger institutional structures, especially those around gender and sexuality.

Creating mash-ups requires great patience and editing skills, both of which represent a modern iteration of a production skill long associated with female labor—film editing. In the early decades of Hollywood film, studios initially sought after and then discarded women from cutting rooms because, as editor Walter Murch explains,

> "[editing] was something like knitting. It was something like tapestry, sewing. That you took these pieces of fabric, which is what film are [sic] and you put them together. It was when sound came in that the men began to infiltrate the ranks of the editors because sound was somehow electrical, it was technical, it was no longer knitting" [qtd. in Apple].

Although mainstream editing histories work to bring editors into the light, quotes like Murch's also help contextualize why women's labor is hidden. Good editing makes film look effortless, so all editors' work is overlooked. Moreover, historical film narratives often assume male dominance and include only female extraordinariness, overlooking how editing remains one of the film industry professions most open to female workers and advancement. Though women never completely disappeared from editing, as Murch suggests, this assumption about women's innate inability to wield technology repeats itself in vidding histories "as if it were the recent invention of men, rather than the longstanding practice of women," as well as in popular discourses regarding women and the Internet (Coppa qtd. in Jenkins, "Gender and Fan Culture"). Moreover, as will be explained later, these gendered ideas about technology are deep-rooted in Lifetime's digital expansions and self-assigned role as digital teacher within its mash-up venture and throughout its overall history.

One of the ways in which fandoms, feminism, and uses of technology overlap is in the history of vidding. As Francesca Coppa argues, though remixing seems to be a new phenomenon, vidding practices extend back to 1975 with "What Do You Do with a Drunken Vulcan," when Kandy Fong clicked through *Star Trek* stills on a slide projector in precise time with a fan-written folk song at *Star Trek* fan conventions (Coppa, "Women" sec. 3.1–3.3). In the wake of Fong's vids, vidder communities formed, but were largely underground due to fears of prosecution due to copyright violations or fears of being misunderstood by those outside their communities (Jenkins, "Fan Vidding"). In addition to their largely female makeup, there are many ways in which vidding reflects feminist practices. Women worked in collectives to teach one another to use editing technology, assemble vids, and distribute them. Feminist historian Francesca Coppa elaborates:

> One of the great stories of vidding is that it's a sort of female training ground. Fandom in general has been great for women teaching women technological skills: Web design, video editing, coding, Photoshop. It's such a great site of grassroots peer group learning. Vidders want to teach other people to do it [qtd. in Walker par. 35].

Vidders experienced pleasure in interacting with one another while making new videos from material they loved (Coppa, "'Pressure'" par. 1). In addition to the feminist means of production, the vids themselves overwhelmingly recontextualize popular texts with feminist readings. Dominant educational philosophies assume that girls will read masculine narratives, but boys will not read feminine ones. As a result, girls learn how to interpret male-focused stories whereas boys completely discount female-focused ones (Jenkins, *Textual Poachers* 114). In a sense, girls become culturally bilingual, and vidders tap into this skill set when they deconstruct dominant meanings and propose alternative ones. The mash-up is a particular subset of vid, that, according to Paul Booth, "takes data from two or more different inputs and mixes them together in such a way as to create a unique, third form without loss to the meaning of the originals," which requires an additional level of comprehension (sec. 1.2). These vids depend on the mixing of texts and requires viewers have additional knowledge in order to make the resulting vid legible.

In addition to making vids, the community flourished by trading their creations. Before the digital era, vidders shared their vids with other interested fans via mail trading (Ulaby par. 9). While technological advances such as computers and editing software may have decreased the need to create vids together, the vidding community still provides an infrastructure for women to help other women succeed, create, and express themselves. Currently, Internet distribution through websites like YouTube and Vimeo provides even greater opportunities for sharing and expanding the vidding community.

## Women as Consumers: Lifetime's Branding and Website History

The advent of the Internet not only changed vidding processes, it made media producers more aware of fan activities, including female vidding production. As a result, corporations and media producers, including Lifetime, began incorporating female fans into their business models to further propagate interactive experiences with their brands, but on their own terms.

This targeting of female fans was not new historically. Since the advent of radio and television, advertisers and networks had identified women as their majority audiences during the daytime hours as well as the primary purchasing agents within the home. Programming designed for them, the soap opera, was serial in nature, highly repetitive, and filled with melodramatic elements. As stated by Jackie Byars and Eileen Meehan, "Melodrama, whether packaged as fiction or reality, clearly draws a strong female audience and remains the vital force in women's television" (18) and is and has been a central tenet to Lifetime programming. Moreover, incorporating melodramatic elements into primetime programming, once the explicit domain for male viewers, reflected women's growing importance as media consumers, especially in the 1980s. By this time, women gained even more notice as a purchasing demographic when, as a result of the women's movement and Reaganist pro-privatization and deregulation economic policies, more previously homebound women entered the workforce. After the success of shows like *Cagney and Lacey* amongst upscale workingwomen, advertisers and networks realized there was another viable untapped market to exploit (D'Acci 169). These social and economic changes, in turn, coincided with the advent of cable television. Cable offered consumers the ability to opt in to additional programming, and networks sprung up and fought to serve this sought-after, affluent subscriber base to advertisers hungry to sell products to them. Lifetime, a joint venture between Hearst publications, Disney, and Viacom, launched in 1984 as a means of connecting with upscale female viewers and consumers.

As the 1980s progressed, the number of cable stations increased, so the need to stand out and be easily definable becomes increasingly important. From its launch, the network has had a long history of defining itself in relation to its core demographic. Although Lifetime established itself as a destination for women's programming, the network never clearly identified the ideal Lifetime woman and was careful not to be outwardly feminist. Instead, the network based its initial brand on offering the "feminine side of television" (Byars and Meehan 13). Although Lifetime's underlying ambiguousness and refusal to narrow down their idea of womanhood allowed them to reach broader audiences, it also resulted in disjointed programming. In 1989, as Lifetime began refining itself in the cable realm, senior vice president of marketing and communications Marge Sandwick explained Lifetime's programming decisions: "All we had was a mishmash of programs aimed somewhat at women, but there was no cohesive vision. We weren't sure about our reception out there. We feared people would see us as either the Feminism channel or the Betty Crocker channel" (qtd. in Wilson 115). Though the network initially aired a mixed bag of programming intended to connect with women, including cooking shows, exercise shows, and medical shows, the network eventually found a stronger branded identity via its rebroadcast of made-for-television movies. Lifetime went on to produce its own films, building on the female-focused tropes and using them to express the network's branded identity as a destination for traditionally-understood ideas of "women's programming." In their 1995 deconstruction of the network, Jackie Byars and Eileen Meehan explain that Lifetime's original made-for-TV movies

> revolved around a strong, competent woman who overcomes adversity. Generally, the films involve a social issue believed to be of particular concern to women: domestic violence, sexual harassment, adoption, AIDS, or rape. Female protagonists generally work within the system to correct some injury, often in a professional capacity. Most of the actresses cast in these original movies are white and middle-aged. Actresses like Blair Brown, Stephanie Zimbalist, Christine Lahti, and Cathy Lee Crosby typify Lifetime's vision of female protagonists as fully adult women with weaknesses, soft edges, and strong emotions. This emphasis on emotions inflects Lifetime's productions with a distinctly melodramatic edge, regardless of genre. Lifetime consistently focuses on the personal and familiar, even when the setting is institutional. Systemic challenge is rare; solutions are generally personal [Byars and Meehan 26].

Ideologically, refocusing larger social issues onto the individual helps reinforce current political economies and cultural hierarchies, drawing attention away from a call for systemic change, particularly economic, that might threaten the interests of cable and network businesses. Moreover, the generic tropes of the Lifetime movie specifically worked to reinforce patriarchal structures where women are deemed to be family caretakers. Without these ideological boundaries, Lifetime would have had a harder time lining up potential advertisers for its programming. These films aired in primetime, after both the white-collar business day ended and feminine responsibilities such as making dinner, childcare, and home upkeep had largely been completed for the day. Though the women in Lifetime movies of this period were often heroic as they overcome seemingly overwhelming obstacles in their way, they likewise reinforced the driving message that for women to be successful, they needed to tend to responsibilities both in and out of the home. The need to include consistent ties to both the public and domestic spheres helps explain why Lifetime could not quite create a further niche or cohesive network brand beyond "woman." The only thing executives continued to agree on was that Lifetime wanted upscale women, especially workingwomen, to watch their network because their eyes attracted premium advertising dollars (Wilson 115). Not taking a definitive stand on exactly who their ideal woman was allowed Lifetime to bundle all women together as it expanded its brand reach. Once the network established itself as a destination for women's programming, the network could tweak its programming in order to further refine what women wanted without too narrowly defining who that woman was.

Despite not taking a definitive stand on feminism, Lifetime vastly expanded its branded digital presence from the late 1990s through 2009, and an examination of its popular website suggests how implicitly the network defined its ideal woman. During this time, Lifetime's website expansion mirrored its aggressive programming expansion as the network fought to maintain its standing as a women's entertainment behemoth. In March 2009, mylifetime. com reported attracting three million monthly users and highlighted how the site was one of the top 25 online gaming sites for women (Lifetime Networks, "About Lifetime" par. 31). In considering the site's acquisitions history, the Lifetime woman transformed from one who needed the network for Internet literacy to one interested in watching and creating video, playing internet games, shopping, and reading about style, beauty, health, relationships, and celebrity. However, in line with pervasive gender stereotypes, any connection to hard news, politics, science, or technology was notably absent. Rather than providing a platform where women could actively engage with one another, Lifetime instead created multimedia destinations for them to more passively and individually escape their lives.

As cable historian Megan Mullen points out, by 2000, most cable networks had diversified their media presence to include "their own interactive and coordinated websites," (Mullen 2). Lifetime was ahead of this curve as Lifetime Digital launched in 1996 under CEO Carole Black (1999–2005) to expand its brand and entertainment slate into the digital space (Lifetime Networks, "About Lifetime" par. 6). Lifetime's connection with female audiences, especially middle-aged and senior women, put the network in a prime position to guide viewers into the digital realm and could do so in a way that furthered the network's brand. In 2000, Lifetime further expanded their digital presence and established a precedent where the network asserted itself as a guide for presumably technologically inept female viewers to experience the Internet when it entered an agreement with women.com. Later ivillage.com, women.com was a top Internet destination for women at the time, so the partnership created promotional opportunities for each on multiple media platforms, while increasing Lifetime's presence on the Internet (Saunders). Moreover, women.com carried several Hearst publications, which created additional synergy between Lifetime and one of its partial owners. This association was further compounded when *Lifetime Magazine* debuted in 2003, providing additional context for the ongoing magazine aesthetic that still remains part of Lifetime's branded web presence (Hall par. 9). These media extensions were designed to be additional opportunities for advertisers to reach audiences, and the familiarity of the Lifetime brand likewise drove audiences from one platform to another in order to consume more and more content, which in turn strengthened their relationship with the larger network brand.

In a move further gendering its web extensions, Lifetime partnered with QVC in 2002 to incorporate a long assumed feminine pastime—shopping—into their website (Lifetime Networks, "Lifetime/QVC"). Creating associations between Lifetime and QVC eased users into the practice of Internet shopping because QVC and Lifetime were trusted brands. Furthermore, since each network had similar demographics, viewers familiar with one were will likely to be familiar with the other. In 2008, when the Lifetime Movie Mash-Ups tool was also active elsewhere on the site, the store function included purchasing guides (like how to buy a flat screen television or facial moisturizer) as well as topical guides (like how to dress like Michelle Obama). Although Lifetime's current website only sells DVD versions of its most current original movies and series, considering the QVC partnership and past construction of the online store shows how Lifetime positioned itself a bridge between female users and larger changes in digital consumption and behaviors.

Lifetime underwent major expansion again under Andrea Wong's tenure as CEO (2007–2010). Changing the website's URL from lifetimetv.com to mylifetime.com in 2007 signaled a more direct connection between user and cable network. Also in 2007, Lifetime partnered with website/blog publisher Glam Media and linked Glam Media's extensive lifestyle websites and blogs with Lifetime's website. This joint venture commissioned new content for Lifetime's website including introducing a "Style and Beauty" section as well as increased video and gaming opportunities (Glam Media). Likewise, Lifetime also acquired the ParentsClick network, an aggregated network of blogs featuring MomBlogNetwork.com, giving those users increased readership by directing their web traffic while specifically highlighting and subsequently creating brand associations between Lifetime, women, and blogging (Lifetime Networks, "About Lifetime" par. 36–7). Throughout Lifetime's numerous expansions, one must remember the network's ultimate driving force:

> The real success of Lifetime's brand extensions will be measured in how well the company can convert brand strength into advertising dollars. Having a presence in television, print and online opens the door to the development of integrated marketing packages that can grab a bigger share of an advertiser's budget [Hall par. 11].

These acquisitions represented Lifetime's multifaceted approach to increasing their digital presence, and each one approached a slightly different segment of its audience in order to expose and curate their experiences with constantly changing technologies. The Lifetime audience is older women (both in and out of the home) who may be interested in technology but are unsure of how to use it or participate in digital culture. Lifetime in turn provided them with a solution to this problem by teaching users to engage with technology, but in a way that further reinforced and articulated the network's brand. The network even announced it as such in a 2008 press release proclaiming that Lifetime would "expand its leadership position as the only media company offering a singular branded 360-degree experience for women—featuring a consistent, powerful brand across all platforms—with a diverse array of new digital initiatives" (Lifetime Networks, "Lifetime Networks Expands Leadership Position"). This suggests that the network saw women's affinity for the channel as an opportunity to use the brand to then drive them to seek out further opportunities while providing a familiar and safe way to explore digital tools and behaviors. Lifetime became their access point to technology, and as such, the network influenced how women interact with the Internet by framing their experiences.

## Appropriating Women Producers: Lifetime Movie Mash-Ups

As part of the network's 2008–2009 digital initiatives, Wong expanded the website again in 2008 by joining with Gotuit to launch Lifetime Movie Mash-Ups, an online software program allowing viewers to re-edit and create their own Lifetime movies by reassembling clips from a selection of initially fifteen, and eventually thirty five, fully intact original Lifetime-produced movies (Business Wire). Examining Lifetime's Movie Mash-Ups offers a unique look at the convergence of brand, gender, and technology. Incorporating the mash-ups into the website suggests Lifetime's promotion of female creativity and empowerment in the tradition of vidders, but the mash-ups' restrictions reflect how they were primarily a branding tool rather than an outlet for creative expression or engagement with larger internet communities.

In line with Lifetime's digital expansion and efforts to provide branded opportunities to introduce new Internet phenomenon including Internet shopping, blogging, and casual gaming, Lifetime took advantage of the larger cultural interest in video creation and distribution sites like YouTube. In the case of Lifetime Movie Mash-Ups, Lifetime intended to show women how to navigate and assemble web-based video editing software, presumably to engage their aging audience on a new platform while hoping to simultaneously attracting younger viewers to the site, and eventually, the network.

When users initially navigated to the Lifetime Movie Mash-Up extension, an instructional video immediately popped up automatically. Reminiscent of 1950s-1960s instructional videos in both style and narration, the black and white how-to video flickered and included crackling sounds as if it were an old film. Presenting the directions in this way reinforced Lifetime's self-imposed role as technological teacher. The instructional video blended old familiar technology that users were already familiar with—movies—while introducing the new element—editing web video—as a means of disarming user fears about managing technology. Within the tutorial, the screenshots depicting the mash-up interface and creation process were the only parts of the video in color, suggesting that the creative process not only breaks up but also adds life to users' otherwise mundane daily tasks. The video also depicted Lifetime's historical interest in the upscale workingwoman as the tutorial took place in an office. As opposed to the vidding community where mostly female collectives taught each other about the technology and software needed to make vids, a male omniscient narrator jovially explained how to use the software. This choice in narrator reinforced Lifetime's continued fear of aligning itself with feminism. Lifetime users learned from an unseen male authority, which reinforced patriarchal constructs where men weld power and access to institutional and technological structures. Moreover, the single woman learning a skill from an unseen man likewise erased the feminist means of production and community creation that were central to development of historical vidding culture. Likewise, in line with the patriarchal ideology of Lifetime's brand, the video implicitly suggested how women needed to segment their time in order to continuously prioritize the needs of others over themselves and their responsibilities to their families above all.

Within the video, an animated blonde woman named Susan leads users through the verbal instructions. Susan wears glasses, has slightly messy hair, and works in an office where she is shown carrying large stacks of files between a filing cabinet and the copier. Viewers do not learn that Susan even has a computer at work, which could alleviate the need for so many paper files, until she starts making her mash-up. At this early point, the Lifetime network is Susan's—and thus the user's—only access point to technology, and the entire reason to own and use a computer. As the video progresses, Lifetime further asserts its larger commercial interests in and connections to conventional feminine beauty standards. As soon as Susan begins clicking through the mash-up process, her glasses are gone and her hair is far neater. Her improved physical appearance coincides with her pleasurable mash-up experience and escape into fantasy. Note that Susan is shown interrupting her workday to create a video, not her home life. This portrayal simultaneously reiterated that the workingwoman remained Lifetime's favored demographic while still privileging the sanctity of the home and woman's place in it. At its conclusion, the instructional video reminds users that "with the Lifetime Movie Mash-up tool, you too can escape into your very own Lifetime movie," but positioning Susan at work conveyed that women might be able to escape at work, but they should not escape their domestic responsibilities (Lifetime Networks, "Lifetime Movie Mash-Ups").

After watching the instructional video, users could then login using their Lifetime accounts and begin making videos. In March 2008, users could choose from thirty-five original Lifetime made-for-television movies. Each movie was broken up into smaller scenes, and users had the option of leaving those scenes intact or cutting them further. If they cut a new scene, users chose where they wanted scenes to start and stop, and then add a title, description, and metadata tags to organize their particular scenes within their account as well as adding their newly created scene to a communal receptacle. When users were ready to assemble their mash-ups, they dragged the scenes they had created or pulled from the larger pool into a tool bar in the order they liked. Mash-ups could be assembled using scenes from any of the available films in any order users wanted.

Although users could cut and rearrange scenes from various different movies, they could not remove the existing sound or add their own soundtracks. A significant part of a vid's criticism comes from fusing images with music because music creates the thematic foundation for vidders' central arguments. In contrast, Lifetime's mash-up software made it very difficult for users to criticize or radically reinterpret the material because it limited how users could deconstruct and rebuild. Lifetime allowed users to place intertitle cards between scenes to create context, meaning, and some semblance of narrative cohesion between otherwise disjointed scenes. However, Lifetime again limited this freedom. Users could not create their own intertitles, but were forced to rely on those Lifetime created for them. More than anything, these restrictions suggest that Lifetime was very concerned with how their material was repurposed. By stripping users of substantial agency, Lifetime ensured that its brand-defining made for television movies could not be manipulated to present alternative readings. As mentioned, the Lifetime movie genre was—and still is—heavily invested in mapping larger cultural issues onto the individual in order to maintain larger political economies and cultural hierarchies, especially patriarchal social structures. The network's livelihood within larger economic structures depends on it presenting the dominant viewpoint. If Lifetime allowed users greater ability to reconceptualize and recontextualize their films, the results could have undermined the core values supporting the network's brand and business model.

Once users created their mash-ups, they could post and share them with the Lifetime community. Although the community repository or user-created mash-ups disappeared when Lifetime removed the tool in its entirety sometime in late 2009, at the time, it included all completed videos made by all users. The user-created videos were of varying length (ranging from less than a minute to over four hours), but were more similar than different. Many of the videos were clearly experimentation or mistaken postings like XandraSkye's "Mash-Up No. 1," which is comprised of five title cards. XandraSkye does not incorporate any scenes, suggesting that the user was playing with the interface and accidentally posted it, especially because the title card sequence does not make sense: "'Cue flashback…' 'The plot thickens…' 'Now for a change of pace…' 'That bitch!' 'Oh my!'" (XandraSkye). Many of the mash-ups are not really mash-ups at all, but reassemblies of the source movies in their exact order. These attempts represent either a complete misunderstanding of mash-ups, which are the intercutting of at least two different source texts to form a new narrative, or were a creative way to watch intact Lifetime movies. Although Lifetime posted some of its made for television movies in their entirety elsewhere on the website, those titles were not included as part of those available to mash-up. Notably, user-created videos did not include commercials like the movies available on the website or any of the content on the Lifetime Television Network. Reassembling the movies in their exact order could be a subversive way for users to view them, but without access to the show's website or possible message boards from the time, it is impossible to know with what intent viewers created and consumed the mash-ups. It is also interesting to consider whether or not this possible subversion contributed to the end of the website application, especially in light of Lifetime's July 2015 decision to offer its original movie catalog as an over-the-top monthly subscription service as an application called the Lifetime Movie Club (O'Connell). The movie catalog is so instrumental to Lifetime's larger brand that it is the aspect of the network's holdings that Lifetime feels is in highest demand and most easily monetized.

Other longer mash-ups followed the same pattern where they present scenes from one specific title, but omit or repeat certain scenes. For example, tinkerbell459's seventy-two-minute mash-up "Hush" features scenes exclusively from the Tori Spelling Lifetime movie of the same name. However, instead of telling the story chronologically, tinkerbell459 begins her mashup with a scene from the last third of *Hush*, follows the film to its narrative conclusion, and then jumps back to the very beginning and continues mixing scenes from the first two-thirds of the film. Although scenes throughout are not chronological, the film's narrative is still apparent because outside of rearranging the order, the scenes remain largely intact. "Hush" does not radically alter *Hush* or offer viewers who have seen it any new perspective. Moreover, the scenes tinkerbell459 uses in "Hush" are identical to how Lifetime broke down scenes from *Hush*. Although tinkerbell459 reassembled the scenes differently, the user did not make any further edits to the scenes provided. "Hush" and other similarly long mash-ups do not utilize their length to present anything new, but rather retell the stories from the source material (tinkerbell459). Alejandra6969's "what really happened" is almost four hours long and is, as the user describes it, "a movie filled with thrillers," (Alejandra6969). Like "Hush," "what really happened" seemingly arbitrarily puts scenes together, but does incorporate scenes from different movies. Like tinkerbell459, Alejandra6969 does not alter (or shorten!) any of the material, nor does she seem to put it together in a cohesive way that is understandable to other viewers without prior knowledge of any of the available titles. This latter point does connect Lifetime Movie Mash-Ups to larger fan vidding traditions, because, as Paul Booth explains, for mash-ups to be legible, "viewers much be knowledge about both sources, as well as the convergence of them, in order to make sense of the final product" (Booth sec. 1.2). But in execution, although "what really happens" suggests that climactic plot twists will be put together, that is not the case as it features several exposition scenes without revealing any major information. Even though "what really happens" suggests user potential in the mixing of texts, its larger legibility in combining pieces does not go much further than being able to identify the component pieces. This illegibility could have been corrected with some unifying component, like a single piece of music in the tradition of song vids. Instead, these typical examples represent the extreme difficulty in creating new narratives using the Movie Mash-Up tool because of the software's inability to remove sound in order to create cohesion amongst the disjointed images.

However, there are a limited number of mash-ups in the spirit of vids in that users edit material and use what they need in order to convey a point of view and serve viewers' specific interests. As mentioned previously, it was difficult to create anything cohesive from very disjointed material, which was not made easier by Lifetime's software limitations. The most successful, and frequently appearing, mash-ups spliced together sex scenes from various Lifetime movies.[1] Rachel+C's "Sex, Sex & Sex" epitomizes this type of mash-up: characters spanning different films are not introduced and there is no narrative context. The sex scenes across the available films do not have dialogue, and are largely scored with alto saxophone music, which unifies scenes in the vid tradition. Moreover, arranging the clips thematically allows viewers a clearer understanding of what users are conveying because, especially in these cases, these mash-ups are primarily image based. Viewers do not need to know or understand what is happening in the rest of the movie in order to understand the mash-up. Additionally, "Sex, Sex & Sex's" tagline succinctly states, "Why do we like Lifetime movies? Hmmm…. Watch and see!" This sums up the idea of escape into fantasy repeated throughout Lifetime's website and programming, and a type of escape offered to Lifetime viewers (Rachel+C). Mash-up makers like Rachel+C curated what they believed to be the most pleasurable scenes as those most inherent to their understanding of the Lifetime brand. Her introduction underscores the association between user and brand as it evokes it. Rachel+C creates a video using the Lifetime Movie Mash-Up that directly reflects Lifetime's articulation of pleasures to audiences.

That being said, though Rachel+C may be using the Lifetime branded tool to mash-up Lifetime movies and share them with the Lifetime community, users like her also offer counter-hegemonic avenues into consuming Lifetime's brand. "Sex, Sex & Sex" and other vids like it offered the most feminist potential as they presented a record of female sexual agency and desire, which are rarely part of or associated with mainstream television. Mash-ups highlighting the sex scenes represented an alternative reading of Lifetime movie narratives as they removed all of the surrounding issues and commentary that reinforce societal norms to focus solely on pleasure. They offer a counter-imagining of contemporary womanhood by going against cultural pressures dictating that women be normatively feminine and in service of others over themselves. Moreover, the ability to share the mash-ups and its component scenes with a larger community facilitates the potential for finding likeminded people and organizing in the spirit of feminist vidders. Though mash-ups like this engage with implicit pleasures within the Lifetime brand, bringing these pleasures to light threatens the larger economic and social structures the network depends on for its very livelihood.

## Conclusion

In the late 2000s, Lifetime utilized its vast digital expansion to widen its reach and service women's entertainment needs on multiple platforms. The network's Internet acquisitions suggest that Lifetime wanted to assert itself as the access point for women to interact with unfamiliar technologies in an unthreatening, fun way. However, Lifetime's conflicted position as teacher and as a commercial media company demands scrutiny. Lifetime may create new opportunities for inexperienced users to explore the Internet, but one must remember that everything from programming to the communal message boards, Internet games, and movie mash-ups all serve as vehicles to entice users to cultivate a relationship with the larger network brand.

One cannot consider Lifetime Movie Mash-Ups without also thinking about branding. Celia Lury defines brands as "a set of relations between products and services" as well as "a set of relations between products in time," which further stresses changes in business models that depend on recognizing common themes, images, and concepts in order to unify user experiences (Lury 1–2). Branding is a direct response to increased consumer awareness, so rather than sell products, brands sell lifestyles that people cannot embody without purchasing products. Lifetime made its material available and suggested users were free to play with it in the tradition of vidders. However, although Lifetime provided instruction and software to make vids, their restrictions make it nearly impossible to critically challenge or talk back to the network, and these limitations ultimately protected Lifetime's brand. In order to challenge Lifetime's programming as well as its underlying branded ideas of womanhood, users need to take their interest and skill set elsewhere. Users could not challenge the status quo because the software's limitations prevented it. Allowing users to manipulate the video and audio files too much took control away from Lifetime and disrupted the unified image that Lifetime presented on its network and throughout its website. Moreover, Lifetime Movie Mash-Ups may have been the first experience that many users have with editing and creating videos on their computers. The limited scene selections and tendency towards long scenes instead of short cuts to create new ideas could be a product of ignorance. Users may not have had much experience watching vids either because they did not know where to access them or that they existed at all. Despite its limitations, Lifetime's Movie Mash-Ups can serve as introductory experiences for women interacting with technology in creative ways. Perhaps experimenting with the software will inspire some users to challenge themselves with more complex software, material, or ideas, allowing them a closer comparison to the established feminist vidding community.

Although there is no existing discourse on why the mash-ups vanished, I suspect that they no longer fit with Lifetime's evolving version of its brand. As historian Megan Mullen argues, "even those networks that targeted specific audience constituencies ... found themselves continually having to broaden their scope so as to capture the largest possible audience—precisely the imperative that has driven commercial broadcast television throughout its entire existence" (152). The network's acquisition of the juggernaut reality competition show *Project Runway* from Bravo in 2009 suggests not only larger changes in network programming, but in its branded identity. *Project Runway* aired its first Lifetime season in summer 2009, and this marked the point where the network made substantive programming changes as it moved away from its television movie fare to feature more reality-based programming. In reexamining the network's preferred history in its current incantation of "About Lifetime" on its website, which appears to have been written in 2009, there is no mention of Lifetime Movie Mash-Ups at all, but several references to the acquisition of *Project Runway* specifically as the turning point for the network in its present mode. Moreover, in describing its digital offerings, Lifetime now has a more contained message. The network now highlights the digital communities it has made for moms to communicate, as opposed to women without children or potentially without household responsibilities to commune over pleasures offered by Lifetime movies (Lifetime Networks, "About Lifetime"). The complete erasure of the tool from its website and larger official history, even one written immediately before the tool disappeared, further enforces how the needs of the brand will always take precedence over the needs or wants of the user.

## NOTE

1. This type of mash-up comprised seven of the thirty-four pages of mash-ups.

## WORKS CITED

Alejandra6969. *What Really Happened. Lifetime Movie Mash-Ups.* User Mash-Up. 2009.
Apple, Wendy. *The Cutting Edge: The Magic of Movie Editing.* 2004. DVD.
Booth, Paul J. "Mashup as Temporal Amalgam: Time, Taste, and Textuality." *Transformative Works and Cultures* 9 (2012): n. pag. Web. 3 Mar. 2015.
Business Wire. "Lifetime Networks Selects Gotuit for New Mash-Ups Site at www.MyLifetime.com." *Business Wire.* N.p., 19 May 2008. Web. 9 Mar. 2009.
Byars, Jackie, and Eileen R. Meehan. "Once in a Lifetime: Constructing the 'Working Woman' through Cable Narrowcasting." *Lifetime: A Cable Network "For Women."* Spec. issue of *Camera Obscura: A Journal of Feminism, Culture, and Media Studies* 33–34 (1994–1995): 13–41. Print.
Coppa, Francesca. "'Pressure'—a Metavid by the California Crew." *In Media Res.* NYU DLTS, 2008. Web. 8 Mar. 2009.
_____. "Women, *Star Trek*, and the Early Development of Fannish Vidding." *Transformative Works and Cultures* 1 (2008). Web. 5 Feb. 2015.
D'Acci, Julie. "Defining Women: The Case of *Cagney and Lacey.*" *Private Screenings.* Ed. Lynn Spigel and Denise Mann. Minneapolis: University of Minnesota Press, 1992. 169–200. Print.
Glam Media. "Lifetime Networks Partners with Glam Media to Develop New Vertical Media Network." *Glam Media.* Mode Media Corporation, 12 Nov. 2007. Web. 8 Mar. 2009.
Hall, Lee. "*Lifetime* Put Brand on Female Demo." *Television Week* 4 Apr. 2004. Print.
Jenkins, Henry. "Fan Vidding: A Labor of Love (Part Two)." *Confessions of an Aca-Fan.* N.p., 2008. Web. 12 Aug. 2015.

_____. "Gender and Fan Culture (Round Fourteen, Part One): Francesca Coppa and Robert Kozinets." *Confessions of an Aca-Fan.* N.p., 2007. Web. 27 Feb. 2009.

_____. *Textual Poachers: Television Fans & Participatory Culture.* New York: Routledge, 1992. Print.

Lifetime Networks. "About Lifetime." www.MyLifetime.com. Lifetime Entertainment Services, LLC, 2009. Web. 6 Mar. 2015.

_____. "About Lifetime." www.MyLifetime.com. Lifetime Entertainment Services, LLC, 27 June 2007. Web. 1 Mar. 2009.

_____. "About Lifetime." www.MyLifetime.com. Lifetime Entertainment Services, LLC, 2015. Web. 12 Aug. 2015.

_____. "Lifetime Movie Mash-Ups." www.MyLifetime.com. Lifetime Entertainment Services, LLC, 2008. Web. 1 Mar. 2009.

_____. "Lifetime Networks Expands Leadership Position as the Only Media Company Offering a Singular Branded 360-Degree Experience for Women With Wide Array of New 2008–09 Digital Initiatives." MyLifetime.com. Lifetime Entertainment Services, LLC, 14 Apr. 2008. Web. 21 Jan. 2015.

_____. "Lifetime Television and Global-QVC Solutions to Launch Online Retailing Business and Direct Response Campaigns Featuring Items Related to the Network's Programming." *Internet Retailer.* www.MyLifetime.com. Lifetime Entertainment Services, LLC, 16 July 2002. Web. 8 Mar. 2009.

Lury, Celia. *Brands: The Logos of the Global Economy.* International Library of Sociology. London: Routledge, 2004. Print.

Mullen, Megan Gwynne. *The Rise of Cable Programming in the United States: Revolution or Evolution?* Austin: University of Texas Press, 2003. Print.

O'Connell, Michael. "Lifetime Launching Over-the-Top App for Original Movies." *The Hollywood Reporter.* Hollywood Reporter, 2 July 2015. Web. 12 Aug. 2015.

Rachel+C. *Sex, Sex & Sex. Lifetime Movie Mash-ups.* User Mash-Up. 2009.

Saunders, Christopher. "Women.Com, Lifetime Team in Promotional/Ad Deals." *ClickZ.* ClickZ Group Limited, 2000. Web. 10 Mar. 2009.

Schley, Stewart. "More Women Want Lifetime Movie Network." *Multichannel News* 21 June 2008: n. pag. Print.

tinkerbell459. *Hush. Lifetime Movie Mash-ups.* User Mash-Up. 2009.

Ulaby, Neda. "Vidders Talk Back to Their Pop-Culture Muses." *National Public Radio.* NPR.org, 2009. Web. 26 Feb. 2009.

Walker, Jesse. "Remixing Television: Francesca Coppa on the Vidding Underground." Reason.com. Reason Foundation, 18 July 2008. Web. 27 Feb. 2009.

Wilson, Pamela. "Upscale Feminine Angst: Molly Dodd, the Lifetime Cable Network and Gender Marketing." *Lifetime: A Cable Network "For Women."* Spec. issue of *Camera Obscura: A Journal of Feminism, Culture, and Media Studies* 103–132 (1994–1995): 103–130. Print.

XandraSkye. *Mash-up No. 1. Lifetime Movie Mash-ups.* User Mash-Up. 2009.

# "One day you're in and the next day you're out"

## Making Project Runway Work from Bravo to Lifetime

### Emily Witsell

On August 6, 2015, the fourteenth season of the competitive fashion design reality show *Project Runway* premiered on Lifetime. Since its debut on the network in January 2009, *Project Runway* has become a staple of Lifetime's schedule. The season six opener, the first episode that aired on Lifetime, became the network's highest-rated series premiere ever with 4.2 million viewers and the highest-rated reality show of the year for any cable network. This number was a 32 percent improvement over the previous season's premiere, which had aired on Bravo one year before (Levine 5). Ratings for the show have fluctuated in the years since, recalling host Heidi Klum's oft-repeated injunction that "In fashion, one day you're in, and the next day you're out," but the fourteenth season opened to a solid audience of 1.6 million viewers, so it is clear that audiences still consider *Project Runway* "in" after nearly a decade of episodes (Bibel). This loyal audience was what Lifetime was counting on when it made the bold move to purchase rights to the show's sixth and subsequent seasons from Bravo at a price of one million dollars per episode. Bravo, the arts and entertainment network that had developed the show, made it into a ratings juggernaut that captivated the attention of what is widely considered to be the "right" kind of viewer for advertisers: young, affluent, and culturally savvy. While *Project Runway* was a runaway success for Bravo, it was unclear whether Lifetime, a network with a reputation for airing melodramatic made-for-television movies, original drama series, and syndicated sitcoms aimed at women, would be able to translate that success by enticing Bravo viewers to the network and convincing Lifetime viewers to accept reality television. This essay explores the varying audiences drawn to Bravo and Lifetime, the appeal of *Project Runway* for these two groups, and how Lifetime has tweaked an incredibly successful product to appeal to a wider audience.

The premise of *Project Runway* remains essentially unchanged from the formula it created for its first season on Bravo: a group of aspiring fashion designers compete in weekly challenges to create outfits based on parameters set by the judges. The challenges have brief timelines, ranging from just a few hours to two days, a small budget for materials, and frequently incorporate a twist, such as the requirement to use unconventional materials purchased from a grocery store or to work in teams. In the first season, designers were asked to sketch and construct a wedding dress based on the requests of a client, design an outfit for a presenter to wear to the Grammy's, and reimagine a modernized uniform for a postal service worker, among other tasks. In the workroom, the designers interact with their mentor, Tim Gunn, who offers advice and criticism. A model walks the runway wearing the completed outfit before a panel of judges that includes the host of the show, former supermodel Heidi Klum, two regular judges from the fashion world, and a guest judge, who may be a celebrity, designer, or client. Each week, one designer is eliminated with Klum's now-iconic dismissal of "Auf Wiedersehen." The top three (or sometimes four, if the judges deem the talent pool to be particularly strong) designers present collections at New York Fashion week in front of an invited audience, with the ultimate winner receiving prizes that typically consist of a cash award to put toward starting a fashion line,[1] the opportunity to sell his or her designs at a popular store, a car, and a vacation. The model who worked with the winning designer in the final runway show would be photographed for an editorial in a magazine (first *Elle*, then *Marie Claire* in later seasons) along with an article about the winning designer.

The formula of creative people competing to prove that they are the best at their craft has been tried frequently in reality television, to mixed results. For every success, such as Bravo's cooking challenge *Top Chef* (2006–) or SyFy's contest for makeup artists *Face/Off* (2011–), there are legions of short-lived shows that failed to resonate with audiences. What is it that makes *Project Runway* successful while other fashion shows, including some of *Project Runway*'s many spin-offs, have failed? The opening of the first episode of season fourteen promised viewers "action … drama … fun … and tears!" Tim Gunn, the show's mentor and beloved character, avowed that "this group of designers had me pulling my hair out!" This opening monologue was set against a montage of designers crying, arguing, laughing, and looking stressed. Almost as an afterthought, host Heidi Klum reminds the audience that yes, there will also be fashion design: "fashion that inspires us and fashion that excites us, and some fashion that scares us." Finally, the viewer is invited to hop on board the "roller coaster ride" that is *Project Runway* ("Mad Dash Mayhem"). While part of *Project Runway*'s success has been attributed to the show "focusing on its contestants' talent rather than on stunts" ("*Project Runway* in Limbo"), it is clear that Lifetime believes that its contestants' personalities, drama, and conflict are just as compelling at the fashion displayed on the show.

The prizes and the show's focus on the creative process drew a strong pool of experienced and novice designers, because, as Jane Lipsitz, executive producer of *Project Runway* during the show's Bravo run, claims, "there isn't an outlet or an opportunity like this ... for designers on a national scale" (Aurthur E1). As the show gained popularity, later seasons featured more established designers who saw *Project Runway* as a vehicle to jumpstart or reinvigorate their careers; season four runner-up Rami Kashou, who ran a successful design studio with clients like Jessica Alba before coming on the show, said, "I think that *Project Runway* can introduce my work to a larger audience" ("Sew Us What You Got").

Just as young and unestablished designers saw an opportunity to open their doors to new clients, part of *Project Runway*'s appeal to the audience is that the show pulls back the curtain on the insular world of fashion. The show let everyday Americans into what executive producer Desiree Gruber calls the "invite-only world" (qtd. in Bruce), which especially appealed to a young, affluent audience who, despite their socioeconomic standing, were unlikely to attend fashion week or go behind the scenes of a fashion icon's studio. Nina Garcia, one of the show's regular judges and longtime fashion editor at *Elle* and *Marie Claire* magazines, reflects that "*Project Runway* came at a time when the [fashion] industry was going through a kind of democratization.... People wanted to know how the designers worked" (qtd. in Mell 26). Thus, the audience and the designers both benefitted from the arrangement, leading to a steady supply of both viewers and potential contestants even as *Project Runway* entered its eleventh year on the air in 2015.

The success of *Project Runway* could not have been predicted given its beginnings on Bravo. In 1980, Bravo began its life as the first television channel dedicated to film and the performing arts ("About Us"). NBC Universal acquired the channel in 2002, and Lauren Zalaznick took the reins as president in 2004 with an eye toward changing the network's content and audience (Feuer 186). At the time of *Project Runway*'s premiere, Bravo was reeling from the runaway success of reality show *Queer Eye for the Straight Guy* (2003–2007), which helped rebrand the network as a destination for young, socially progressive professionals. *Project Runway* debuted on the cable network in 2004, where it would run until Lifetime purchased the show in 2008. *Project Runway* was conceived by Bravo as part of its new strategy to reach "a small but affluent audience, the kind that advertisers covet" (Dominus MM38). Bravo identified its audience as "urban gay men and single female professionals" (Dominus MM38), and *Project Runway*'s contestants were largely drawn from a similar pool.

*Project Runway* got off to a rough start on Bravo, where its series premiere was seen by only 345,000 viewers (Aurthur E1). Zalaznick marketed the program by playing the first three episodes nonstop through the winter holiday season, hoping to gain an audience by catching viewers searching among the channels during their holiday breaks (Dominus MM38). The gamble worked: viewers tuned in to the marathons, and by the end of the show's first season, the viewer numbers had grown to 1.2 million ("*Project Runway* in Limbo"), and the show had been nominated for an Emmy award in the category for outstanding reality competition (Aurthur E1). Bravo and *Project Runway* ultimately reached the most desired demographic of advertisers, women aged 18 to 49, and its viewers were among the most educated and upscale of any network (Dominus MM38). Audiences were drawn by the network's "knack for flattering the viewers' sense of their own good taste" (Dominus MM38). Clearly, the show was popular with audiences and advertisers, and a second season was quickly ordered.

Reality television was certainly not new to the American television viewer, who had seen *Survivor* (CBS, 2000–present) and *Big Brother* (CBS, 2000–present) on network television for years, but Jane Feuer argues that Bravo reinvented itself and the reality television genre in the early 2000s with *Queer Eye* and *Project Runway*, shows that "assume a definition of celebrity that includes talent, whether for dressmaking or cooking, that defies Daniel J. Boorstin's definition of 'celebrity' as being famous for being famous" (186). *Project Runway* announced its membership in the club of talent-based reality shows from the very first episode, when designers were charged with making a glamorous outfit for a night on the town using only materials purchased from a grocery store with a $50-budget ("Innovation"). A large part of the show's appeal is seeing how designers solve the problem set before them in a creative and innovative way. Each season, designers were asked not just to show the judges and viewers their point of view as a designer, but also to push their limits, creating outfits for all occasions, from haute couture to avant-garde to ready-to-wear outfits for major commercial fashion lines. When the designers were drawn out of their comfort zones, whether they rose to the occasion or floundered, the process was interesting to watch.

Andrea Wong, CEO of Lifetime Networks, arrived at the network in 2007 with plans to reinvigorate the flat or falling ratings of Lifetime's programming (Sacks 39). Wong, who had worked on reality shows such as *Dancing with the Stars* (ABC, 2005–present) and *The Bachelor* (ABC, 2002–present), asked Harvey Weinstein, whose Weinstein Company owned *Project Run-*

*way*, if there was any way Lifetime could acquire the rights to the show once its five-season contract with Bravo expired. Weinstein saw the opportunity to create "one of the biggest smash hits of all time on cable TV" if "the hipster from Bravo's audience followed us and the housewives on Lifetime could fall in love with us" (qtd. in Sacks 40). A long legal battle concerning whether NBCUniversal should have been given first right of refusal for *Project Runway*'s future seasons followed, and the show's future seemed in jeopardy as courts ordered Lifetime to not promote the show while the case was mediated. Finally, after years of legal wrangling, the Weinstein Company admitted fault, and the two entities settled out of court, with Weinstein paying damages to NBCUniversal (Bruce). The move to Lifetime also meant a change in production companies. Wong brought in Bunim/Murray, best known for their work on the genre-making reality show *The Real World* (MTV, 1992–present), to replace former production company Magical Elves, who chose to remain with Bravo and NBCUniversal (Bruce).

Lifetime's acquisition of *Project Runway* harkened back to the network's earlier strategy of purchasing known products to re-air on the network, such as made-for-television movies and sitcoms like *Designing Women* (CBS, 1986–1993) and *The Golden Girls* (NBC, 1985–1992). With *Project Runway*, Lifetime bought a current property with a built-in fan following, much in the same way it had purchased the sitcom *The Days and Nights of Molly Dodd* from NBC in 1988 and produced additional episodes to air on Lifetime (Hundley 176; Wilson 104).

Lifetime was confident that they could draw *Project Runway* fans to the network to watch the show; as Tim Gunn told the media, a "DVR doesn't know the difference" as to whether a show is aired on one station or another (qtd. in Sacks 41), so Lifetime felt confident that *Project Runway* fans would tune in to the show on Lifetime. At the same time, Lifetime would have to draw its regular viewers to *Project Runway*: in the weeks before the show debuted on Lifetime, research showed that only four percent of the network's viewers were aware of *Project Runway*'s existence, never mind that the show was coming soon to their beloved network (Sacks 41). However, the great overarching question surrounding Lifetime's acquisition of *Project Runway* was whether the network could successfully woo their new audience to the network's other programming and translate *Project Runway*'s success into better overall ratings for the flagging network. It was evident that there was a disconnect between the established *Project Runway* viewer and the Lifetime viewer that the network would have to bridge in order to earn a return on the investment it had made in the show.

During the premiere of season six, the network attempted to draw new Lifetime viewers to other shows, airing commercials for popular returning shows *Army Wives* (2007–2013) and *Drop Dead Diva* (2009–2014), along with the new (and ultimately short-lived) sitcom *Sherri* (2009) during the show (Levine 5). To win over new fans for *Project Runway* from its existing pool of viewers, Lifetime created one of the biggest marketing campaigns the network had ever seen, which they hoped would make up for the months-long injunction against advertising that they had been under while the legal case between the networks was argued (Schwartz 24–27). The advertising campaign reached out to women who had never seen the show by presenting them with fans of all ages talking about their love for *Project Runway*, emphasizing that the show was not only aimed at fashion insiders but at people just like them ("To the Nines"). Unlike Bravo, which emphasized *Project Runway*'s ability to give viewers a glimpse into an elite world, Lifetime communicated that anyone could participate in fashion and have an opinion about style, quality, and runway appeal—quite a powerful statement made to Lifetime's older audience, who were told by advertisers that their opinions were less valuable than those of 18- to 34-year-olds.

While Lifetime clearly stated, both in relation to *Project Runway* and in general, that they remained committed to providing "television for women" even after they dropped that phrase as their official tagline in 2012, the network refused to explicitly define exactly who the Lifetime woman was, though demographic data showed that the typical Lifetime viewer was older than 34 and belonged to an upscale social class. This lack of limitations benefitted Lifetime when it acquired *Project Runway* because the network did not need to bend the show to conform to a certain demographic's expectations. David Hillman, vice president for reality programming at Lifetime and an executive producer for *Project Runway*, stated that the show brought Lifetime a "younger, more affluent demographic" (qtd. in Mell 165), but the show's impact on the network had even broader implications: "It's allowed us to create new shows that appeal to today's contemporary woman. In many ways, I feel it's allowed Lifetime to make its brand hipper, bolder, and more relevant" (qtd. in Mell 165). One thing Lifetime gained when it acquired *Project Runway* was a show with a young, diverse cast. Designers on *Project Runway* have come from all walks of life and represented varying ethnicities, sexual orientations, nationalities, and gender expressions. Though Lifetime had already featured quite a bit of diversity in many of its shows, such as the racially diverse cast of *Army Wives* and *Any Day Now* (1998–2002), viewers drawn to Lifetime by *Project Runway* may have been surprised and pleased to find similar representation of contemporary America among Lifetime's other shows.

The legal battle that surrounded *Project Runway*'s move to Lifetime created tension and worry among its diehard fans, which can be summarized succinctly in the words of Jon Carroll: "There was some extremely boring and contentious disagreement between Bravo and the Weinstein Co., which wanted to move the program to Lifetime, the channel of women-in-peril movies, and hire a new production company to run it. Well, litigation, countercharges, blah blah, but in the end *Project Runway* ended up on Lifetime, where it is the same, but different" (E12). Fans, bloggers, and media critics expressed concerns over many aspects of the move, including Lifetime's reputation to the show's new shooting location of Los Angeles, but gender and sexuality were at the core of many fans' anxieties about the move.

Critics noted that Lifetime's discourse surrounding the acquisition of the show focused on the show's appeal to women, while *Project Runway*'s audience on Bravo included a large proportion of men, both gay and straight (Shafrir). Meredith Wagner, Lifetime's executive vice president of public affairs and corporate communications, painted a welcoming picture, calling the network "inclusive" and stating her hope that men would follow the show to Lifetime, but she still reiterated, "We really love women. And we care about women. We put them first" (qtd. in Shafrir), indicating that while men were welcome to join in, women would still be the priority in terms of programming and advertising. This put male fans of the show in the position of having to fit into a new community which they perceived to be less concerned about their needs and desires than Bravo had been.

Another frequently-raised concern was sexuality: *Project Runway* featured a large number of gay designers, to the point that straight men on the show often talk about being in the minority among the contestants. Bravo's reputation as a gay-friendly network in comparison to Lifetime's image as a network for housewives from middle America certainly increased some viewers' anxiety about the move. Some wondered if Lifetime would censor contestant interviews that referred to sexual orientation or reduce the voices of gay men to those of "an accessory in the new Lifetime, around for camp value and being able to tell you if your butt looks big, but with no programming around them" (Shafrir), while others wonder if "Lifetime will cast saps and nice ladies instead of crazy gay guys" (Sicha 55) to appeal Lifetime's older female viewers. Since reality television was an important factor in normalizing LGBT (lesbian, gay, bisexual, and transgender) visibility and was one of the first locations that allowed gay and lesbian people to be themselves, rather than playing a stereotype, on television (Gamson 228–229), viewers' unspoken concern lay in the possibility that progress made in the fight for realistic representation for gay characters on television would be set back by the move to Lifetime.

Perhaps these fears were overblown or even the result of stereotypical thinking; when Lifetime purchased the rights to *Project Runway*, it was already employing Bravo alumni Carson Kressley, one of the stars of Bravo's breakout hit *Queer Eye for the Straight Guy*. Kressley's makeover show, *How to Look Good Naked*, ran for two seasons in 2008 and focused on building women's self-esteem in addition to providing them with a new wardrobe

(Shafrir), so Lifetime had already demonstrated that it was not opposed to putting gay characters on the channel. Indeed, many of Lifetime's original movies had dealt with sexual orientation explicitly, including *Any Mother's Son* (1997), which told the story of a mother searching for answers after her gay son was murdered during his navy service, to *What Makes a Family* (2001), about a lesbian woman who fights for custody rights to her daughter after her partner dies, to the story of the murder of a transwoman, *A Girl Like Me: The Gwen Araujo Story* (2006). Despite popular perception, Lifetime has not shied away from bringing gay and lesbian characters to the small screen, and *Project Runway* was no different. Joshua Gamson writes in 2014 that both the Lifetime and Bravo versions of *Project Runway* have succeeded in creating a comfortable space for LGBT designers and fans:

> A particular social world, inhabited by gay men and women, becomes visible; the rare straight male designer struggles socially as an outsider, literally unable to even get some of the jokes. Here, homosexuality is neither a singular clichéd role nor a source of dramatic conflict. Instead, one sees between gay men, between gay men and women, and between women various kinds of dramatic gay back-stories (a contestant cries to his boyfriend, another misses his son, another gains the courage to come out as HIV positive) and interpersonal drama that are unrelated to sexual identity. That is, one sees a version of collective queer life, in which there are many sorts of "gays," in which heterosexual masculinity is irrelevant or even scorned, in which nonsexual intimacy between men and women is central, and in which gay men build nonsexual friendships and enmities [239].

It seems that an element of stereotyping and panic was at play when critics and fans wondered if Lifetime would erase the gay presence on *Project Runway*, and the network assuaged fears by not intervening in a successful formula: they simply allowed *Project Runway* to continue casting talented characters regardless of sexuality and encouraged the cast to express themselves openly on the show, just as they had on Bravo.

It is clear that a large part of, if not the main reason for, Lifetime's motivation for to purchase *Project Runway* was a very heated desire to appeal to a younger viewer. Lifetime's audience skewed older than Bravo's in 2008, with a large portion of its audience aged over 55. This demographic is less desirable to advertisers than the 18–34 age group that *Project Runway* typically attracted. Sarah Banet-Weiser believes that this endless hunt for the "right" viewer is contrary to cable networks' original mission: "It seems like the narrowcasting and niche marketing that was part of the promise of cable is going back to the broadcast model, where they are all going for a similar audience, 18- to 34-year-olds" (qtd. in Salkin ST2). While Lifetime presents itself as a network that welcomes all women, it is also a business that relies on advertising dollars to sustain itself. A show that draws younger women who are perceived to have more buying power would draw more advertising money, which could then theoretically support original programming for a more diverse audience. Of course, Lifetime hoped that their current demographic of older women would also watch *Project Runway*, bringing the number of viewers even higher, but they depended on drawing the lucrative 18- to 34-year-old crowd that other networks were also courting for the network's continued success.

The audience that Lifetime hoped to draw from Bravo was not only defined by their youth and affluent socioeconomic status: Bravo had carefully cultivated an online presence for *Project Runway*, and Lifetime could expand upon the digital presence that the audience had come to expect from its show. For the show's second season, Bravo had partnered with then-hip social networking site MySpace.com to stream a ten-minute preview of the season premiere before the show's debut in December 2005. Bravo targeted MySpace.com because of the site's appeal to younger consumers, the ability of users to share interesting content with one another, and the fact that the site's users skewed toward artists, musicians, and other creative types who would appreciate the show's emphasis on talent and design. The promotion translated to a large bump in traffic to the network's own website, bravotv.com (Whitney, "Bravo's Viral" 11). By the third season, viewers could sign up to have text messages from their favorite contestant sent to their phones during the episode with gossip and insight into the challenges (Brown 17). *Project Runway* also provided Bravo with its first opportunity to engage in home viewer voting; during the third season finale, the audience was invited to vote on the designs and the judges' decisions in real time, with the results displayed onscreen during the broadcast. Though the results did not affect the outcome of the competition, each person who voted was entered in a competition to win a video iPod (Hibberd 5). *Project Runway's* audience was clearly comfortable with technology, as was furthered demonstrated by the show's season three finale episode ranking among the top thirty iTunes downloads at the time (Whitney, "iTunes Effect" 40).

Lifetime continued the practice of engaging viewers through what came to be called "second screen" technology—that is, the use of a computer, tablet, or mobile phone to interact with content presented on television during a show's initial airing. Viewers were invited to vote in polls during the broadcast, which Evan Silverman, senior vice president for digital media at Lifetime, says brings excitement to a recorded program. Perhaps more importantly, in the era of ubiquitous DVR usage, being able to vote in polls and see the results on screen immediately encourages viewers to watch the primetime broadcast rather than delaying viewing until later. Not only does this attract more viewers for the all-important ratings numbers, but Lifetime receives money from advertisers only when the ads are viewed within three days of the episode's premiere (Dreier). Thus, the interactive features both help the viewer feel more engaged with Lifetime's programming and brings revenue to the network.

To further entice *Project Runway* viewers to Lifetime's digital world, during season six, myLifetime.com provided for the first time full streaming episodes the same week that the episode aired, in addition to on demand options through cable providers. Behind-the-scenes clips aimed to create a sense of intimacy and participation among the website's visitors ("Lifetime Digital"). Among the website's featured videos were extended judging commentaries, which revealed every moment of the judges' critiques with the designers, which can be interpreted as a rare moment of transparency in the reality television world and an attempt to create a sense of authenticity and reassure viewers that the show is not being tampered with by Lifetime producers ("Lifetime Digital"). In the same season, Lifetime debuted a centralized social media hub, The Project Runway Buzz Room, which aggregated Twitter and Facebook messages that used hashtags about *Project Runway* and added content from designers, models, former show participants, and bloggers ("Lifetime Digital"). All in all, Lifetime encouraged viewers both new and old to interact with the show and the Lifetime website in order to create an engaged audience who would tune in each week in time to bring in advertising dollars, then bring their eyes to the website to view additional advertising.

By the time Lifetime purchased *Project Runway*, the show had a history of successful product tie-ins and corporate partnerships. In the debut season on Bravo, product partners included Banana Republic, Cotton, and L'Oréal Paris ("*Project Runway* in Limbo"). Sponsors had the opportunity to weave their products into the fabric of the show by mentoring designers in a challenge, such as the Banana Republic challenge in season one, or by providing their products for competitors' use, as in the Bluefly accessories wall or the L'Oréal Paris makeup room. One of the prizes offered in to the winner throughout the Bravo seasons was a fashion spread in *Elle* magazine, where one of the show's judges, Nina Garcia, held the title of fashion director. The partnership saw *Elle*'s circulation and advertising rates jump dramatically from 2008 (Smith and Nitke 8). Lifetime was able to draw its own pool of sponsors to the show and continued the practice of integrating product placement ranging from luxury cars to fast food restaurants into the weekly challenges, as well as offering prizes sponsored by major brands including HP, Lexus, and Lord & Taylor.

When Lifetime purchased the rights to *Project Runway*, Lifetime executives promised fans that no changes would be made to the heart of the show in interviews in major outlets like Entertainment Weekly ("Project Relaunch") and television advertising on Lifetime. New showrunners Bunim/Murray were also given the dictate to not alter the already-successful product that Lifetime had purchased (Schwartz 25). Producer Sara Rea confirmed these instructions in a 2013 interview, saying,

"The directive that we got from Lifetime when Bunim/Murray took over the show and I became the showrunner was, 'We want the same exact show. We didn't buy this show to change it. It's successful.' So it was the same, the same, the same. We heard that to the point of ad nauseam, to be honest. But then a few seasons later, we got to start making changes and updates" [qtd. in Eakin].

Jonathan Murray, executive producer with Bunim/Murray, agrees with Rea's interpretation of events and adds that "our goal was to understand how our show DNA fit into Lifetime's DNA. How to keep the show authentic to the original fans and blend that to bring in more viewers" (qtd. in Bruce). Early reviews confirmed that the formula of the show felt essentially unchanged in season six, from the challenges to the contestant pool, which featured "several archetypes without whom competitive reality television could not thrive" (Bellafante C1).

While it was reassuring fans that nothing would change with their beloved show, Lifetime marked its intention to expand the *Project Runway* brand by airing a two hour special, *Project Runway: All-Star Challenge* immediately before the premiere of the long-delayed season six. This show served two purposes: first, it reassured nervous viewers that the Lifetime appreciated the same things about *Project Runway* as its loyal audience, namely, the characters. Eight former Runway contestants competed in this single-night event for a prize of $100,000, with season two finalist Daniel Vosovic winning the competition. The reappearance of familiar faces competing in familiar challenges provided continuity for viewers. Memorable characters from previous seasons would also be featured on Lifetime's website in the form of blogs recapping and critiquing the show, including Nick Verreos and Andrae Gonzalo from season two and Chris March from season four, providing a link between Bravo and Lifetime for the audience ("Lifetime Digital"). Secondly, the all-star show demonstrated that Lifetime would experiment with *Project Runway* spin-offs that expanded the Lifetime brand, with the next example of this strategy coming mere hours later in the form of *Models of the Runway*, a half-hour companion show that documented the experiences of the models who worked with the designers on the main show.

The show's models had been featured on *Project Runway* in the Bravo years to varying extents; a challenge occasionally featured the models as the designers' clients, and early seasons featured a model selection at the beginning of the show, in which the previous week's winning designer could select which model he or she would like to work with that week. Lifetime's *Models of the Runway* expanded the models' role in the show and gave audiences a glimpse into the world of working models, including the competing professional priorities of the models on the show, who were often shown going on auditions or being offered modeling jobs that would interfere with their *Project Runway* schedule. Heidi Klum hosted and acted as a mentor to the models, sometimes giving the models tips or discussing the profession with them. This show was likely an attempt to draw more women to *Project Runway* by showing more of the entirely-female model group and giving the audience a glimpse into what is often imagined as a glamorous profession.[2] At the end of each episode, model selection for the following episode occurred, meaning that *Project Runway* viewers who skipped *Models of the Runway* would miss what had always been an important part of the show; Lifetime must have hoped that this would entice viewers to watch the entire half hour in addition to *Project Runway*'s hour. However, ratings for *Models of the Runway* were not as good as the network had hoped, and the show was cancelled after two seasons. The half hour that had been allotted to *Models of the Runway* was used to extend *Project Runway* to an hour and a half in length, where it remains today. Heidi Klum stated that the network would use the extra time to show viewers more of what goes on behind the scenes of the show, including longer judging sessions and more attention to the "stories" on the show, such as arguments between designers and sewing struggles (Nguyen).

After *Models of the Runway* was cancelled, the models disappeared into the background of *Project Runway*. With the additional half hour, the audience still does not see much of the models, as model selection has been eliminated from the show. The only times in which the models are mentioned on the show are in relation to design problems: sometimes a model is bigger or smaller than a designer expects, leading to problems with the fit of a particular outfit, for example. Although the designers are seen chatting with their models, the emphasis on the relationship between designers and their models that was a recurring theme through *Project Runway*'s early seasons is notably absent in later seasons. The models are thus reduced to little more than an apparatus for clothes, which some would argue is the model's traditional role in fashion. As with many short-lived reality TV shows, *Models of the Runway* was never released on DVD, even as a special feature on the season six *Project Runway* DVDs. The experiment that brought women to the forefront and presented modeling as hard work and an often less-than-glamorous profession was erased from the network's website and the collective memory of the audience.

After its record-breaking premiere on Lifetime, ratings for *Project Runway*'s sixth season dropped nearly a third over the course of the season, falling below past seasons' viewer numbers. While some decline was certainly expected as new viewers who sampled the show decided not to continue watching, critics lobbed a volley of complaints at Lifetime's new gem. The show's move from New York to Los Angeles, intended to accommodate Heidi Klum's desire to be closer to family and to engage the celebrity fashion culture that is unique to Los Angeles, meant that regular judges and show cornerstones Nina Garcia and Michael Kors could not regularly participate as business commitments kept them in New York. The audience felt the absence of the pair's colorful and cutting commentary, while the series overall suffered from a lack of consistent judging as guest judges looked for different things each week and did not develop relationships with the designers. Indeed, some commentators even remarked that the guest judges did not seem to be able to intelligently talk about a fashion—a skill that the regular judges had honed in their years of work on the show—and sometimes seemed lost as to the parameters of the challenges the designers had been given (Carroll E12). Lifetime executives were aware of the challenges the location presented, and while they appreciated the opportunities that the Los Angeles location presented them, such as working on red carpet looks in the city that invented the red carpet, the show returned to New York the next season, where it remains to this day. "New York was and is such a huge character in itself on the show ... that year, we were missing a character," judge Michael Kors reflects (qtd. in Mell).

The season six designers themselves were criticized for being too reserved: "Where's the Santino? Or even the Christian?" laments Jennifer Armstrong (12), referring to the colorful characters of the previous seasons. However, as the season was filmed, the designers were aware of the legal battles surrounding the show, and the question as to whether the show would ever be allowed to air dampened the mood in the workroom considerably. In fact, the finalists were not even allowed on the runway to introduce their collections at Fashion Week for fear of spoiling the final results, so the top three designers missed an important opportunity to speak directly to the fashion community that had been afforded to all the previous seasons' finalists (Stetler C3). The 13-month hiatus also meant that the fashion shown on the show was a year out of date, which in the world of fashion can bring drastic changes in popular styles, leading to the fear that the runway show would seem outmoded (Armstrong 12). Lifetime made moves to correct some of the problems critics identified, moving the show back to New York City for the seventh season, and trusting that the perceived problems with the contestants' lack of enthusiasm and performance that arose from the show's legal troubles would disappear in subsequent seasons.

Lifetime did allow *Project Runway* to evolve over the course of its tenure on the network. In season twelve, the producers made a change that at least made a gesture toward the idea of making the judging as fair as possible: the introduction of the anonymous runway show. In previous seasons, the judges were aware of which designer created which look during the runway show, which allowed their knowledge of the designers' previous work to influence their scores for the current week. By implementing anonymous judging, the show—and Lifetime—allow the designers a fresh chance to impress the judges each week, free from any preconceived notions. This move, combined with Lifetime's earlier efforts to put the full judging sessions online for viewers to peruse, suggests that Lifetime wants to promote a transparency and fairness that rarely exists in everyday life.

Another change made in the twelfth season played on the popularity and respect the audience has long had for show mentor Tim Gunn. Unlike previous seasons, Tim Gunn was allowed to interact with the judges after the runway show, explaining the creative process as he witnessed it in the workroom and answering judges' questions, increasing his influence on the proceedings and adding a more human dimension to the judging. The show also introduced a new element, the Tim Gunn save, which allowed him to override the judges' decision and keep one designer in the competition after he or she was chosen for elimination one time per season. While the save was perhaps intended to allow a strong contestant who experienced one bad week the chance to stay in the competition, the initial results suggest that Gunn used the save to reward good people, rather than good designers; in the first season when the save was in play, Gunn chose to save Justin LeBlanc, a designer who had yet to see great competitive success during the season but who had a compelling backstory due to being a Deaf designer who had formed many friendships with the other designers. Whether Gunn saw potential for great design or potential for great ratings in LeBlanc, the designer made good on his save and reached the finals of the season. In the following season, Gunn upped the drama by saving a designer not immediately after the runway show, but the at the beginning of the episode following her elimination. Once again, the saved designer, Char, had not particularly distinguished herself as a designer, but Gunn felt her absence left "a void in the workroom" ("Priceless Runway"). Again, the saved designer made the finals and presented a collection at Fashion Week, though her results in the remaining challenges usually left her near the bottom of the pack. Gunn said in 2012 that *Project Runway* "teaches that good qualities pay off. Working hard, playing nice and not being a diva" (qtd. in Bruce), and it seems that Gunn used his power to reinstate contestants to reward those who he perceived as having these qualities. Without a doubt, the Tim Gunn save added an element of drama and tension throughout the season, first as viewers wondered whether Gunn would use his save on this week's eliminated contestant, then as the audience watched the saved designer closely to see if he or she would put the second chance to good use through the remainder of the season. Thus far, the two "saved" contestants seem to have benefitted from Gunn's demonstration of faith in their abilities and returned to the workroom with a new sense of confidence.

There have certainly been changes to *Project Runway*'s formula since the show moved to Lifetime that create drama and tension within the show, but whether these changes are part of the natural evolution of a reality program that has been on the air for over a decade or are the artificial result of producer influence is not clear. Executive director David Hillman argues that the production team has not interfered in the show's direction, but he says, "I personally love it when something surprising happens, like Mya quitting in Season 7 and Gretchen winning in Season 8. It polarized the audience, which again reinforces the authenticity of the show and its subjective nature. It's not produced drama. This stuff happens organically" (qtd. in Mell 165). There is much in this quote that reveals Lifetime's current perspective on *Project Runway*. First, Hillman believes that a divided audience benefits the show, and that conflict between the viewers is an authentic state. In this way, Lifetime at least gives lip service to the idea that there is no one authentic way to be a woman—at least, a woman consuming fashion. Women will have different opinions, and they have the freedom to express those opinions within and without the spaces Lifetime has created for discussion and community. In encouraging discussion and personal expression, Lifetime encourages women to own their opinions and state their preferences to each other and the network.

Hillman emphasizes the subjective nature of the show, with the implication that women are expected to think for themselves and pick their favorite designers, just as the judges do, and if their choices vary from those of the judges, that does not mean that the viewer is uneducated or unsophisticated; that women are encouraged to reject the idea of a single authority who can determine which opinion is the correct one is a powerful message. An example of this idea of subjectivity is the fan favorite competition, in which viewers can vote to award a cash prize to their favorite designer of the season; there are no parameters to the competition, so women can choose to vote for the nicest designer, the one who creates the most wearable fashion, the most outrageous character, or simply a designer that the viewer relates to, giving the viewer power to communicate to the network and the world what she holds dear, which could be very different from the judges' opinions. Finally, the concept of organic conflict is particularly interesting. Women have traditionally played the role of mediators, minimizing and smoothing over conflict at home and at work. Hillman and *Project Runway* tell women that conflict is a part of life, and women can, and should, disagree with authority and defend their choices, as the designers explain their work on the runway, without losing their place in Lifetime's network for women.

In the press release advertising season fourteen, a clue to *Project Runway*'s future appeared without comment: one of the featured guest judges for the season is Hannah Davis, who is listed as "Sports Illustrated swimsuit model and host of *Project Runway Junior*" ("Lifetime's *Project Runway* Announces"). *Project Runway Junior* is a spin-off show set to debut in the fall of 2015 that will feature teens aged fourteen to seventeen, with Tim Gunn acting as mentor and season four winner Christian Siriano as a regular judge

("About *Project Runway Junior*"). Lifetime's goals for this series appear to be twofold: by featuring two well-known *Project Runway* cast members, Lifetime hopes to engage longtime fans while also bringing in a young tween or teen audience, who can imagine themselves competing on the show. Even after *Project Runway: Threads*, a show where teens and tweens competed in a single-episode fashion design competition, failed, Lifetime did not give up on the idea of teen designers, and *Project Runway Junior* will be a season-long competition that more closely follows the formula established by the original series. Time will tell if the show finds an audience compelling enough to keep it on the air, as Lifetime has demonstrated clearly with its various *Project Runway* spin-offs that they are not afraid to cancel a show that fails to live up to expectations, even if it is linked to a known and popular brand. When the world of modeling proved unpopular, *Models of the Runway* was replaced with an extra half hour of *Project Runway*'s known brand. Fans of Bravo's original series were treated to a show featuring two of its most popular character in *On the Road with Austin & Santino* (2010), while a new show based on jewelry design copied *Project Runway*'s formula, *Project Accessory* (2011), failed to capture the magic of the original show. Though many *Project Runway* spin-offs have been launched and cancelled, Lifetime continues to search for more ways to capitalize on the unprecedented success of the show by targeting women with different interests, demonstrating again that Lifetime sees itself as a gathering place for women at different points in their lives who can gather around good television.

## Notes

1. First season winner Jay McCarroll declined his winnings, saying that the contract required that the Weinstein Co. own a ten percent stake in his future brand. This clause was removed from future winners' contracts (Senior).

2. Ironically, the show recalls *Project Runway* creator Harvey Weinstein's initial concept for the show, which was to be called *Model Apartment* and feature models rather than designers. Later, the initial plans for *Project Runway* eliminated the models from the show altogether before landing on the current formula (Bruce).

## Works Cited

"About *Project Runway* Junior." www.MyLifetime.com. Lifetime Entertainment Services, LLC, n.d. Web. 5 Aug. 2015.

"About Us." BravoTV.com. Bravo Media LLC, n.d. Web. 5 Aug. 2015.

Armstrong, Jennifer. "*Project Runway*'s Problems." *Entertainment Weekly* 6 Nov. 2009: 11–12. Print.

Aurthur, Kate. "Another Catwalk for Fashion Series." *New York Times* 6 Dec. 2005: E1. Print.

Bellafante, Ginia. "Designers, Start Your Engines for Season 6." *New York Times* 20 Aug. 2009: C1. Print.

Bibel, Sara. "Thursday Cable Ratings: Republican Presidential Debate Wins Night,

*The Kelly File, The Daily Show, Teen Mom 2, Project Runway* & More." *TV by the Numbers*: Zap2It/Tribune Digital Ventures, 7 Aug. 2015. Web. 23 Sept. 2015.

Brown, Karen. "Bravo Fashions Mobile, Interactive *Runway* Fare." *Multichannel News* 10 July 2006: 17. Print.

Bruce, Leslie. "'Fashion Is Not for Sissies': An Oral History of *Project Runway*'s First 10 Years." HollywoodReporter.com. The Hollywood Reporter, 18 Aug. 2012. Web. 5 Aug. 2015.

Carroll, Jon. "The Problem with *Project Runway*." *San Francisco Chronicle* 30 Sept. 2009: E12. Print.

Dominus, Susan. "The Affluencer." *New York Times Magazine* 2 Nov. 2008: MM38. Print.

Dreier, Troy. "Get Your Second Screen Off My First Screen." *Streaming Media* Apr. 2014: 19. Print.

Eakin, Marah. "What Goes On Behind the Scenes at *Project Runway*?" *AV Club*. Onion Inc., 13 Oct. 2013. Web. 5 Aug. 2015.

Feuer, Jane. "'Quality' Reality and the Bravo Media Reality Series." *Camera Obscura* 30.88 (2015): 185–195. Print.

Gamson, Joshua. "'It's Been a While Since I've Seen, Like, Straight People': Queer Visibility in the Age of Postnetwork Reality Television." *A Companion to Reality Television*. Ed. Laurie Ouellette. Malden, MA: Wiley Blackwell, 2014. 227–246. Print.

Hibberd, James. "Bravo Extending *Runway* Finale." *Television Week* 6 Feb. 2006: 5–18. Print.

Hundley, Heather. "The Evolution of Gendercasting: The Lifetime Television Network—'Television for Women.'" *Journal of Popular Film and Television* 29.4 (2002): 174–181. Print.

"Innovation." *Project Runway*. Bravo. 1 Dec. 2004. Television.

Levine, Stuart. "*Runway* Sews Up Record for Lifetime." *Daily Variety* 24 Aug. 2009: 5. Web.

"Lifetime Digital to Provide Unprecedented Level of Coverage for New Season of *Project Runway* and the All-New *Models of the Runway*." *PR Newswire*. N.p., 20 Aug. 2009. Web. 5 Aug. 2015.

"Lifetime's *Project Runway* Announces Season 14 Designers & Guest Judges Including Bella Thorne, Tracee Ellis Ross & Kiernan Shipka." *TV by the Numbers*. Tribune Digital Ventures, 7 July 2015. Web. 9 Aug. 2015.

"Mad Dash Mayhem." *Project Runway*. Lifetime. 14 Nov. 2007. Television.

Mell, Elia, ed. *Project Runway: The Show That Changed Fashion*. New York: Weinstein Books, 2012. Print.

Nguyen, Hahn. "*Project Runway* 8: Heidi Klum Talks New Format, New Twist and Guest Judges." *Zap2It*: Zap2It/Tribune Digital Ventures, 15 July 2015. Web. 4 Oct. 2015.

"Priceless Runway." *Project Runway*. Lifetime. 4 Sept. 2014. Television.

"*Project Runway* in Limbo." *Mediaweek* 21 Feb. 2005: 6+. Print.

Sacks, Danielle. "The Escape Artist." *Fast Company* 138 (2009): 39–43. Print.

Salkin, Allen. "In Bed with *Runway*: A Lifetime Story." *New York Times* 13 Apr. 2008: ST2. Print.

Schwartz, Missy. "Project Relaunch." *Entertainment Weekly* 5 June 2009: 24–28. Print.

Senior, Jennifer. "The Near-Fame Experience." *New York Magazine*. New York Media LLC, 6 Aug. 2007. Web. 5 Oct. 2015.

"Sew Us What You Got." *Project Runway*. Bravo. 6 Aug. 2015. Television.

Shafrir, Doree. "Lifetime, in Search of Makeover, Lures Klum, Gunn and Gays." *New York Observer* 30 Apr. 2008. *LexisNexis.* Web. 15 Sept. 2015.

Sicha, Choire. "Relax—It's Just TV." *Advocate* 1 July 2008: 53–55. Print.

Smith, Stephanie D., and Barbara Nitke. "Fashion Television Continues Steady Growth." *Women's Wear Daily* 19 Aug. 2009: 8. Print.

Stetler, Brian. "*Project Runway* Battle Dampens Fashion Week." *New York Times* 21 Feb. 2009: C3. Print.

"To the Nines: Dissecting Lifetime's *Project Runway* Catwalk." *CableFAX* 26 Aug. 2009. *Business Insights: Essentials.* Web. 5 Oct. 2015.

Whitney, Daisy. "Bravo's Viral *Project.*" *Television Week* 12 Dec. 2005: 11–18. Print.

_____. "Programs Feeling the iTunes Effect." *Television Week* 27 Mar. 2006: 40. Print.

# PART II

# Original Episodic Programming

# Feminizing Militainment
## Post/Post-Politics on Army Wives

### Mary Douglas Vavrus

Writing in *Television Week*, *Army Wives* creator and executive producer Katherine Fugate explains the program's broad appeal: "At its core, *Army Wives* is about love: love of our families, our friends, our country.... America's presence in Iraq is controversial. Some might wonder how a show can thrive against that backdrop. But our show isn't about Iraq. It's about relationships and people who make sacrifices" (12). The relationships Fugate references here are not simply those friend, family, and romantic relationships that form the core of the program; implicitly, she also points to the relationship between the program's producers and the Pentagon, a type of strategic alliance characteristic of Lifetime—the network of *Army Wives*. Such alliances have had a mixed record overall for Lifetime, but its partnership with the Department of Defense's (DOD) Pentagon Entertainment Office was integral to the success of this program that brought Lifetime its highest ratings during its seven season run (2007–2013).[1]

In this essay—a feminist analysis of the discourse and political economy of *Army Wives* across its seven seasons—I argue that the program's portrayal of military life at Fort Marshall results chiefly from this partnership and constructs a postfeminist, postracial Army that advocates military solutions to resolve problems that women and girls face. *Army Wives'* infusion of contemporary martial themes into a woman-identified serial drama fits well with Lifetime's telefeminism and fulfills the Pentagon's mandate that its supported projects serve to recruit as well as entertain.

Through storylines including those that tout joining the Army as a smart career move for women, particularly those of color; promote the GI Bill as a life-enhancing benefit for service women; reward military men when they eschew patriarchal behavior and embrace women as their equals; and illuminate the problem of gender violence while obscuring the power relations that underpin it, *Army Wives* produces a regime of representation about military life and war. With the conventions of militainment, this post-political regime obscures the military's gravest threats, constituting service instead as a difficult but responsible life choice for women and girls. *Army Wives* follows a core group of five women and one man: psychiatrist Roland Burton, married to Lieutenant Colonel (later promoted to Colonel) Joan Burton. The women in the core group are Claudia Joy Holden (wife of Brigadier General Michael Holden, later promoted to General), Denise Sherwood (wife of Major Frank Sherwood, later promoted to Lieutenant Colonel), Pamela Moran (wife and ex-wife of Chase Moran, Delta Force), and Roxy LeBlanc (wife of Private First Class Trevor LeBlanc, later promoted to Sergeant). Although seasons six and seven saw the group change with different wives added—including a lesbian couple (Charlie and Nicole, an officer)—and subtracted from the mix with Claudia Joy's death and Pamela's move to California, *Army Wives* maintains the focus on their relationships to one another.

Media texts such as *Army Wives* cohere around historically specific objects of knowledge to form what Stuart Hall calls a regime of representation. Hall argues that in order to understand how such a regime works, analysis must account for intertextual constructions: the "accumulation of meanings across different texts, where one image refers to another, or has its meaning altered by being 'read' in the context of other images"; in other words, "the whole repertoire of imagery and visual effects through which 'difference' is represented at any one historical moment" ("The Spectacle of the Other" 328). Elsewhere, Hall notes that the media representations such a regime comprises are not reflections or simple re-presentations of the object(s) around which they cohere; rather they constitute the meanings of these objects through discourse ("The Work of Representation" 44–45). This Foucaultian perspective is premised on the idea that discourse produces the knowledge we can have about objects. Following Hall, I argue that *Army Wives'* regime of representation constitutes particular meanings about military life and war with a damage control and recruitment mission. The program's rendering of the military to elide both racism and sexism constructs a post-political Army that can appeal to both the Pentagon and commercial sponsors at a juncture when public support for the military and the wars in Afghanistan and Iraq is waning (Keeter). I have argued that, given its timing, *Army Wives'* "central role … is to naturalize and normalize historically specific ideologies about Army gender politics and the wars in Iraq and Afghanistan" ("Lifetime's *Army Wives*" 93). This is a significant factor in the damage control the program accomplishes: as it foregrounds military benefits while downplaying the violence and death inherent to military life, *Army Wives* constitutes a benevolent military, supportive of soldiers, their kith and kin.

Meeting military families as she toured Army posts with Tanya Biank convinced Katherine Fugate that *Army Wives* resonated with their experiences:

> A young Army wife told us she watches each new episode with her husband, who was severely burned from the waist up, as she sits on the edge of his hospital bed. A newly widowed woman, who lost her husband to a sniper attack, told us the series has "saved her life." Other wives told us the camaraderie on the show gets them through the long months when their husbands are deployed and they become single mothers, running a household on their own [Fugate 12].

Army wives at Fort Drum watching the program with a *New York Times* reporter echo Fugate's account; although the Fort Drum viewers quibble over some details, the group "mostly found *Army Wives* entertaining, well-acted and able to shed some light on their real lives." Explaining the stakes of the program, one of these wives laments, "people don't understand what our lives are like.... I guess that's why we want this show to get it right. We take this so personally" (Lee E8). Such accounts of actual Army wives offer one rationale for the program's use of post-politics: the push to understand military issues through a personal lens displaces critical attention from actual sources of power (e.g., the Pentagon) and on to the lives of individuals and their families (Vavrus, "Unhitching" 223). Thus I refer to *Army Wives* as post-political to emphasize how its narratives discourage interpretation of various issues and even the military itself as political (that is, resulting from human actions, policies, institutions, and laws that can both reproduce and remedy identity-based oppression), and instead keep viewers' eyeballs trained on their personal stories. Using relatable themes that transcend those specific to military life and obscuring the power relations of those topics it does take up—rape, for example—*Army Wives* produces a post-political regime of representation that works to obscure patriarchy and racism in the military and larger society and burnishes the Army's image by casting it as a kindly *paterfamilias*.

## Feminizing Militainment

In describing *America's Army*, a video game developed by the Pentagon to recruit and train soldiers, Singer notes that it signals a cultural "transformation [that] has taken place over the last decade—largely escaping public scrutiny, at modest cost relative to the enormous sums spent elsewhere in the Pentagon budget, and with little planning but enormous consequences": the emergence of "militainment" (91). The term militainment was "first coined to describe any public entertainment that celebrated the military, but today it could be redefined to mean the fascinating, but also worrisome, blurring of the line between entertainment and war" (Singer 92). Stahl examines a diverse array of popular culture produced since September 11, 2001, such as video games, films, reality TV, and even children's toys that fit a definition of militainment; each of these products translates "state violence ... into an object of pleasurable consumption," making such "violence ... not of the abstract, distant, or historical variety but rather an impending or current use of force, one directly relevant to the citizen's current political life" (6). Most of these products are interactive in one way or another, a feature Stahl believes to be crucial for pushing the "discourses of militainment" to burrow "deeper into the capillaries of the subject, working internally to intensify a prescribed posture toward state violence and thereby widen the 'coalition of the willing'" (140).

Producing militainment is a carefully orchestrated process benefiting both the Pentagon and media industries. Robb traces it back to the beginning of the film industry in the United States, calling it out as "Hollywood's dirtiest little secret ... a devil's bargain that's a good deal for both sides." Film and TV producers generally like the arrangement because

> [m]illions of dollars can be shaved off a film's budget if the military agrees to lend its equipment and assistance. And all a producer has to do to get that assistance is submit five copies of the script to the Pentagon for approval; make whatever script changes the Pentagon suggests; film the script exactly as approved by the Pentagon; and prescreen the finished product for Pentagon officials before it's shown to the public [25].

For the military, the ultimate goal of such "mutual exploitation" (Bennett) is spelled out in the pages of *A Producer's Guide to U.S. Army Cooperation with the Entertainment Industry*: to "aid in the recruiting and retention of personnel" (qtd. in Robb 26). On PBS's *Newshour*, a military liaison officer underscores the important role these productions play in recruiting, noting that a Youth Attitude Tracking Survey conducted twice by the Pentagon "found that young men of recruiting age cited movies and television as the primary source of their impressions about the military. So it's very important [for showing] what the possibilities are and to see what being a soldier would be like" (PBS). Today all branches of the military actively shape military-themed media productions; each branch as well as the DOD maintains a liaison office in Los Angeles, while the DOD's main entertainment media division operates from the Pentagon (Smith). Phil Strub, Pentagon liaison since 1989, reports, however, that Pentagon influence is waning in Hollywood as a result of Special Forces operations increasing while "big combat arms are being pared down" (Bennett).

Debruge identifies *Army Wives* as one of the TV programs that has received DOD assistance, an arrangement confirmed and celebrated in a bonus feature from the season two DVD set, entitled "Operational Intelligence: Getting the Army's Support." This eight-minute segment features executive producers and cast members alike gushing with gratitude for the "realism," "plausibility," and "authenticity" DOD support brings to the program; for example, Brian McNamara, who plays General Michael Holden, believes this authenticity allows *Army Wives* to "honor the people we're portraying." DOD liaison staff likewise appreciates *Army Wives'* representation of military life; Project Officer Master Sergeant Kanessa Trent explains that Army entertainment staff approached the program's producers about providing DOD support once they realized the program "was touching hearts, that people were watching it." *Army Wives'* arrangement (and, after it, that of *Coming Home*[2]) exemplifies Burston's point that "it is no longer always productive to think about cultural power and military power separately.... With the advent of militainment, the intricate relationships between popular cultural forms and military technology have all become rather difficult and confused" (93). Given the DOD's support for the program, it is no surprise that *Army Wives* epitomizes militainment: its very premise blurs the line between entertainment and war while its sexualized, conventionally attractive cast members, lush sets, and actual military equipment and personnel all play roles in translating state violence into objects of pleasurable consumption.

By constructing Fort Marshall as a world apart from vexing problems of geo- and identity politics, the program is an attractive venue for airing both pro-military sentiments and securing commercial sponsorship. To achieve its distance from what Ono refers to as "icky historical abominations" (227), the program manages different oppressions by not invoking them (in the case of racism), by constituting them to suggest they are mainly irrelevant and no longer require attention from the political movements historically associated with them (in the case of sexism and homophobia[3]), or by discrediting actions of those characters who hold explicit political positions (in the case of anti-war and Black power activism). Post-politics thus enable *Army Wives* to both serve as a Pentagon public relations campaign to recruit women and girls and to counter critiques of the military and the wars in Iraq and Afghanistan (Vavrus, "Lifetime's *Army Wives*"). In this way, the program works much as Hasian believes the film *Zero Dark Thirty* does: as a "patriotic commodity, firmly convinced that women can act in empowering ways that take-for-granted the fruits of activism without any continued engagement with any lingering structural inequalities" (237).

*Army Wives'* post-politics in turn serve as a boon to the Lifetime network, enabling it to secure partnerships with sponsors such as Proctor and Gamble, Hallmark, and Ford Motor Company that wish to "augment their commercials by becoming a prominent part of the program" (Lafayette, "Ford Deal") but wish to distance themselves from controversial aspects of military service. A scene that takes place during the second season offers an example of this. Roxy's friend and boss at the Hump Bar, Betty, has completed a round of treatment for breast cancer and learned that it was unsuccessful. She decides to leave for California for more treatment at a "great cancer center there," and breaks the news of her move to Roxy early one morning in front of Roxy's house. Betty loads her luggage into the trunk of a gleaming black convertible with wide pink racing stripes; Roxy admires the car as the camera pans it and stops briefly to reveal "MUSTANG" written into the pink stripe at the bottom of the passenger door, sitting just below the pink ribbon-festooned silver mustang horse—the logo that identifies this model of car. Betty tells Roxy that she's always wanted a convertible and this one is special to her: as part of the Warriors in Pink edition, it "supports breast cancer research and whatnot. Thought it might bring me some good karma" ("Thicker Than Water"). This subplot allows *Army Wives* to both showcase a Ford product absent any war references and bestow it with the halo that accompanies corporations' associating themselves with the pink ribbon of the Susan G. Komen Foundation's breast cancer awareness campaign. King's research on the pink ribbon campaign shows how it has worked to construct the disease and support for curing it as outside of politics and even fashionable, so that all sorts of corporations from Yoplait yogurt to Ford Motor Company can comfortably (and profitably) associate themselves with it. Breast cancer has been "naturalized *as* uncontroversial by the dominant form of activism that has grown up around the disease," King argues, "particularly insofar as this work has disarticulated breast cancer from broader issues, such as the fundamental inequality of the American health care system or environmental degradation" (112, italics in original).

The program's post-politics evident in this scene and so many others are therefore vitally important for producing a representational regime that increases the likelihood of women enlisting in military service as it fulfills the commercial dictate that TV programs attract and deliver to sponsors eyeballs of the right ("affluent") kind. Meehan and Byars demonstrate that in an effort to "gain legitimacy," throughout its history Lifetime has formed institutional alliances with organizations whose missions relate to program content; such alliances "have the effect of both defusing feminist critiques of capitalism and legitimating the participants by granting them institutional status within each other's spheres of influence" (35). Such is the case with *Army Wives*, which typically pulls its punches when it comes to criticizing either the military or questioning the profit-maximizing imperative of commercial media.

Suturing issue advocacy and support into dramas is a long-standing strategy at Lifetime. In 1999, then Lifetime executive Carole Black crafted Lifetime as a "support network intended to empower women" (Hundley 178). Black wanted Lifetime to be "'not only about entertaining and informing, but advocacy and support as well. I want us to have the best shows, but we also have a unique opportunity to make women's lives better'" (qtd. in Hundley 178). Marketing research by Lifetime's top programmer during Black's tenure, Dawn Tarnofsky-Ostroff, revealed that viewers loved such programming: "These women identify with drama. The [heroines] are women who overcome obstacles, and I think women love to see women triumph" (180). Andrea Wong, who took over at Lifetime just prior to *Army Wives'* debut, observed that the success of the program owed to how it "really connected with women, really resonated with women.... [I]t's obviously the right time for a show like Army Wives" ("Wong Polishes Lifetime's Brand" 23). Echoing Katherine Fugate's vision of the program, Wong averred that "our show is more than just entertainment. We believe that on a higher level, we are embracing the stories of real people, of real sacrifice." Embodied by *Army Wives*, the formula was again successful. Soon after Wong's arrival and owing mainly to the success of *Army Wives*, Lifetime achieved the distinction of being the top cable network of 2007 in two prized demographic groups of women: ages 18–49 and 25–54 (Lafayette, "Andrea Wong's" 22). Strong ratings during *Army Wives'* first season demonstrated that it could attract female eyeballs—some of recruitment age—and keep them trained on the program.

Like other Lifetime fare, *Army Wives* is a serial drama that features protagonists being "terrorized, abused, or threatened" (Hundley 180). To make it Army-specific, the program integrates "real world" military events, issues, political figures, and organizations intertextually, ultimately reconstituting them as post-political. Intertextuality such as this offers one more means by which viewers can use media to negotiate the meaning of military life throughout a tumultuous period for the wars in Afghanistan and Iraq, and includes such issues as sexual assault (not, however, of its own troops by its own troops), domestic violence, torture (enacted *on* Pamela Moran's Delta Force husband Chase, but not *by* him or any other member of the military—an especially unlikely scenario given the findings of the 2014 Senate torture report), suicide, sexual harassment, breast cancer and the pink ribbon campaign, post-traumatic stress disorder (PTSD), Don't Ask Don't Tell (DADT), and child adoption by a lesbian couple. Actual politicians who have worked on military issues also appear on *Army Wives*. In 2010, vice presidential spouse Jill Biden appeared on the program as herself to promote the military family support initiative she and Michelle Obama had created, South Carolina governor Nikki Haley made a cameo appearance, and, when they were running for president, both Barack Obama and John McCain appeared in bumpers to promote the program before the 2008 season began. Viewers can participate in intertextual processes using the Lifetime web site and *Army Wives* pages to, for example, connect with military organizations such as the USO and Operation Homefront, interact with other fans of the program in chat rooms, watch video clips of the actors discussing how they played their respective roles, and vie to receive prizes from the *Army Wives* Gives Back program. Through this program, Lifetime donated money to Operation Homefront, brought Army spouses from Fort Stewart to an Outback Steakhouse luncheon, and sponsored visits by the program's actors both to Walter Reed Hospital to meet injured soldiers and to the homes of real Army wives to deliver gifts from T-Mobile, Ford, and JC Penney, among other sponsors ("Army Wives Gives Back").

Many of these intertextual activities are commercial in nature, a factor that allows cross-pollination between the military and *Army Wives*' corporate sponsors. This is an environment ideal for post-politics, which typically privilege consumerism over political activism. For example, I have defined postfeminism as a "revision of feminism that encourages women's private, consumer lifestyles rather than cultivating a desire for public life and political activism" (*Postfeminist News* 2). Similarly, Squires defines the "postracial mystique" as a reduction of the "social and political aspirations" of the Civil Rights movement "to consumer and individual choice [and] ... market-oriented freedoms rather than a transformation of the society and common understandings of our humanity, our relations with each other, our responsibilities to each other, regardless of race, color, or creed" (15). This fundamental characteristic of postracial/postracist and postfeminist regimes of representation thus makes them ideal for Lifetime and the DOD, particularly as they intersect to produce a view of the military cleansed of the racism and sexism that, in reality, continue to dog both the military and the civilian world.

## Postfeminist Army

Although examples abound of *Army Wives*' "postfeminist sensibility" (Gill 254), I want to examine what I believe are the two most prevalent means by which it "posts" feminism: by personalizing systemic gender violence such as domestic abuse and rape and by rendering invisible the military's own epidemic of sexual violence, *Army Wives* deflects attention from the patriarchal power and misogyny that legitimate and perpetuate such violence at a moment when the prevalence of domestic and sexual violence by military personnel was just coming to light. By the program's final season, newspapers, film, and Capitol Hill lawmakers were all publicizing the military's sexual assault problem, but within *Army Wives*' *mise en scène,* the issue was conspicuously absent.

A soldier abusing his wife or other family member is the typical means by which domestic violence is written into *Army Wives* episodes. Narrative arcs in *Army Wives*' seven seasons include Denise being abused by her son, Jeremy, and learning from Roxy how and why to fight back against him; Army wife Marilyn being abused and finally killed by her husband, who also kills

Claudia Joy and Michael Holden's daughter Amanda when he blows up the popular Hump Bar; Pamela Moran (formerly a police officer) being stalked by a listener to her radio program; and in an episode featuring Wynonna Judd (which included a contest to win Wynonna prize packages), Army wife Marisol revealing that her husband is abusing her, which prompts the wives to help her escape.

In response to these scenarios, *Army Wives* offers domestic violence remedies that comprise fighting back by acquiring self-defense skills, jailing abusers, and contacting organizations that help domestic violence survivors. All of these strategies are important for dealing with domestic violence, and all derive from feminist principles and activism. But the episodes that advance such remedies neither identify gender violence as an expression of patriarchal power, nor challenge men to stop it. And although the program treats violence survivors sensitively, viewers should not "mistake concern for victims with the political will to change the conditions that led to their victimization in the first place" (Katz 6). Instead of burdening women with the responsibility for remedying the violence they experience, Katz believes we must challenge "those aspects of male culture—especially male-peer culture—that provide active or tacit support for some men's abusive behavior" (7). Such a critique of patriarchal power is absent from the military's policies dealing with sexual assault, according to the documentary film *The Invisible War*, and it is unlikely to appear on Lifetime, which, since its beginning, has relied on "telefeminist programming formulae that defuse any basic structural challenges to patriarchy and its institutions," according to Meehan and Byars (34).

Refusal to confront "patriarchy and its institutions" occurs clearly in a storyline spanning two episodes—"Safe Havens" and "Payback"—which feature the attempted rape of Claudia Joy Holden by family friend and visiting Chilean diplomat, Paolo Ruiz. Paolo holds the key to negotiating a lease on land that the Pentagon seeks in order to expand a strategically important Army post and must be appeased if the deal is to take place. Throughout "Safe Havens" Paolo flirts overtly with Claudia Joy, exclaiming repeatedly about how beautiful she is. As the episode progresses, he becomes increasingly daring and attempts to rape Claudia Joy on a couch in the Holdens' home. When he finds her home alone, Paolo announces happily that his President has renewed the lease agreement; Paolo suggests they celebrate with the wine he has brought with him into the room. Claudia Joy declines to drink, at which point Paolo attacks her. She struggles against him as he tears at her clothes, eventually reaching around for the wine bottle beside the couch and breaking it over Paolo's head. The episode ends with a brief scene of determined-looking Pamela at the shooting range, aiming her gun at the camera as she prepares to take on her own stalker—a man whose threats to Pamela increase over the course of several episodes ("Safe Havens").

"Payback" begins with a sequence of Paolo lying unconscious on the floor, Claudia Joy calling the military police (MPs), and an ambulance taking Paolo away as Michael storms into the home among the MPs stationed outside. When Claudia Joy tells him what has happened, Michael becomes outraged and tells her he wants to prosecute. Cleaning up the broken glass and ice on the floor, Claudia Joy tells him, "It's over. Let it be over." She assures him that the attack did not go "far at all," and urges him to drop his pursuit of Paolo: in addition to Paolo being "connected" and having diplomatic immunity, "we're in the middle of a very sensitive lease negotiation. We need them more than they need us…. The only punishment this bastard is going to get is a champagne bottle to the head." Michael protests to Claudia Joy that she should forego such stoicism, "You're not a soldier!" In return she exclaims, "I became one the day I married you!"

Growing increasingly frustrated, Michael realizes that the situation is untenable; he must satisfy the Pentagon—which has sent explicit instructions for him not to press charges and to attend the lease signing ceremony, as per Paolo's mandate—yet he feels he must avenge the attack on Claudia Joy. Deciding to act, Michael confronts Paolo in a dark, shadowy room at the jail where three MPs stand guard. Michael stands in front of the table where Paulo sits and casts a long shadow, head bandaged; Paolo calmly insists, "Michael, this is all a misunderstanding. Claudia Joy was being so friendly. It was a mistake." Michael corrects him: "It was an attack. On my wife." Invoking a pernicious rape myth, Paulo replies: "Sometimes signals are not what they seem. Occasionally no means something else." Michael walks toward Paulo, looking menacing as he shouts, "My wife!" Paulo pulls back, telling him, "Nothing happened. I got what I deserved. I will go home, confess to my wife, and get even worse…. Okay? You have my word." He also reports that "my president" would like "this kept quiet." Michael: "And you just walk away, like nothing ever happened." Paulo returns with "That's how it is sometimes in world politics." As he starts to walk away, Michael tells him ominously, "Not in my world," and walks out of the room.

Further into "Payback," Pamela, Roxy, Claudia Joy, and Denise sit on Claudia Joy's porch discussing their various experiences being threatened and attacked. Claudia Joy ruminates that if she hadn't been able to reach the champagne bottle, "I would not have been able to defend myself." Roxy reveals that she, too, had been attacked once, but "thank god he was drunk because that was the only way I got outta there. And I started kickboxing class the next day!" Pamela, a former police officer still dealing with a stalker who is becoming increasingly threatening, says, "Well I know how to defend myself and it doesn't always help. That's why I got a gun."

The last sequence of scenes includes a reluctant Michael dressing to attend the lease signing ceremony; he tells Claudia Joy that he can see she's suffering. Claudia Joy turns to face him:

> "Okay, you're right! I'm not okay! I'm mad as hell, I'm ashamed and I didn't do anything wrong. But we can't let him know that! We can't give him the satisfaction of thinking what he did is going to change the way we live our lives. That's what he wants. That's what rape—even attempted rape—is about: power. I need you to go because I don't want him to hold any power over us…. The Army needs that land in San Pasqual and they're not going to lose it because of what he did to me."

The storyline concludes with Michael knocking on Paolo's hotel room door after the ceremony is over, and, when Paolo answers it, punching him in the nose. Paulo falls backward onto the floor with blood on his face and Michael, jaw set, stalks away down the hallway.

In this episode, Claudia Joy, especially, provides a perspective on rape and domestic violence—one that gestures weakly toward second wave feminism with her emphasis to Michael that rape is a means of exerting power over people who have done nothing to invite such a display. Questions about where that power comes from and why some men exercise it whereas most do not are never answered, let alone asked. The wives' porch conversation reveals that threats of violence from men are common among women and abuse can come from friends and family members; this, too, is an important insight resulting from feminist activism. But more pointed feminist analyses of gender violence—that it is almost always used by men to "dominate, punish, or degrade" victims (Benedict, *Virgin or Vamp* 15)—is absent from Claudia Joy's explanation. The only solutions on offer here are for a survivor to pretend as if the attack did not bother her, to become skilled at self-defense, or to own a gun. Although this storyline would have been ideal to call out and challenge the patriarchal system underpinning gender violence, it fails to do so; it neither illuminates the ways in which sexual violence has been used historically as a form of patriarchal oppression (Benedict, *Virgin or Vamp*; Cuklanz; Katz; Meyers; Nettleton), nor explores the military's role in perpetuating and enabling such violence within its own ranks. Making such a critique would likely lose support of the DOD, an organization that has proved ineffective at solving or even curbing the epidemic of sexual assault plaguing every one of the military's branches.

Sexual violence against service women[4] has been widespread since 2001 when women began mass deployments to Afghanistan with their male compatriots, but only sporadically documented in news reports before the release of *The Invisible War* (see, for example, Herdy and Moffeit's *Betrayal in the Ranks* [2004] or Benedict's *The Lonely Soldier* [2009]). In 2010, Congress member Jane Harman noted provocatively that "a female soldier in Iraq is more likely to be raped by a fellow soldier than killed by enemy fire" (qtd. in

Gibbs), but despite these attempts to publicize it, the problem was cloaked by radio silence. Across the few media accounts documenting sexual assault by troops on other troops, a clear pattern emerged: when women reported their attacks using military channels, the commanders to whom they reported typically responded by protecting the accused and dismissing or downplaying victims' claims. Such stories were so widespread—across all branches of the military and from the top to the bottom of the military hierarchy—they suggested the Department of Defense was either unprepared to deal with the wave of service women who were deployed after September 11, 2001, or criminally negligent in dealing with sexual assault of military personnel (or perhaps both).

Despite clear evidence of a persistent sexual assault problem throughout the military, the soldiers depicted in *Army Wives* experience no such assaults or even threats of such assaults. For survivors, their families, and friends, such a storyline arguably would have enhanced the program's authenticity and verisimilitude; its absence speaks volumes about the DOD's position on military sexual assault. Claudia Joy's vague explanation to Michael that rape is about power neither identifies rape as a symptom of structural patriarchy nor implicates the Pentagon in enabling the continuation of military sexual assault. Claudia Joy's decision to not push for a more thorough investigation of Paolo (although she tells Michael "he's probably been getting away with it for years") could serve as a cautionary tale for other survivors of military sexual assault deciding whether or not to report their assailants. Better that your husband defends your honor than demand that the Army change.

This is an *Army Wives* pattern: identifying sexual and domestic violence as problems but then refusing to analyze the system that causes such violence to persist.[5] During season one, Denise and Frank Sherwood's son Jeremy is abusing his mother by hitting her, and when she learns that he is continuing to do it "even after Michael [Holden] talked to him," Claudia Joy tells her, "I don't know what to tell you ... except that I'm here for you" ("The Art of Separation"). Nothing is wrong with supporting friends who are the victims of gender violence; likewise, nothing is wrong with Denise learning self-defense techniques so that she can fight back against future attacks or Roxy learning to kick box or Pamela carrying a gun (although evidence shows that Pamela is more likely be victimized with the gun than be able to use it against her stalker [Gerney and Parsons]). *Army Wives*' missed opportunities force women to continue to shoulder the burden of transforming such a culture of misogyny, letting men and the institutions that enable their predatory behavior off the hook. Absent solutions that go after causes rather than treat symptoms, *Army Wives* proves to be inadequate before the task of stopping gender violence; instead it illustrates how a postfeminist approach to such violence may actually aid in its proliferation.

## Postracial Army

In addition to being infused with a military-friendly, postfeminist sensibility, *Army Wives* portrays military life as postracial: devoid either of scenarios where race is a salient category of identity or of instances of racial discrimination. This is particularly odd considering that Fort Marshall is located in South Carolina, where, during the time of *Army Wives'* run, the Confederate flag—symbol of loyalty to antebellum institutions, including slavery—flew over the state Capitol building. Ono asserts that postracism like that in *Army Wives* is the "perfect elixir to help society forget about the icky historical abomination known as racism"; it

> beckons its unknowing subjects to embrace and live within a mental habitus of preracial consciousness.... Postracism disavows history, overlaying it with an upbeat discourse about how things were never really that bad, are not so bad now, and are only getting better [227].

In a pithy affirmation of postracism, Indian-American South Carolina governor Nikki Haley remarked during a gubernatorial debate in 2014, "I can honestly say I have not had one conversation with a single CEO about the Confederate flag.... We really kind of fixed all that when you elected the first Indian-American female governor.... When we appointed the first African-American U.S. senator, that sent a huge message" (qtd. in Edwards). It was only after white supremacist Dylann Roof killed nine African Americans inside of a historically significant AME church in Charleston on June 17, 2015, that the Confederate flag's status in South Carolina began to change; on July 10, Governor Nikki Haley authorized the removal of the flag from its spot on the state Capitol building. Prior to the shooting, Roof had posed for a photograph holding the Confederate flag and a gun; in an internet manifesto Roof claimed to want to use the shooting to initiate a race war (Apuzzo). Up until the slaying, Haley had no problem with the Confederate flag because, according to her, CEOs did not object to it; thus she had endowed *them*—privileged white men, most likely—with the right to determine whether South Carolina should continue to fly it. In her statement, Haley likewise shrugs off any suggestion that racism persists in South Carolina; because the executive office is led by a woman of color and an African American man represents the state in the Senate, there can be no racism there. Haley's statement parallels what Ono and others have noted about media coverage of Barack Obama's presidency: "That a Black man became the president of the United States implies that past racial barriers to occupying that office are now gone. Racism is passé. Today, anything—even tremendous political and international power—is possible" (228). That it took a tragedy rooted in white supremacy to affirm that the flag still operates as a symbol of intense racial hatred is a morbid demonstration that the U.S. is far from being postracist.

To its credit, *Army Wives* has had a racially diverse cast throughout its seven seasons, especially the last two. For example, cast members of color play characters Joan and Roland Burton, who are intelligent and competent, wise and professionally ambitious; Latino Hector and African American Quincy are good soldiers, loyal to the military if not always to their spouses; African American and lesbian, Charlie is a compassionate leader of the Fort Marshall community center's youth programs; and the extras appearing in every episode suggest that today's Army is racially diverse. Beyond this, however, the program's portrayal of people of color consistently lacks any indication that they encounter racial discrimination either within the Army or without; on the contrary, *Army Wives* portrays the Army as a color-blind meritocracy where qualified officers like Joan Burton lead battalions with nary a hint of racial resentment from the white soldiers subordinate to them or racial discrimination from higher ranking white officers. Such color blindness is a hallmark of postracial discourses and is prevalent in the white ranks of the Army as well. For example, Dempsey and Shapiro's examination of racial and ethnic discrimination in the Army reveals that Hispanic and African American soldiers report they experience a great deal of discrimination, but that it goes unnoticed among the mostly white officer corps.

An illustration of *Army Wives'* color blindness comes in the depiction of Joan Burton as a more talented warrior-strategist than her white male rival, Evan O'Connor (later shown to be both dishonest and incompetent). Evan taunts Joan as they prepare to lead opposing teams in the annual war games exercise at Fort Marshall, telling her, "I guess we're finally going to find out who the better man is." Joan remarks, demeaningly, that unlike her, Evan is a "pencil pusher. Let me remind you, I've commanded more than a desk in my career. I know what it takes to lead in combat, and believe me, you don't have it." She leans in toward him and asserts, menacingly, "I'm gonna kick ... your ... ass" ("Onward Christian Soldier"). This scene, Joan's winning performance during the subsequent war games exercise, and numerous other episodes that showcase her intelligence and heroism construct Joan as an ideal Army officer whose race is never a consideration in whether others will respect her authority.

In general, *Army Wives* renders race relations unproblematic by casting the Army as a benevolent *paterfamilias*. For example, successive episodes "Duty to Inform" and "Need to Know Basis" show white Trevor LeBlanc embodying such a paternal role as he works with Joan Burton to recruit a promising African American high school girl. This narrative arc begins after Joan assigns Trevor to be a recruiter—a position he is dubious about after being awarded a Silver Star medal. Trevor starts his new duty by trying to talk to a high school track team training in the town square; he scares them away, but the next day African American Vanessa Jones returns to the recruiting office to see Trevor. Trevor asks her, "Have you thought about what you want to do after high school?" "Work I guess," she replies. Trevor pushes her to consider the Army: "This is your time, Vanessa. You gotta make decisions for yourself…. The Army can give you choices you never thought you'd have." He invites her to candidate physical training (PT) sessions the next morning, to which she reluctantly agrees to go ("Duty to Inform").

The story continues in "Need to Know Basis," when Vanessa fails to appear at a PT session, even after excelling at the first one. Although Trevor is disappointed with Vanessa, instead he sells the Army to Martinez: an overweight, out-of-shape Latino man. Trevor encourages Martinez to continue to train. "There's a warrior inside you," Trevor insists. "You're just setting him free." After the PT session has ended, Trevor visits Vanessa's dilapidated home, where a car sits in the front yard, falling apart and rusting. Vanessa's sister answers the door, explaining that she is Vanessa's legal guardian after their mother abandoned them. Reluctantly she tells Trevor where Vanessa works, but warns him, "She don't have time for the Army. She needs to work!" She slams the door in Trevor's face as he thanks her for her time.

Trevor visits Vanessa at the burger joint-bowling alley where she works behind the counter. Angry, she tells him, "I got no time for playin' soldier, okay?" Trevor tells her, "We can work around your schedule…. And as far as money goes, once you sign up, the Army'll pay for your college." "College?" she asks incredulously. "How 'bout next month's electric?" Trevor continues undeterred, telling Vanessa about the signing bonus and concluding with "I'm talking about your life, Vanessa." "What you know about my life, LeBlanc?" Vanessa rebuffs Trevor, telling him, "I got customers." Unsettled, he tells her, "If that's how you feel, I'm gonna need my [Army-issued PT] t-shirt back…. Yeah, that's government property and if you're not going to enlist, I need it washed and folded and back on my desk by 1500 hours. Tomorrow." He walks away, angry that he has lost a promising recruit.

Later, Vanessa walks into recruiting office and drops her t-shirt on Trevor's desk. "Okay—we done?" she asks. Trevor looks away and rifles through some papers as Joan walks through the door. Everyone in the office stands up and salutes her. "I'm looking for prospect Vanessa Jones," she announces. "Here," Vanessa answers weakly. "I'm Lieutenant Colonel Joan Burton. Sargeant LeBlanc suggested we talk. Let's take a walk, okay?" As they walk, Vanessa asks, "People always stand up for you like that?" Joan replies, "Oh yeah. I'm a Lieutenant Colonel. I'm in charge of 1,400 soldiers." Incredulous, Vanessa asks, "For real? And they gotta listen to you?" Joan laughs, "For real. They have to take orders from me." Joan compliments Vanessa on her sprinting time, and tells her,

"You know, track was my way out of the Southside.... Southside of Chicago. Grew up in the projects and my parents split when I was six. Raised myself more or less. In high school, most my friends were on their way to getting pregnant or in jail. Me, too ... except for one thing: I was fast. So my track coach told me about an ROTC scholarship where I could go to college for four years and then do anything I want. He opened a door that I didn't know existed. I always dreamt about going to college but thought it was out of reach.... I guess I fell in love with the Army. Been around the world a couple of times, got married, had a baby all while serving my country. It's a great feeling" ["Need to Know Basis"].

Vanessa tells her, "I don't have the grades to go to college. I'm barely gonna graduate from high school next month." Turning to face her, Joan says,

"Look, Vanessa. You don't have to be me. But you do have to be you. And you have to choose. There's a world of possibilities past the end of your block. But you're gonna have to make this happen. Sergeant LeBlanc says you have everything it takes to be an outstanding soldier. You could start a whole new life for you."

Vanessa, appearing bewildered, asks, "He said that about me?" Joan replies with a decisive "He did," and hands Vanessa her business card: "My email's on there. Let me know how you do." Joan then gets into a waiting car, door opened by her driver. Vanessa looks down at the card and up at Joan, waving as the car drives away, music swelling to end the scene.

The storyline ends with Trevor walking into Joan's office, where he tells her, "Prospect Jones is on board, ma'am.... I'm not sure what you said to her, but she brought her papers in right away." Joan looks at him admiringly: "So your first recruit. That's a big one. How does that feel?" Trevor replies, "It really feels really good. I think I'm helping this girl to change her life." Joan affirms him: "Hmmm—that's pretty powerful stuff.... Now you have a responsibility, Sergeant. See her through" ("Need to Know Basis").

Although this one is far from the only narrative arc that showcases *Army Wives*' postracial politics, it is particularly illustrative of how well they can work when woven together with postfeminism as militainment. Throughout the scenes this storyline comprises are overt statements of the many benefits of the Army: health benefits for the enlistee and all dependents, college tuition coverage through the G.I. Bill, a path out of poverty, and so forth, all expressed through a paternalistic narrative of a white man and an African American, postfeminist officer shepherding a poor African American girl through the process of enlistment. *Army Wives* recognizes no structural barriers to racial or gender equality, for example, erasing any suggestion that Vanessa's or Joan's poverty could have roots in racist housing and education policies or wage discrimination (the wage gap for African American women remains large: the average African American woman earns 64 percent of a white man's salary ["By the Numbers"]). Instead of exploring these or any other possibilities, the poverty conditions of each are attributed to their respective parents' abandonment, thus allowing the Army to step in and act as both parental substitute and social safety net. And what a generous parent it is, making Joan fall in love with it and presenting Vanessa with a means to live out the American Dream.

## Marching Orders

Since conscription ended in 1973, the U.S. military has relied on an all-volunteer force; during this same time, the portion of the federal budget allocated to military spending has progressively increased, resulting in a "permanent defense establishment" (Thorpe 5).[6] These shifts help to explain both the DOD mandate that its supported projects recruit prospects and legitimate the military as they entertain, and why *Army Wives* proved to be a good investment.

Attempts such as this one to fix the meaning of the object of media representations illuminate the power inherent in the process. Stuart Hall reminds us that even regimes of representation that become dominant—such as that which assigned negative meaning to the military pre–*Army Wives*—can be intervened into and altered, if the intervention "locates itself *within* the complexities and ambivalences of representation itself, and tries to *contest it from within*" ("The Spectacle" 342, italics in original). As I have shown, *Army Wives* works as just such a strategy for contesting negative views of the military with a serial drama that locates itself amidst the "complexities and ambivalences" of military discourses, foregrounding the personal lives of military personnel and their families and resolving problems they encounter with a mixture of social support, military benefits, and instruction in self-care (particularly self-defense). Although *Army Wives* received its marching orders in 2013, by then it had done the work for which it had been tasked by Lifetime and the Department of Defense: personalize the military, portray the Army sympathetically … and do it all with love.

## Notes

1. *Army Wives* is an adaptation of *Under the Sabers: The Unwritten Code of Army Wives*, a book by Tanya Biank that followed the lives of four Army wives at Fort Bragg. The book emerged from Biank's work as a military reporter for the *Fayetteville Observer*, where she covered nearby Fort Bragg and a series of murders that occurred on and around it during 2002.

2. When *Army Wives* proved successful, in 2011 Lifetime introduced a military reality program—*Coming Home*—that immediately followed *Army Wives* and featured military men and women returning home to surprise their families in various contrived settings. *Coming Home* ran for two seasons before its 2012 cancellation.

3. See Elias (in press) for analysis of *Army Wives'* post-gay politics.

4. As *The Invisible War* and some other accounts make clear, men are also the victims of sexual assault. Assaults on men are "quite common," and extremely underreported; the Government Accountability Office notes that the DOD has been slow and unprepared to respond to male victims as well (Olson).

5. Research by both Meyers and Nettleton shows that such a pattern of omission is typical of media coverage around domestic violence.

6. In 2015, for example, defense spending is expected to reach $600 billion (Preble).

## Works Cited

Apuzzo, Matt. "Dylann Roof, Charleston Shooting Suspect, Is Indicted on Hate Crime Charge." *New York Times* 22 July 2015. Web. 8 Aug. 2015.

"Army Wives Gives Back" (bonus feature). *Army Wives: The Complete Second Season.* Buena Vista Entertainment, Inc. 2009. DVD.

"The Art of Separation." *Army Wives: The Complete First Season.* Writ. Katherine Fugate. Dir. Patrick Norris. Buena Vista Home Entertainment, Inc., 2008. DVD.

Benedict, Helen. *The Lonely Soldier: The Private War of Women Serving in Iraq.* Boston: Beacon Press, 2009. Print.

_____. *Virgin or Vamp: How the Press Covers Sex Crimes.* New York: Oxford University Press, 1992. Print.

Bennett, Laura. "The Pentagon's Man in Hollywood: I'm a Eunuch." *The New Republic* 21 Dec. 2012. Web. 14 Mar. 2015.

Biank, Tanya. *Under the Sabers: The Unwritten Code of Army Wives.* New York: St. Martin's Press, 2006. Print.

Burston, Jonathan. "The Slippery Slopes of 'Soft Power': Production Studies, International Relations, and the Military Industrial Media Complex." *The International Encyclopedia of Media Studies.* Ed. Angharad N. Valdivia. *Volume II: Media Production.* Ed. Vicki Mayer. Malden, MA: Blackwell, 2013. 83–104. Print.

"By the Numbers: A Look at the Gender Pay Gap." *Career and Workplace.* Association for American University Women, 18 Sept. 2014. Web. 10 Aug. 2015.

Cuklanz, Lisa M. *Rape on Prime Time: Television, Masculinity, and Sexual Violence.* Philadelphia: University of Pennsylvania Press, 2000. Print.

Debruge, Peter. "Tanks a Lot, Uncle Sam." *Variety* 22 June 2009: 1, 30. Print.

Dempsey, Jason K., and Robert Y. Shapiro. "The Army's Hispanic Future." *Armed Forces and Society* 35.3 (2009): 526–561. Print.

"Duty to Inform." *Army Wives: The Complete Third Season.* Writ. T.D. Mitchell. Dir. Emile Levisetti. Buena Vista Home Entertainment, Inc., 2010. DVD.

Edwards, David. "SC Governor Defends Confederate Flag at Statehouse: Not 'a Single CEO' Has Complained." *Raw Story.* N.p., 15 Oct. 2014. Web. 4 Jan. 2015.

Elias, Liora P. "Lesbian and Gay Civil Rights in a Post-Gay Era: 'Don't Ask, Don't Tell' and Its Repeal As Seen in Lifetime's Army Wives (2007–2013)." *Living Room Wars: American Militarism on the Small Screen.* Ed. Anna Froula and Stacy Takacs. New York: Routledge, in press. Print.

Fugate, Katherine. "*Wives* Puts a Face on Military's Unsung Heroes." *Television Week* 11 Aug. 2008: 12. Print.

Gerney, Arkadi, and Chelsea Parsons. "Women Under the Gun: How Gun Violence Affects Women and 4 Policy Solutions to Better Protect Them." Center for American Progress, June 2014. Web. 8 July 2014.

Gibbs, Nancy. "Sexual Assaults on Female Soldiers: Don't Ask, Don't Tell." *Time* 8 Mar. 2010. Web. 12 Oct. 2013.

Gill, Rosalind. *Gender and the Media*. Cambridge, UK: Polity, 2007. Print.

Hall, Stuart. "The Spectacle of the Other." *Discourse Theory and Practice: A Reader*. Ed. Margaret Wetherell, Stephanie Taylor, and Simeon J. Yates. London: Sage Publications, Ltd. 2001. 324–343. Print.

_____. "The Work of Representation." *Representation: Cultural Representations and Signifying Practices*. Ed. Stuart Hall. London: Sage, 1997. 13–74. Print.

Hasian, Marouf. "*Zero Dark Thirty* and the Critical Challenges Posted by Populist Postfeminism During the Global War on Terrorism." *Journal of Communication Inquiry* 37.4 (2013): 322–343. Print.

Herdy, Amy, and Miles Moffeit. *Betrayal in the Ranks* [Digital newsbook]. Denver: The Denver Post, 2004. Print.

Hundley, Heather. "The Evolution of Gendercasting: The Lifetime Television Network—'Television for Women.'" *Journal of Popular Film and Television* 29.4 (2002): 174–181. Print.

*The Invisible War*. Dir. Kirby Dick. New Video Group, Inc. 2012. DVD.

Katz, Jackson. *The Macho Paradox: Why Some Men Hurt Women and How All Men Can Help*. Naperville, IL: Sourcebooks, 2006. Print.

Keeter, Scott. "Trends in Public Opinion About the War in Iraq, 2003–2007." *Pew Research Center*. Pew Charitable Trusts, 15 Mar. 2007. Web. 7 June 2010.

King, Samantha. *Pink Ribbons, Inc.: Breast Cancer and the Politics of Philanthropy*. Minneapolis: University of Minnesota Press, 2006. Print.

Lafayette, Jon. "Andrea Wong's Lifetime Project." *Television Week* 3 Sept. 2007: 1, 62. Print.

_____. "Ford Deal Drives 'Wives' Storyline." *Television Week* 2 June 2008. Print.

Lee, Felicia R. "Watching Army Wives Watching *Army Wives*." *New York Times* 28 June 2007: E-1, E-8. Print.

Meehan, Eileen R., and Jackie Byars. "Telefeminism: How Lifetime Got Its Groove, 1984–1997." *Television and New Media* 1.1 (2000): 33–51. Print.

Meyers, Marian. *News Coverage of Violence Against Women: Engendering Blame*. Thousand Oaks, CA: Sage, 1997. Print.

"Need to Know Basis." *Army Wives: The Complete Third Season*. Writ. Elizabeth Jacobs. Dir. Allison Liddi-Brown. Buena Vista Home Entertainment, Inc., 2010. DVD.

Nettleton, Pamela Hill. "Domestic Violence in Men's and Women's Magazines: Women Are Guilty of Choosing the Wrong Men, Men Are Not Guilty of Hitting Women." *Women's Studies in Communication* 34.1 (2011): 139–160. Print.

Olson, Wyatt. "Federal Watchdog: DOD Slow in Addressing Sexual Assault of Men." *Stars and Stripes*. N.p., 19 Mar. 2015. Web. 22 Mar. 2015.

Ono, Kent. "Postracism: A Theory of the 'Post-' as Political Strategy." *Journal of Communication Inquiry* 34.3 (2010): 227–233. Print.

"Onward Christian Soldier." *Army Wives: The Complete Third Season*. Writ. Tanya Biank, Katherine Fugate, Jennifer Schuur, and T.D. Mitchell. Dir. Carl Ludwig. Buena Vista Home Entertainment, Inc., 2010. DVD.

"Operational Intelligence: Getting the Army's Support" (Bonus feature). *Army Wives: The Complete Second Season*. Buena Vista Home Entertainment, Inc., 2009. DVD.

"Payback." *Army Wives: The Complete Second Season*. Writ. Tanya Biank and Katherine Fugate. Dir. John Kretchmer. Buena Vista Home Entertainment, Inc., 2009. DVD.

PBS Newshour. "U.S. Military Helps Create Hollywood Films on War and Warriors." *Pbs.org*. Public Broadcasting Service, 6 Oct. 2006. Web. 14 Mar. 2015.

Preble, Christopher. "U.S. Military Spending: A Lot? Or a Lot More?" *Newsweek*. 8 Feb. 2015. Web. 30 Mar. 2015.

Robb, David. *Operation Hollywood: How the Pentagon Shapes and Censors the Movies*. Amherst, NY: Prometheus, 2004. Print.

"Safe Havens." *Army Wives: The Complete Second Season*. Writ. Tanya Biank and Katherine Fugate. Dir. Lloyd Ahern. Buena Vista Home Entertainment, Inc., 2009. DVD.

Singer, P. W. "Meet the Sims … and Shoot Them." *Foreign Policy* 178 (Mar./Apr. 2010): 91–95. Print.

Smith, Steven Donald. "Hollywood, Military Cooperation Often Mutually Beneficial." *Defense.gov*. US Department of Defense, 21 Aug. 2006. Web. 14 Mar. 2015.

Squires, Catherine R. *The Post-Racial Mystique: Media and Race in the Twenty-First Century*. New York: New York University Press, 2014. Print.

Stahl, Roger. *Militainment, Inc.: War, Media, and Popular Culture*. New York: Routledge, 2010. Print.

"Thicker Than Water." *Army Wives: The Complete Second Season*. Writ. John E. Pogue. Dir. Tawnia McKiernan. Buena Vista Home Entertainment, Inc., 2009. DVD.

Thorpe, Rebecca U. *The American Warfare State: The Domestic Politics of Military Spending*. Chicago: University of Chicago Press, 2014. Print.

Vavrus, Mary Douglas. "Lifetime's *Army Wives*, or I Married the Media-Military-Industrial Complex." *Women's Studies in Communication* 36.1 (2013): 92–112. Print.

_____. *Postfeminist News: Political Women in Media Culture*. Albany: State University of New York Press, 2002. Print.

_____. "Unhitching from the 'Post' (of Postfeminism)." *Journal of Communication Inquiry* 34.3 (2010): 222–227. Print.

"Wong Polishes Lifetime's Brand." *Broadcasting and Cable* 16 June 2008: 3, 23. Print.

# "In Extremis"

## Unnatural Selection in Lifetime's Speculative Fictions

### Lisa K. Perdigao

While Lifetime has represented "Television for Women" since its premiere in 1984, its recent turn to the supernatural and science fiction in its original series presents complicated messages about women's roles in contemporary society.[1] Writing in 2002, Heather Hundley notes, "The Lifetime cable network did not just magically appear; it evolved over sixteen years of planning, programming, personnel changes, and an increasing commitment to *narrowcasting*, or, more precisely, to *gendercasting*" (175). For a network that began with—or at least was shaped by—"true life" movies, magical realism and science fiction seem to be an unlikely fit. Given its history, Lifetime's turn to speculative fiction in the past two years with *Witches of East End* (2013–2014) and *The Lottery* (2014) appears to be anomalous to the network's vision. *Witches of East End* and *The Lottery* promote a problematic message for women: rather than highlighting progress, a story of evolution shared by the network and its viewers, these series reinforce antiquated ideas about what women were always meant to be.

The two series depict women as static characters, unchanged and unchanging over time. Adapted from Melissa de la Cruz's novels, *Witches of East End* portrays "hysterical" women who are doomed to replay the roles always already prescribed to them. The future of the Beauchamp women is already written, dictated by the past. Conversely, *The Lottery*, with its look to the future, offers a society where women's "natural" roles have been negated. Created by Timothy J. Sexton, who co-wrote the screenplay of Alfonso Cuarón's *Children of Men* (2006), *The Lottery* depicts a society where men hold the keys to the future. Women are not merely erased from the story of procreation; they are cast as incubators for a dying society. As depicted within and between the

95

two series, Lifetime is engaged with contemporary issues in the real world—perhaps most notably women's rights over their bodies. Where the network's slogan "Your Life. Your Time." emphasizes a celebration of women's roles in the twenty-first century, these series counter a story of becoming—a realization of women's potential. However, part of that stagnation can be attributed to the network itself. In the fall of 2014, Lifetime cancelled *Witches of East End* after two seasons and *The Lottery* after its first season. The title of *The Lottery*'s final episode, "In Extremis," suggests a way of reading the two series. *Witches of East End* and *The Lottery* highlight how women on Lifetime are in extremis; they are in an extremely difficult situation, facing extinction on the very network that once championed their causes.

With its cancellation, *The Lottery* episode "In Extremis" serves as the series' resolution, offering a final reflection on the series' future on the network. While *Witches of East End* has a longer gestation period, with plot and character arcs that take the characters from a contemporary East End, New York, to a fictional Asgard, it also suddenly came to a close in fall 2014. At the end of its second season, *Witches of East End* appears to be poised for a third season, with the introduction of new plot lines, including a pregnancy, two deaths, and body-switching. With contemporary television series existing "on the bubble," constantly under the threat of extinction, Lifetime's experiments with the two series highlight the limits and possibilities of sustaining both its female characters and its female audience. The cancellation of *Witches of East End* led to a fan campaign initiated in social media, the Twitter campaign #RenewWitchesOfEastEnd, which boasts a celebrity following (most notably star Jenna Dewan Tatum's husband Channing Tatum), and an iPetition. In contrast, *The Lottery* ended not with a bang but a whimper. Following the adage of life imitating art, and perhaps reflecting the network's vision, the viewer responses seem in tune with the series' content: the Beauchamp women continually die and are reborn while *The Lottery* struggles to create new life within a dying population. Individually and collectively, the series—and their cancellations—offer timely reflections on women's power within traditionally patriarchal systems, including network television.

## *"Over, and over, and over, and over"*: Witches of East End's *Essentialist Nature*

On the surface, *Witches of East End* and *The Lottery* share little more than their places within Lifetime's fall 2014 programming and notice of cancellation; however, the two series similarly begin with meditations on reproduction. In the pilot episode of *Witches of East End*, Ingrid Beauchamp's (Rachel Boston) friend Barb (Kellee Stewart) is struggling with infertility.

She comes to Ingrid after learning that her last attempt at in-vitro fertilization (IVF) has failed; as she and her husband have run out of money for another round, she says that getting pregnant would take a "miracle" ("Pilot"). Ingrid, a librarian and Ph.D. candidate writing a dissertation on witchcraft and occult practices in post–Revolutionary New York, offers to perform a fertility spell, unaware that she—and her family—has a history of witchcraft. What is initially viewed as a game, with a spell taken from the Internet and homemade witches' hats, becomes real and introduces the possibilities of witchcraft into Ingrid's life. However, antiquated ideas about women's natures are introduced at the same time.

*Witches of East End* reflects postfeminist debates about women's past and future roles in society. Stéphanie Genz and Benjamin A. Brabon write that postfeminism is a "concept fraught with contradictions" (1), one being that "postfeminism signals the 'pastness' of feminism—or, at any rate the end of a particular stage in feminist histories—and a generational shift in understanding the relationship between men and women and, for that matter, women and themselves" (3).[2] As *Witches of East End* begins, it depicts a younger generation—Ingrid and her sister Freya—learning about its family's history and, specifically, the roles that the Beauchamp women historically played. The women struggle to understand and define their own past(s), present, and future in these contexts. While they realize the potential that they did not know existed, they also find themselves conscribed to replay the same roles that they—and the generations of women before them—have played in the past.

The Beauchamp family history presented to Ingrid, her sister Freya (Jenna Dewan Tatum), and the viewer reinforces traditional gender roles and dualistic thinking. Their mother, Joanna (Julia Ormond), and aunt, Wendy (Mädchen Amick), are "cursed," and we learn in season two that their grandfather, Asgardian King Nikolaus (Steven Berkoff), is responsible. The revelation of their grandfather's rule in Asgard and power over his daughters highlights the patriarchal order that underlies—and perhaps undermines—the series. In season two, Joanna and Wendy fight their newly embodied father, challenging, most notably, his attacks on their roles as daughters and women. Wendy, the shapeshifter, is cursed like the cat that she transforms into: performing as the proverbial cat, she has many lives, but they will eventually run out. As King Nikolaus tells her, the curse reflects her "nature"; she is "catlike"—cold, a predator, and only gives love when it suits her purpose ("For Whom the Spell Tolls"). He says that because she is not a "selfless nurturer" like her sister Joanna, his curse rendered Wendy unable to have children ("For Whom the Spell Tolls"). He would not inflict *that* curse on her children.

In contrast to Wendy, Joanna, the "selfless nurturer," suffers a different curse; unlike Wendy, she is immortal but similarly "doomed." As Joanna tells Wendy, "having children is my curse," "immortality with endless mother-hood" ("Pilot"). Explaining to Wendy why she did not tell her daughters about their gifts in this lifetime, Joanna says,

> "I just got sick of it, the endless cycle. I watched my girls grow up, grow into their gifts. And then they die because of it. And before I'm even done mourning, the cycle starts up again. I'm suddenly nine months pregnant with Ingrid. And then soon after comes Freya. And once again my girls grow up, they practice magic, and then, one way or another, they die by its hand, over, and over, and over, and over. I've given birth to them and watched them die over a dozen times and neither of them lived past thirty. I am sick of it. I decided this life, for once, they'd be normal" ["Pilot"].

Exploring how power is rewritten in a postfeminist context, Yvonne Tasker and Diane Negra write, "most postfeminist texts combine a deep uncertainty about existing options for women with an idealized, essentialized femininity that evades or transcends institutional and social problem spots" (10). Joanna's description of the "endless cycle" that she and her daughters are trapped within highlights this uncertainty. Their twentieth-century world affords them new opportunities, more independence and autonomy; however, their past is never truly past. Although Joanna does not want her daughters to be "defined by all [their] other lives" ("Potentia Noctis"), she admits that the girls cannot evade their gifts because "it's who [they] are. It's who [they've] always been" ("Today I Am a Witch"). With its premise, *Witches of East End* presents the roles that women are forced to play, especially in relation to men, again and again throughout history.

With King Nikolaus' curse of motherhood and attack on Wendy's nature, the series projects how the patriarchy confines women to roles that are deemed natural. Elizabeth Grosz writes,

> Patriarchal oppression … justifies itself, at least in part, by connecting women much more closely than men to the body and, through this identification, restricting women's social and economic roles to (pseudo) biological terms. Relying on essentialism, naturalism, and biologism, misogynist thought confines women to the biological requirements of reproduction on the assumption that because of particular biological, physiological, and endocrinological transforma-tions, women are somehow *more* biological, *more* corporeal, and *more* natural than men [14].

The series reinforces these ideas as much as it challenges them. Ingrid discovers an old power in a new form: she is able to give Barb a baby. She is both "more biological" and "more natural." IVF—a product of science—is limited, while magic is full of potential. However, when Barb is admitted to the hospital and at risk of losing the baby and her own life, Ingrid worries that the resurrection spell she uses to revivify Wendy is the cause. As Wendy tells Ingrid, magic has a price; balance has to be restored following "universal law" ("Marilyn Fenwick, R.I.P."). The women cannot create out of nothing, as everything originates in nature. Barb and the baby survive, but Ingrid loses her new love Adam Noble (Jason George). Nature and natural law are asserted, held intact. Throughout the series, the characters continually test the boundaries of both the natural world and their own natures, realizing the limitations of their newly discovered powers in the twenty-first century.

Ingrid and Freya learn that their magic originates from different sources, and the map of their powers appears to be drawn by René Descartes, positioned along the lines of the mind/body dualism. Grosz describes the "correlation and association of the mind/body opposition with the opposition between male and female, where man and mind, woman and body, become representationally aligned" (4) and argues that "misogynist thought has commonly found a convenient self-justification for women's secondary social positions by containing them within bodies that are represented, even constructed, as frail, imperfect, unruly, and unreliable, subject to various intrusions which are not under conscious control" (Grosz 13). *Witches of East End* both reinforces and challenges this binary opposition.

Even before their powers are identified in terms of the mind/body split, reason and emotion are associated with their characters, identifying and distinguishing the two women. The pilot episode reveals that Freya thinks she is a psychic and able to read auras. She is continually referred to as emotional and irrational. Yet rather than reinforce stereotypical representations of women, the series recasts the male/female divide in its depictions of the sisters. Ingrid describes herself as a "rational skeptic" ("Pilot"), looking to science rather than the supernatural for answers. The revelation of the sources of their magic makes these associations literal. Freya learns that she is motivated by her emotions and heart, much like her aunt who is driven by instinct, while Ingrid is motivated by her "strength of mind" and intellect. The characterization of the women introduces a shift from a traditional interpretation of the Cartesian dualism that equates women with the body and men with the mind. However, the series also reinforces dualistic—and misogynistic— thinking by highlighting the contrast between the two sisters. And, once the sisters' "nature" is revealed, Ingrid learns that she can never escape her body: as Grosz describes, it is "frail, imperfect, unruly, and unreliable, subject to various intrusions which are not under conscious control" (13).

Although Freya's connection to her emotions is identified as a source of power, she is characterized as *overly* emotional, even irrational, from the series' beginning. In the pilot episode, Freya says, "I feel off. I had the strangest dream last night." The term "off" is recycled throughout the series to describe the women's behavior. Although Wendy refers to the Beauchamp women as "very intuitive," a positive quality, Joanna tells her daughters that Wendy is a "flake" and that they should not trust anything she says ("Pilot"). Even Freya's fiancé Dash Gardiner (Eric Winter) includes the terms "crazy" and "dramatic" when describing what he loves about her. Later, in season two, after Freya calls off the wedding, a literally venomous Dash verbally attacks her, calling her a "lying bitch" ("When a Mandragora Loves a Woman"). A scene from Freya's past depicts a former jilted lover telling her that she "turned out to be a vindictive little witch like all the rest" ("Marilyn Fenwick, R.I.P."). Elaine Showalter says that the terms "hysteria" and "witchcraft" had "always been pejorative" (54) until hysteria "became a positive term for those trying to write the 'her-story' of hysteria, a story that emphasized the cultural construction of women's hysterical symptoms, diagnosis, and treatment" once women found a "public voice" (54). While Showalter's treatment of witchcraft primarily focuses on witch-hunts as examples of mass hysteria, in *Witches of East End*, hysteria and witchcraft are connected, similarly made pejorative.

The series' treatment of Freya is initially that of the hysterical woman. Tracing the origins of the term, Showalter writes, "Throughout most of its medical history, hysteria has been associated with women" (15). Juliet Mitchell echoes Showalter when she writes, "Of all the psychic, mental, emotional or behavioral conditions known to humankind, it is hysteria which has been bound with bands of steel to femininity, and hence very largely to women" (ix). The term comes from the Greek word for uterus, hysteria, an organ that was believed to go "unfettered" and cause the "disorder" (Showalter 15). In this definition, the mind is affected by the body. In a series where curses upon women are "endless motherhood" and infertility, the appearance of the hysterical woman is particularly significant. The uterus is under the control of King Nikolaus, the patriarch. As Showalter identifies, in later centuries, "doctors relocated the centers of hysteria to the nervous system" and women became the "nervous sex, suffering from vapors, spleen, and fainting fits, or eroticized as hysterical nymphomaniacs" (15). In the contemporary world of *Witches of East End*, the women are similarly overly sexualized. They are constantly depicted having sex or dreaming of having sex. As Freya says of her romantic dreams of Killian, "Every night it's the same thing" ("Today I Am a Witch"). Barbara Becker-Cantarino writes, "The definition of the witch relied on an eroticized construct of female behavior that saw women as threatening and in need of control" (170). In the series, "ancient stereotypes" are "pressed into popular service to interpret all women's frustrations as sexual and irrational" (Showalter 10) again and again.

Freya plays this role well, as she appears to be defined by her romantic entanglements. In season one, torn between two brothers, Dash and Killian Gardiner, Freya frets over which is her "soul mate" and continually uses the term "meant to be" when describing each relationship. After asking Dash if he believes in fate, Freya says, "I believe certain things are written in the stars, like us, we're meant to be" ("Snake Eyes"), but at other times she is convinced that Killian is her soul mate. Joanna finally agrees to read Freya's tarot cards after seeing her daughter struggle with her feelings for the two men. Joanna identifies two figures, the Trickster and the Emperor, brothers and mirror images, and tells Freya that they divide her heart. Freya will love both; however, one is her soul mate and the other her destroyer. Joanna says, "Whoever you choose will decide your fate" ("Unburied"). The remainder of the series leaves Freya questioning which brother represents which figure, wondering which will determine her future. Freya has the illusion of choice; choosing the wrong suitor will destroy her.

As Freya finds herself repeatedly drawn to Killian, she begins to realize that they are "star-crossed lovers." On the day of her wedding, her father Victor (Joel Gretsch) produces evidence that confirms she had known Killian before, in San Francisco in 1906. Victor explains the concept of Samsara, a cycle of death and rebirth. He says that he cannot confirm that Killian is her soul mate; she must "look into [her] heart and decide" ("Oh, What a World!"). This news leads Freya to break up with Dash on their wedding day. However, as Freya learns, her love story with Killian follows a prescribed plot. They are "star-crossed lovers," destined and doomed to lose each other every time. In the season two finale "For Whom the Bell Tolls," after believing Freya is dead, Killian drinks poison to break their curse and join her in the afterlife. Wearing a nightgown like the Juliet awoken from her death-like sleep, Freya appears before Killian to restore him to life with a kiss. The series' play with familiar plots demonstrates one of the central tenets of the series: the characters are doomed—or cursed—to reenact previous scripts. As the Lifetime network moves away from reality television to introduce new scripted series, it faces challenges in creating material that reflects a contemporary reality for women. *Witches of East End* is like its characters—struggling to define itself in relation to its past, to traditional, conventional, and even stereotypical representations of women.

The language of fate is a constant and driving force in *Witches of East End*, yet the series appears to be ambivalent about it: the characters continually reassert fate's role and reference the possibility of changing fate. Joanna tells her sister Wendy that she did not tell her daughters who they are because she wanted to change their fate. Although Wendy initially responds that they cannot change fate, she later says, "Every life is completely different" and "history can change" ("Unburied"). After reading Freya's cards, Joanna tells her that there is a shroud around the future because her choice "isn't yet made" ("Unburied"). However, choosing between the two men will determine her fate. She does not control it; the men do.

*Witches of East End* explores and exposes the central tenets of feminist and postfeminist theories in its representations of the characters' fates and destinies. Tasker and Negra argue that the challenges facing feminist media critics of an earlier era centered on the need to make women visible, to denaturalize the construction of women's culture as inherently trivial or banal. The contemporary challenges that postfeminist culture poses for feminist media studies are rather different. Postfeminism displaces older forms of trivialization, generating a sense of newness, yet it also refreshes long familiar themes of gendered representation, demonstrating the ongoing urgency of speaking feminist critique [22].

*Witches of East End*, marketed as a "new" and "original" scripted series, refreshes and repeats longstanding debates about gender and feminism. Although the characters play the same roles "over, and over, and over, and over," each version is purportedly "different." The series performs the critique that is central to postfeminist theory in questioning (if not challenging) the gains made by feminism and, more specifically, the gains made by a network for women.

Shapeshifting is a recurring trope within the series that allows for experimentation with the women's identities. In the pilot episode, a shapeshifter disguised as Joanna murders a man in a park. The wife asserts that she saw Joanna commit the crime, and Joanna has difficulty proving her innocence. However, when the shapeshifter reanimates a former Ingrid, Joanna is able to recognize her as an imposter and destroy her ("Unburied"). The contemporary Ingrid is distinct and unique. Throughout the series, Ingrid and Freya struggle to understand their relationship to their other selves and other lives. When Ingrid and Freya cast spells that allow them to dream of past lives, Ingrid's is a nightmare of that other self, an Ingrid who becomes obsessed with Archibald Browning (Matthew Del Negro) and dark magic. Freya's is the realization, after visiting different forms of herself, most notably one in a fanciful 1970s disco setting ("Boogie Knight"), that she and Killian are soul mates, constantly reappearing in each other's lives. Where Ingrid learns that she is not the worst version of herself, that she is able to "change and grow, keep moving forward" ("Electric Avenue"), Freya realizes that she and Killian are "meant to be." The spell proves that the women are both connected to and distinct from their past selves.

For Freya, her sense of determinacy is rooted in the body. After traveling to an 1848 Baltimore and meeting her former lover Edgar Allan Poe (played by DiTomasso), Freya wonders why no one else sees that it is Killian ("Poe Way Out"). Wendy explains the confusion, saying that Freya recognizes his soul, so to Freya, the men appear identical. The soul is embodied, rendered to Freya and the viewer as a physical manifestation of the contemporary Killian. Although she can read auras, Freya can only recognize the soul in terms of physical appearance. This is further complicated at the end of season two when an imprisoned Dash performs a body-switching spell with Killian. Freya embraces Dash (as Killian) but does not recognize the difference. Dash promises Killian that the spell is "untraceable," and this may be a plot hole, but it is suggestive of the complications of knowing by way of the body.

As *Witches of East End* complicates the mind/body and male/female binaries in its representations of Ingrid and Freya, season two introduces new complications for the patriarchy. At the end of season one, Penelope Gardiner/Athena Browning (Virginia Madsen), mother of Dash and Killian and daughter of Archibald Browning, dies after being revealed as the shapeshifter. With her death, the magic that she took from her sons is restored. The season one finale "Oh, What a World!" depicts Dash, driven by dark magic, murdering his brother and hiding the evidence. Season two restores Killian to the narrative, revealing that he had been saved by a witch (Bianca Lawson) in Santo Domingo. In season two, the brothers struggle with what they have become. After realizing that his CAT scan is identical to Ingrid's and learning that Ingrid has powers, Dash asks, "I'm a witch?" ("The Old Man and the Key"). Ingrid laughs and says, "Technically, a warlock" ("The Old Man and the Key"). She then adds, "You were born this way" ("The Old Man and the Key"), seemingly borrowing from Lady Gaga's anthem for her "little monsters." Like the women, the men struggle with their inheritances—from their grandfather Archibald, a source of dark magic, and their mother, a shapeshifter.

Yet, at the same time, season two introduces Joanna's son Frederick (Christian Cooke) and father King Nikolaus into the narrative, along with the complications brought by the men's presence in the women's lives. The Beauchamp women's history is determined by men, particularly King Nikolaus, but the men are notably absent in season one. In season two, the series examines the relationships between the men and women and the power of the patriarchal order in a contemporary landscape, with a new generation of men. Additionally, Frederick's role as Freya's twin is important, as it further reflects and complicates the gendered binaries at work in the series. Initially, Frederick is viewed as a threat. The characters fear that he is working for King Nikolaus and question his loyalties. When Frederick is revealed to be a host for the grandfather's spirit, the patriarchy is given new life in the next generation. Frederick does his grandfather's work: he attempts to appease the grandfather by finding a new host body, testing potentials by emblazoning the king's sign on their chests and preparing them as vessels. The ritual fails with many male victims before Frederick is forced to attempt it on his female lover Caroline (Anna Van Hooft). Frederick marks her with the grandfather's sign but is unable to complete the ritual because of his feelings for her. While Caroline evades becoming a vessel for the king, she nonetheless bears his inscription. King Nikolaus' power over women's bodies is asserted and restored with this act. After Ingrid and Freya die, Wendy helps Frederick turn her lover Tommy Cole (Ignacio Serricchio) into a host so that King

Nikolaus can resurrect Ingrid and Freya without consequence, without upsetting the "natural" order. Not surprisingly, King Nikolaus is above or outside of nature itself.

The season and series finale "For Whom the Spell Tolls" offers a final challenge to the patriarchy. The women realize that King Nikolaus plans to steal their magic so that he can restore his failing power. Tortured by her father, Wendy tells him, "No matter how much power you steal from us, you'll never be as strong as the three of us together" ("For Whom the Spell Tolls"). At the end of the series, the women are revealed to be the archetypal figures represented in a book, *The Occult History of Sorcery*, which Ingrid discovers while working as a curator. The history of the Beauchamp women depicted in the text casts them in their roles: The Key (Ingrid), The Dagger (Joanna), The Bridge (Wendy), and The Traveler (Freya). The idea that each woman represents a symbol represented within a book introduces new questions for the series. The metaphorical transformation of the women seems to disempower them. While their roles are depicted as recurring "over, and over, and over, and over," here their identities are conscripted in a text that predates them. Their power is literally emplotted. However, the recognition of their roles affords them the power to kill King Nikolaus. Although King Nikolaus initially calls the spell "cute" and affirms that he is "much stronger" than them, he is destroyed by the collective powers of the Beauchamp women. Freya punctuates the point by saying, "We killed the king" ("For Whom the Spell Tolls"). At the end of the series, power is located in the community of women.

This ambiguity about the women's power is compounded by the warlocks' roles. The old empire, Asgard, is defeated; the king is dead. But there is another patriarchy beyond Asgard, one that has roots in an older East End. Dash has access to his ancestor Archibald's spells, and the Browning patriarchy is restored. A contemporary East End suffers a string of murders— those committed by Frederick, under the control of King Nikolaus and Tarkoff (James Marsters), and Dash himself once he is blackmailed with evidence of Killian's supposed death. Dash is arrested and imprisoned for the murders, and his brother, his first would-be victim, pays him a visit. Dash performs a spell to switch bodies with Killian, gaining power over all of the characters. Killian is unable to escape the prison of Dash's body, and the women are unaware that a substitution has been made. Dash (as Killian) leaves the room, joining Freya outside. Another plot twist is the confirmation of Ingrid's pregnancy. The father is either Dash, in a repetition of the Archibald/Ingrid plot of 1906, or the Mandragora, a mythical beast sent from Asgard by King Nikolaus to pursue Frederick. The Mandragora drew its power from Ingrid, using her body to replenish itself. Like Killian, and like her mother before her, Ingrid's body is acted upon, a vessel for whatever dark forces were planned for season three. Paralleling the ending of *The Lottery*, *Witches of East End* leaves its female characters in extremis.

## A Brave New World? The Lottery's *Biological Determinism*

Like *Witches of East End*, *The Lottery* begins with a reproductive crisis. With creator Sexton at the helm, *The Lottery* constructs a "children of men" reminiscent of the 2006 film; however, where the film highlights the struggle to protect a pregnant woman who is the key to the population's survival, in *The Lottery*, science is able to create new life in the form of one hundred embryos. The pilot episode begins with the announcement of an "an alarming drop in worldwide human birth rates" that resulted in infertility. The series, set in the future in 2025, references a fertility crisis that occurred in 2016 and resulted in a "new chapter in human history" ("Crystal City").[3] A montage, mostly composed of news coverage, depicts the aftermath. A poster featuring a blond woman wearing a star-spangled bikini reads "SAM WANTS YOU" and "DONATE AT YOUR LOCAL SPERM CLINIC" ("Pilot"). A reporter states that the last kindergarten has closed its doors; amusement parks and bassinets in a hospital ward are empty ("Pilot").

The images tell the story, but that story is complemented by the male narrative-makers depicted onscreen. Women, like children, are notably absent. In a press conference, Dr. Singh (Raahul Singh), identified by a name-plate, says that "radiation, airborne viruses, contamination, and chemical weapons all may be contributing factors" ("Pilot"). After the title sequence, the president of the United States (Yul Vazquez) is introduced and begins his speech:

> My fellow Americans, we have endured a period of hopelessness without parallel in human history. The global fertility crisis has devastated our most fundamental dreams…. We spent these last five years searching for causes and solutions while living with the possibility of human extinction. Our efforts to solve this mystery have been relentless, and comprehensive, and unsuccessful. Until today. This is the first step on our journey to restore our future, the future of our humanity ["Pilot"].

Shots of the president giving his speech, viewed directly and through various camera and television monitors, are juxtaposed with those of a blond woman being followed by a man. After stopping to watch the end of the president's address, she turns and gasps when she sees her pursuer directly behind her.

The editing that frames *The Lottery* suggests the power dynamics at play within the series. A male scientist and male president are broadcast to an entire population, including Lifetime viewers. The men control the world, and their language shapes it. Conversely, a woman, unidentified by title or name, goes mostly unnoticed by the people around her. Ironically, as the president begins his speech, the credits appear onscreen with the name Marley Shelton given first billing. Shelton plays the role of Dr. Alison Lennon, the scientist who made the breakthrough in the fertility crisis. However, her identity as a scientist is veiled for the first eleven minutes of the episode.

The series plays with the construction of its female lead; she is first cast as a victim and then as a promiscuous woman. The pilot episode flashes back to three days earlier, in Baltimore, Maryland, where Alison (still unidentified) sits at a bar. A man (Ryan Bruce) approaches her, offering to buy her a drink, but she declines. The man tells her, "You know, I fathered a daughter nine years ago. I have her picture" ("Pilot"), identifying the importance of fertility in this environment, including the dating scene. Alison rejects his advances and focuses on finding the man that she seeks, Gregor (Matthew Mandzij). Gregor is initially surprised that Alison is interested in him, but, after they have sex, she tells him, "Women look for the wrong things. I happen to like the premature hair loss. It indicates a high level of testosterone. And your features show Somalian blood. Somalians used to have the highest fertility rate in the world" ("Pilot"). Alison's knowledge of science, which could be the key to preventing extinction, is juxtaposed with a different kind of biological determinism: desperate attempts to become pregnant.

Alison is equally determined when she is depicted at work in the Government Fertility Lab. She rushes into the lab, and Dr. James Lynch (David Alpay), her lab assistant and the male narrative-maker in the scene, announces, "Behold, the first viable human embryo ... in six years" ("Pilot"). Although James is Alison's assistant, he, like Dr. Singh and the president, defines the world of *The Lottery* for the viewers. Similarly, Alison is the lead scientist responsible for the breakthrough, but it is ultimately Director of the U.S. Fertility Commission Darius Hayes (Martin Donovan) who has power in and over the lab. When Hayes asks, "Every other lab in the world has failed. How did you do it?" Alison says that they "in essence ... recreated the environment of a healthy, pre-crisis uterus" ("Pilot"). Alison's phrasing is significant as it highlights how the female scientist is able to simulate a healthy fetus, something that other (male) scientists are unable to do. When Hayes asks about fertilizing more than the original one hundred eggs, Alison is cautious, saying that they need to do more tests. He replies, "I appreciate your diligence, but we'll be taking the lead from this point going forward" ("Pilot"). The government, depicted as a patriarchy rather than a democratic institution, establishes its control over reproduction. When Alison asserts that it is her lab, Hayes says that the lab is financed by the United States government, and a new team will be entering it. Here the lab is rendered as a feminine space reappropriated by a team of male scientists who claim that the space was always already theirs.

The struggle for power over the lab and the embryos is played out in gendered terms. Once her job is completed, Alison is dismissed and denied access to the lab. Although she protests, Hayes replies, "The decision has been made" ("Pilot"). After revealing that he has been asked to continue his work at the lab, James tells Alison that she cannot expect him to "fall on [his] sword," but she counters that it is her sword. James says, "That's why you got fired. You don't know how to play well with others" ("Pilot"). The language in this scene is telling, as the sword, a phallic and traditionally masculine weapon, is exchanged between the two characters. When Alison criticizes James, saying that "playing well with others" is his "specialty" and a "turn-off," James responds, "You know what's a turn-off? My boss using confidential sperm donor lists to find sexual partners" ("Pilot"). Even and especially in the fertility lab, power is both gendered and sexualized.

Once the government "tak[es] the lead," the chain of command is complicated. Hayes reports the results to President Westwood and charts a course of action, suggesting that the Army oversee the operation. Hayes proposes that they use military hospitals, doctors, and female soldiers as surrogates ("Pilot"). Hayes' proposal is that men continue to lead, and the military, depicted as a patriarchal organization with its female soldiers as "surrogates," completes the picture. The president asks for the opinion of the Deputy Secretary (J. August Richards), who replies that it is "reasonable" ("Pilot"). When the president turns to his female Chief of Staff, Vanessa Keller (Athena Karkanis), he refers to her on more familiar terms, asking, "Vanessa, what do you think?" ("Pilot"). Despite her seemingly secondary position as the president's advisor, Vanessa is assertive, replying, "I think we do the exact opposite. Keeping this a secret is a mistake. Let's shout our success from the rooftops" ("Pilot"). Although Hayes says that it is reckless, Vanessa sees it as strategic, a "game-changing event" that will keep their office in control ("Pilot"). Hayes' use of the word "reckless" is suggestive. It contrasts the "reasonable" response from his male Deputy Secretary and recalls Grosz's description of "misogynist thought" that conceives women as "unruly, and unreliable, subject to various intrusions which are not under conscious control" (13). However, her opinion is not discounted.

Vanessa is established as a female narrative-maker in this scene, a single voice in the male-dominated world of *The Lottery*. Yet she does not advocate for women. When she tells the president that she wants to "sell hope" ("Pilot"), it is an ironic reversal from her previous stance. In an earlier scene, she confronts her brother Nick (Michael Irby), who is being held for selling counterfeit fertility drugs. She accuses him of "exploiting desperate women," but he counters by saying that he is "selling hope" ("Pilot"). Nick says, "For fifty bucks, these women they went home feeling better about themselves, like they had a chance at winning something big. Hitting the jackpot. That's all an average Joe wants, a chance at something great" ("Pilot"). When Vanessa suggests the idea for the lottery to President Westwood, she says that every woman will feel like she has "a chance to win the jackpot" and borrows her brother's lines in their entirety ("Pilot"). However, although Vanessa's proposal indicates that the power of reproduction is returned to its citizens, notably the mothers, it remains under the government's control. Selling hope to "desperate women," originally Vanessa's critique of her brother's actions, becomes governmental policy. And, ironically, the lottery at the center of the series is suggestive of Lifetime's work with the series: both provide an illusion of hope and progress for women. That the idea for the lottery is "pitched" by a woman is intriguing, reflective perhaps of the series' origins and development at Lifetime.

Like *Witches of East End*, *The Lottery* is an emplotted narrative that recycles earlier narratives and tropes. The lottery at the series' center is not based on Shirley Jackson's story, but it similarly targets women. As women are cast as incubators, the narrative resembles a classical story with a similar argument: Aeschylus' *Oresteia* trilogy. In Aeschylus' *Eumenides*, Apollo and Athena famously defend Orestes' actions and the role of the father.[4] In *The Lottery*, women are necessary for reproduction: female scientists and biological mothers play central roles. However, the fate of the embryos—of creation itself—is left to a male president and male scientists. Grosz writes, "Female sexuality and women's powers of reproduction are the defining (cultural) characteristics of women, and, at the same time, these very functions render women vulnerable, in need of protection or special treatment, as variously prescribed by patriarchy" (14). *The Lottery*, like *Children of Men* before it, represents a society governed and controlled by men. Despite its scientific advancements, the world of *The Lottery* is entrenched in the past.

Alison's attempts to regain control over her research can be read as fighting for control over the female body. However, the series' argument about women's rights in both domains is ambiguous at best. When Alison locates one of the successful egg donors, she learns that the woman, Brooke Ashton (Amanda Brooks), was a college student "desperate for cash" who considered stripping to pay her bills; Brooke admits, "I had the body for it" ("Pilot"). But she realized that her fertility is more valuable than her sexuality. Brooke embodies Grosz's argument about how "patriarchal oppression" connects "women much more closely than men to the body" and "restrict[s] women's social and economic roles to (pseudo) biological terms" (14). Brooke signed away her parental rights, but she argues that the child is hers. She appears to answer Kathryn Woodward's question if motherhood "more than any other identity, is rooted in biology; where reproduction is a universal fact of nature from which all aspects of maternal identity must follow?" (240) by claiming her status as the child's mother. Alison and Brooke's discussion about rights to the embryo recall Adrienne Rich's categorization of "two meanings of motherhood, one superimposed on the other: the *potential relationship* of any woman to her powers of reproduction and to children; and the *institution*, which aims at ensuring that that potential—and all women—shall remain under male control" (13). Brooke's biological argument does not have currency in this new system.

In the new political climate, the power to reproduce and "mother" is assigned to the patriarchy. When President Westwood asks a female doctor, Dr. Campbell, about how to conduct the lottery, she says,

> From a medical perspective, all I care about is having one hundred healthy, active surrogates willing to adhere to a proper diet and exercise regimen. As for the motherhood part of this, it really isn't a matter for debate. Being a good mother is a subjective thing. I don't know how you could possibly prescreen for that ["Rules of the Game"].

Dr. Campbell's reference to the subjectivity of the term recalls Rich's line "We know more about the air we breathe, the seas we travel, than about the nature and meaning of motherhood" (11).[5] While the female doctor separates biological and environmental factors, the male Director of the Fertility Commission offers a differing opinion. Hayes replies that there are "clearly objective data points" that would predict "stable parenting." He suggests that they define what makes a "great mother" in terms of her "values, her lifestyle, where she went to school, who they're married to" ("Rules of the Game"). Vanessa challenges this idea, asking, "Who are we to decide what makes a good mother? Is she gay, straight, rich, poor, single?" And later, when President Westwood is scheduled to discuss the qualities of a "good mother" with reporters, he admits, "What the hell do I know?" ("Crystal City").

As the concept of motherhood is radically resignified in *The Lottery*, it reflects contemporary debates within feminist and motherhood studies. When President Westwood affirms that they cannot give one hundred embryos to "just anyone," Hayes introduces another question: "What will the government's role be in the children's lives going forward?" He then answers his own question, saying,

> [G]iven the state of the world right now, shouldn't we, in effect, be the mother? ... We can't just relinquish control of the embryos. Our embryos. We need to maintain a certain ownership interest.... Our previous folksy, preconceived notions of motherhood and childhood no longer apply. That ship has sailed ["Rules of the Game"].

Recalling Rich's distinctions between motherhood and mothering, Andrea O'Reilly writes that "the reality of patriarchal motherhood thus must be distinguished from the possibility or potentiality of gynocentric or feminist mothering" (*From Motherhood* 2). Hayes' proposal is that patriarchal motherhood be extended to mothering, as the government will continue its role going forward. O'Reilly argues that "with the advent of the twentieth century, a more policy-based perspective on the institution of motherhood is both judicious and essential" (*Twenty-First Century Motherhood* 3).[6] *The Lottery* makes a similar claim: as "preconceived notions of motherhood and childhood no longer apply," policy must be redesigned.

While Hayes collapses the categories of parent and government, allowing the latter to act upon—and act as—the former, Vanessa attempts to address the complex issues that the lottery raises. Identifying "surrogacy and parenting" as distinct concepts, the Chief of Staff offers a two-part solution: they choose two hundred "biologically viable" surrogates that meet the "agreed-upon medical criteria" and invite them to DC for interviews before choosing the one hundred who they feel would make the best mothers ("Rules of the Game"). When the polls do not change and Vanessa fears that the citizens are not invested, she proposes that the president allow the public to "pick the next generation of mothers" ("Genie"). However, the problems inherent when the government is allowed control over the female body manifest.

Alison is a fitting protagonist in this drama because she seemingly occupies different positions in the nature/nurture, reason/emotion, and mind/body dichotomies. Arguably, these inconsistencies can be read as design flaws; however, they are suggestive of the terms of the debate. Like Brooke, Alison was adopted and longs for the connection found in motherhood. While *The Lottery* more obviously plays out the drama of fertility and infertility than *Witches of East End*, it covers similar ground in representing women as embodied subjects, driven by emotion rather than reason. Grosz writes, "By implication, women's bodies are presumed to be incapable of men's achievements, being weaker, more prone to (hormonal) irregularities, intrusions, and unpredictabilities" (14). Hayes refers to Alison as a "loose cannon," saying that the men "can't control what she does" ("Genie"). After Alison steals an embryo, trying to salvage her work, she is represented as a threat to the state, unpredictable, volatile, and dangerous.

Alison's interest in reproduction is both scientific and personal. These issues are complicated from the series' beginning, as depicted in the competing versions of Alison: victim, promiscuous woman, and scientist. When Alison attempts to steal the embryo to impregnate Brooke and appeals to James for help, she does not cite Brooke's argument that Brooke has rights to the embryo. Instead, Alison considers Brooke the "perfect surrogate" ("Pilot"). The scientist sees nature in a different way and perhaps is more closely aligned with the bureaucrats than she thinks. Alison's and Hayes' ideas about locating a "perfect surrogate" render women as "more biological" and "more corporeal" (Grosz 14) than men.

In *The Lottery*, the viability of a woman's potential is, like the embryos, questionable. As the narrative returns to the president's press conference, he completes his speech by saying that there are one hundred embryos, "one hundred potential children who will require one hundred women to mother them to maturity as the vanguard of the next generation" ("Pilot"). By "executive decree," he institutes a national lottery that offers desperate women eager to conceive the hope of mothering that potential. Borrowing Vanessa's— and, by extension, her brother's—language, the president says that the women will carry a "torch of promise into a brighter future" ("Pilot"). The president's speech is belied by its source and the images concurrently unfolding onscreen. Brooke is killed in her house, and Alison is pursued by one of Hayes' men. Darkness and light, that dichotomous pairing, complements the series' contradictory messages.

In *The Lottery*, men are also victims of the patriarchy. Kyle Walker (Michael Graziadei) is the father of one of the last six children born in 2019, Elvis (Jesse Filkow). Kyle is depicted as a single father struggling to raise a child on his own after his wife, a drug addict, left the family. In the pilot episode, when Kyle drops his son off at school, mothers tell the father that it must not be easy for him as a single father and offer to help take care of Elvis because the boy is important to them. Kyle pulls up to a house where a woman in a white silk nightgown answers the door and says, "Great, I just started ovulating" ("Pilot"). Like the potential donor/suitor that approaches Alison at the bar, Kyle—and his fertility—is viewed as a commodity in this society.

But his power, even though initially depicted as potent, is limited. When Kyle appears at school late to pick up his son, he is greeted by a man and two women, one being the mother he rebuked. As Kyle enters the building, Molly (Nicole Cannon), the mother, says, "I just want what's right for Elvis" ("Pilot"). The man identifies himself and his partner as representing the Department of Humanity (DOH), later identified as an "autonomous" institution ("Genie"). The DOH agents inquire about the suitability of Elvis' biological father and decide to take custody of the boy. The end of the pilot episode affords Kyle new power: he escapes from a hospital with his son and is revealed to be the sperm donor of the embryo that Alison steals. However, the DOH reassumes control over Kyle and his son's lives: Elvis is soon returned to custody despite his father's protests that he is the best caretaker ("Genie"). Like Alison, Kyle's dual roles within the narrative suggest the complexities of the debates about nature vs. nurture and traditional gender roles.

Kyle has currency as the "last man to impregnate a woman," but once Alison tests his sperm, believing that the "secret must be inside of [him] somewhere" ("Greater Good"), she learns its source. James discovers that Kyle possesses a retrovirus, the "Black Death" that supposedly died out in the sixteenth century. Alison identifies the irony of the situation: "So the most fertile man in America has the bubonic plague?" ("Greater Good"). This paradox leads to another: the U.S. government released the sterility virus and created the vaccine that provides protection against it. The institution behind the lottery is a pharmakon, poison and cure. When the president is assassinated in the series finale, the patriarchy does not die. Although he credits *Star Wars*, James sounds like a character from *Witches of East End* when he says, "The Emperor is dead. The forces of evil are gathering power" ("In Extremis"). The hit was planned by Hayes, suggesting that power extends beyond one single man. At its conclusion, *The Lottery* evidences how the patriarchy will outlive the individuals actively working toward change. The other alternative for the future is another "children of men" society: Alison, Kyle, and Elvis escape with an egg donated by a now post-op transgendered man and fertilized by Kyle's sperm. The casualties of *The Lottery*'s system most notably are the women, pawns in the game, left in extremis despite the best efforts of the female characters within the series and behind the Lifetime network.

## Survival of the Fittest?

When assessing the fates of the two series in 2015, Hundley's 2002 comment that the Lifetime network "did not just magically appear" but "evolved" (175) takes new meaning. *Witches of East End* and *The Lottery* present visions of the future that are consistent with Herbert Spencer's "essentially dualistic" evolutionary theory (Prystash 344). Justin Prystash writes that this theory is a "unique amalgamation of science and philosophy" that "assumes that time unfolds, and evolution develops, according to a dialectical process of differentiation and integration, progress and decline, change and stasis" (344). According to Prystash, Spencer's theory remains "incredibly productive" because it "enables imaginative visions of the past and future through narrative recombination of forms" (345). In *Witches of East End*, the same characters are reincarnated over and over throughout time, and in *The Lottery*, the attempt to mitigate overpopulation leads to an infertility crisis. The series recall the theory that presents an "impassable limit," eventually "terminat[ing] evolution itself" (Prystash 345). Stasis is the end game of both series, punctuated by the network's early terminations.

The brief runs of *Witches of East End* and *The Lottery* provide curious case studies for a network built upon an innovative model of gendercasting. *Witches of East End* and *The Lottery* indicate a turning point for the network with their participation in a conversation about what postfeminism means in the context of twenty-first century television. Grosz writes that what is at stake in the struggles between patriarchs and feminists is the "activity and agency, the mobility and social space, accorded to women" (19). As the two series represent the ways that women are shaped by their collective pasts and conceive the future—in relation to and outside of the patriarchy—they reflect the network's vision. The questions that the series raise about women's roles in the past, present, and future are important ones for conceiving the future of a network for women. Lifetime's lineup for 2015 is mostly comprised of reality series, with the exception of *Devious Maids* (2013–) and *UnREAL* (2015–). *UnREAL*, premiering after *Witches of East End* and *The Lottery* ended their runs, can be read as initiating the next generation of Lifetime in its deconstruction of ideas about reality and reality television. Arguably, *Witches of East End* and *The Lottery* began that work earlier by turning to magical realism and science fiction.

Lifetime has established itself as a "pioneer in the growing cable universe to become the preeminent television destination and escape for women" (mylifetime.com), building a network of women, for women, since 1984. However, the industry has changed significantly in the twenty-first century.[7] As Amanda D. Lotz acknowledges, as the post-network era is "still very much defined by uncertainty for both its practitioners and academic researchers," its emerging nature "makes it an invaluable site of study for determining larger patterns, perhaps before they become historical rather than contemporary practices" (41). The production and cancellation of *Witches of East End* and *The Lottery* introduce questions for the network about its vision for the future of women's television. Do the series reach an "impassable limit" by their own designs or did the network cease to evolve? While the possibilities for renewals seem unlikely, the idea that viewers have the potential to shape the future of television is itself a sign of evolution, of progress.

## Notes

1. While the network originated in 1984, the slogan was adopted in 1989 under Pat Fili, senior vice president of programming and production (Hundley 176).

2. Defining postfeminism, Genz and Brabon write, "Loathed by some and celebrated by others, it emerged in the late twentieth century in a number of cultural, academic and political contexts, from popular journalism and media to feminist analyses, postmodern theories and neo-liberalist rhetoric" (1). They explore the term's multiplicity and plurality—including questions about the "passing" of feminism that the term suggests (2–3).

3. Although a work of "science fiction," *The Lottery* is staged in a contemporary reality. Amel Alghrani identifies reproductive advances such as IVF, sex selection, reproductive cloning and embryo selection as "promising to upset the status quo and transform human reproduction" (718).

4. Apollo says, "The mother is no parent of that which is called / her child, but

only nurse of the new-planted seed / that grows. The parent is he who mounts....
There can / be a father without any mother" (Aeschylus 28).

 5. Woodward highlights the competing ideas about motherhood, writing,
"Motherhood is seen as a social institution represented and produced through different symbolic systems, but it is also claimed to be biological and have an essential
nature. Feminist approaches, ranging from Kate Millett's location of the family and
mothers within it as the chief site of oppression of women (1971) and Shulamith Firestone's demands that women be freed from 'the tyranny of reproduction' (1971), to
Adrienne Rich's celebration of motherhood, freed from patriarchal constraints (1977),
challenged assumptions about motherhood, including its idealization within culture"
(241).

 6. O'Reilly cites that "less attention has been paid to how the institution of motherhood is … enacted and enforced through policy, whether governmental, health,
work, or educational" (*Twenty-First Century Motherhood* 3). *The Lottery* ostensibly
answers her call by highlighting how governmental policy regarding reproduction is
(re)constructed in the future.

 7. Lynn Spigel argues that the demise of the U.S. three-network system, the rise
of multichannel cable and global satellite delivery, Internet convergence, the advent
of high-definition TV, technological changes in screen design, digital video recorders,
and new forms of programming have "transformed the practice we call watching TV"
(83). Jason Mittell identifies a "new model of television storytelling" as "Complex
TV," which he argues results from shifts in expectations of "how viewers watch television, how producers create stories, and how series are distributed" (3).

## WORKS CITED

Aeschylus. *The Eumenides*. Trans. Richard Lattmore. *Greek Tragedies*, Vol. 3, 2d ed.
 Chicago: University of Chicago Press, 1991. 4–41. Print.
Alghrani, Amel. "The Human Fertilisation and Embryo Act 2008: A Missed Opportunity?" *Journal of Medical Ethics* 35.12 (2009): 718–719. JSTOR. Web. 15 Mar.
 2015.
Becker-Cantarino, Barbara. "'Feminist Consciousness' and 'Wicked Witches': Recent
 Studies on Women in Early Modern Europe." *Signs: Journal of Women in Culture
 and Society* 20.1 (1994): 152–175. JSTOR. Web. 15 Mar. 2015.
"Boogie Knight." *Witches of East End*. Lifetime. 10 Aug. 2014. *Vudu*. Web.
"Crystal City." *The Lottery*. Lifetime. 17 Aug. 2014. Television.
"Electric Avenue." *Witches of East End*. Lifetime. 3 Nov. 2013. *Netflix*. Web.
"Genie." *The Lottery*. Lifetime. 10 Aug. 2014. Television.
"Greater Good." *The Lottery*. Lifetime. 3 Aug. 2014. Television.
"For Whom the Spell Tolls." *Witches of East End*. Lifetime. 5 Oct. 2014. *Vudu*. Web.
Genz, Stéphanie, and Benjamin A. Brabon. *Postfeminism: Cultural Texts and Theories*.
 Edinburgh: Edinburgh University Press, 2009.
Grosz, Elizabeth. *Volatile Bodies: Toward a Corporeal Feminism*. Bloomington: Indiana
 University Press, 1994. Print.
Hundley, Heather. "The Evolution of Gendercasting: The Lifetime Television Network—Television for Women." *Journal of Popular Film and Television* 29.4 (2002):
 174–181. Web. 20 Oct. 2014.
Lotz, Amanda D. "Textual (Im)Possibilities in the U.S. Post-Network Era: Negotiating
 Production and Promotion Processes on Lifetime's *Any Day Now*." *Critical Studies
 in Media Communication* 21.1 (2004): 22–43. JSTOR. Web. 15 Mar. 2015.
"Marilyn Fenwick, R.I.P." *Witches of East End*. Lifetime. 13 Oct. 2013. *Netflix*. Web.

Mitchell, Juliet. *Mad Men and Medusas: Reclaiming Hysteria*. New York: Basic, 2000. Print.

Mittell, Jason. *Complex TV: The Poetics of Contemporary Television Storytelling*. New York: New York University Press, 2015. Print.

"Oh, What a World!" *Witches of East End*. Lifetime. 15 Dec. 2013. *Netflix*. Web.

O'Reilly, Andrea. Introduction. *From Motherhood to Mothering: The Legacy of Adrienne Rich's*

*Of Woman Born*. Ed. O'Reilly. Albany: State University of New York Press, 2004. 1–23. Print.

_____. Introduction. *Twenty-First Century Motherhood: Experience, Identity, Policy, Agency*. Ed. O'Reilly. New York: Columbia University Press, 2010. 1–20. Print.

"The Old Man and the Key." *Witches of East End*. Lifetime. 20 July 2014. *Vudu*. Web.

"Pilot." *The Lottery*. Lifetime. 20 July 2014. Television.

"Pilot." *Witches of East End*. Lifetime. 6 Oct. 2013. *Netflix*. Web.

"Poe Way Out." *Witches of East End*. Lifetime. 28 Sept. 2014. *Vudu*. Web.

"Potentia Noctis." *Witches of East End*. Lifetime. 10 Nov. 2013. *Netflix*. Web.

Prystash, Justin. "Sexual Futures: Feminism and Speculative Fiction in the Fin de Siècle."

*Science Fiction Studies* 41.2 (2014): 341–363. *JSTOR*. Web. 20 Mar. 2015.

Rich, Adrienne. *Of Woman Born: Motherhood as Experience and Institution*, 2d ed. New York: W.W. Norton, 1986. Print.

"Rules of the Game." *The Lottery*. Lifetime. 27 Aug. 2014. Television.

Showalter, Elaine. *Hystories: Hysterical Epidemics and Modern Media*. New York: Columbia University Press, 1997. Print.

"Snake Eyes." *Witches of East End*. Lifetime. 24 Nov. 2013. *Netflix*. Web.

Spigel, Lynn. "TV's Next Season?" *Cinema Journal* 45.1 (2005): 83–90. *JSTOR*. Web. 25 Mar. 2015.

Tasker, Yvonne, and Diane Negra. Introduction. *Interrogating Postfeminism: Gender and the Politics of Popular Culture*. Ed. Tasker and Negra. Durham: Duke University Press, 2007. 1–25. Print.

"Today I Am a Witch." *Witches of East End*. Lifetime. 20 Oct. 2013. *Netflix*. Web.

"Unburied." *Witches of East End*. Lifetime. 17 Nov. 2013. *Netflix*. Web.

"When a Mandragora Loves a Woman." *Witches of East End*. Lifetime. 17 Aug. 2014. *Vudu*. Web.

Woodward, Kathryn. *Identity and Difference*. London: Sage, 1997. Print.

# Part III

# Original Movies

# "She needs some food"

## Eating Disorders, Lifetime and the Made-for-TV Movie

EMILY L. NEWMAN

Anorexia Nervosa. Self-starvation. Usually it's found in an adolescent who feels she has no control over anything in her life, so she denies her hunger in order to have control of at least one thing–her body. Also has something to do with the fear of growing up, of sexuality. Anorexic girls lose their breasts, stop having periods. In general, they revert to a childlike system. It's a very serious disease. Last year, 5,000 girls died from anorexia nervosa.... It's not caused physically. I think it's spreading because of everybody's preoccupation with thinness. Look at your fashion magazines. The models look like six-week-old cadavers. Half the country is dieting, with a lot of casualties.

That is how eating disorders are defined to a young sufferer's parents in *The Best Little Girl in the World* (1981). But of course the doctor is speaking to more than the parents; he is defining a mysterious disorder to a primarily unin-formed public. Airing originally on ABC on May 11, 1981, this film was undoubt-edly made to accompany the rising public interest and awareness of eating disorders. Until the 1970s, knowledge surrounding anorexia and eating disorders was primarily limited to the medical community (Brumberg, *Fasting Girls* 255). It was not until 1980 that the *Diagnostic and Statistical Manual of Mental Dis-orders*, the book used by health care professionals to help with diagnoses, added anorexia nervosa (Martin 22). Furthermore, substantial changes in the approach to treating anorexia came in 1979, when psychiatrists reclassified bulimia from being one of the symptoms of anorexia to being its own distinct diagnosis of anorexia. This was followed by bulimia being classified as a disease in itself in 1985 (Vandereycken 14; Brumberg, *Fasting Girls* 14). By recognizing bulimia and anorexia as separate diseases, psychiatrists were acknowledging both the need for more awareness of eating disorders and their increasing prevalence.

It was not just doctors who created more awareness of society's shrinking female body size; it was the rise of the diet and exercise industry in the 1970s. In less than a year after its release, *Dr. Atkins' Diet Revolution* (1972) had sold one million copies, and by 1977, Weight Watchers had recruited nine million people (Seid 166–168). Additionally, Jane Fonda popularized aerobics, founding her own studio in 1979 and creating the first aerobics home video ever produced, *Jane Fonda's Workout*, in 1982 (Fonda 391–394). The attention to health consciousness, coupled with the changes to diagnoses, undoubtedly prompted more public attention to eating disorders. Throughout the 1970s, articles on the topic periodically appeared with gradual frequency the mainstream media. By 1975, eating disorders, and increasingly their diagnoses, were no longer rare; rather, they were more and more common (Bruch viii). As bulimia and anorexia became part of the public consciousness, they also became the subject of newspaper features, celebrity tell-alls, and made-for-television movies.

That first movie, *The Best Little Girl in the World*, was based on a book of the same name by Steven Levenkron, originally published in 1978. A psychotherapist specializing in eating disorders, Levenkron wrote the novel based on his own experiences and interactions with patients. Describing the text, Katherine Oldis sees several direct messages emerge: "The anorexic *feels* she doesn't belong; she must learn to verbalize her feelings and needs; she fears gaining weight because that's easier than being rejected; and she'll stay sick until she feels assured of the affection and attention she craves" (86). In both the text and movie, Levenkron demonstrates his nurturant-authoritative approach, which is a combination of offering patients support, guidance, and ground rules. He elaborates:

> We are nurturing that patient, being authoritative with her, and helping her to become dependent instead of independent. The message is: It is OK to be dependent; it is making progress to be dependent; you will still be loved even if you have need; it's marvelous to have mastered your independence but your basic education in dependence is lacking [243].

The movie, then, while it does show the main character's increasing captivation with their daughter's weight and weight loss, also focuses significantly on her and her family's therapy sessions and breakthroughs. The therapist provides comfort and structure for the patient, even promising her that she will get better.

In these repeated interactions, both Levenkron and director Sam O'Steen emphasize the depiction of therapy and recovery in their story, setting the stage for later made-for-television movies. In part because filmmakers are dealing with severe and traumatic subjects, crafting a cathartic ending allows the viewer to process what they have seen and offer some sense of hope.

These films also attempt to be current with the times, emphasizing various types of therapy and changing viewpoints, as well as showcasing the way that the disorder has progressed with advances in technology. We can see then that beginning in the early 1980s, television movies took on the task of educating the public on eating disorders and treatments. With a heavy dose of moralizing, these films reflect the developing research and psychological approaches as well as the changing cultural understandings and technological advancements affecting discussions concerning eating disorders.

Most of these films have at some point appeared on the television network Lifetime. What is unique about this set of twelve made-for-TV movies on the subject, is that even if they were created by another major network (ABC or NBC, for example), eventually they would end up airing on Lifetime, or its partner network Lifetime Movie Network. Because these films focus on women and eating disorders (an issue that primarily concerns women), it is logical, then, that they eventually air on a network whose most famous slogan was "Television for Women." Regardless of where the movies aired originally, I argue that they are perceived to fall into primarily two categories: a major network movie-of-the-week geared towards young adults or a Lifetime film. Yet these films in actuality fit into *both* categories because of their repetitious re-airing on Lifetime network and their presentation of content. In their often melodramatic and over-the-top performances, these films share major plot points and characteristics, which are explored in depth in this essay. Furthermore, and beyond that, Lifetime has actively worked to expand its young adult audience by producing and airing a number of different films aimed at young women, such as *The Choking Game* (2014), *The Pregnancy Project* (2012), *Girl Fight* (2011), *Pregnancy Pact* (2010), *Girl Positive* (2007), and *Too Young to Marry* (2007). In that line of thinking, where these films originally aired is not terribly significant, as these movies live on in re-airings or even just in public perception. These films epitomize the Lifetime brand.

The Eating Disorder made-for-television movie ends up following a fairly strict formula. Through an examination of these repeated narrative events, the history and development of these films can be charted. Additionally, it is worth comparing these films to an HBO episode of *Lifestories: Families in Crisis* and a British television movie, *Catherine*, to see their very different approaches, particularly in light of the similarity of the "Lifetime" film. Moreover, in the mid–2000s, new Eating Disorder films were not produced, instead, documentary television specials and series dominated the market. After these examinations and comparisons, conclusions can be made about the impact of these films on society, and in particular young women.

## Eating Disorder Film Tropes

### "You're running heavy."

In almost every Eating Disorder film, there is a moment when the lead character is told she should lose weight—whether it be to look better, to help her perform, or to advance her career. In 1996, *Dying to be Perfect: The Ellen Hart Peña Story* told the true story of an Olympic-caliber athlete who struggled with bulimia for over ten years. In the first few minutes of the film, Ellen is shown running a long distance. As she finishes, her coach berates her for being too slow. She asks about certain aspects of her running to which he bluntly replies, "You're running heavy," prompting Ellen to offer to lose five pounds over the upcoming spring break. His reply confirms, if not worsens her insecurities, telling her it would be better if it was eight pounds. The next scene in the film shows Ellen thinking about her future and mindlessly eating. When she realizes this, she is disgusted. She spits out what she has in her mouth, and while her sister tries to convince her that she would just run it off the next day, Ellen quickly leaves the room and throws up.

While the coach telling her to lose weight doesn't immediately start her bulimia, it certainly seemed to push her. Coupled with family stress and pressure to succeed in all areas of her life, Ellen requires extensive therapy and treatment to actually process her eating disorder. For many of the young women in these films, it takes just a little push—a dance teacher saying she could jump higher if she was a few pounds less or a family member who jokes about her size. These events, while seemingly tiny, and perhaps even insignificant to the character speaking them, touch a particular nerve in the fragile woman.

### "If you put it in, it stands to reason you can take it out."

Typically, the lead character in these movies doesn't come to anorexia or bulimia on her own. Instead, she relies on someone to show her the ropes. In films like *When Friendship Kills* (1996), *Perfect Body* (1997), *Dying to Dance* (2001), *Hunger Point* (2003), and *Starving in Suburbia* (2014), an important friend or confidant helps the lead character by showing her how to vomit or teaching her tricks to suppress her hunger. Just as important as teaching them *how* to lose weight, the friends also teach them how to outwit their doctors and parents. In *Dying to Dance*, when the ballerinas found out there is to be a mandatory weigh-in with those under 90 pounds being put on medical leave, the women rush around the locker room trying to figure out what to do. Frantically, they variously shout "Put on as many tights as you can!" "Stuff your bra!" One girl even goes so far as to shove a role of quarters into her bun. In a way, this camaraderie is useful for the women. Confiding in one another allows them to find a place that they "fit"—a community that many of them are struggling to find.

*Sharing the Secret* (2000) even takes its title from this type of action. Beth, just 14 years old, has actually been anorexic for years before the movie begins. At a sleepover, the girls are joking around. Eating a piece of candy, Beth looks like she is bleeding from her mouth. While her friends laugh, when she offers one a piece, her friend declines because "it has calories." This shifts the conversation, and one very slender girl mentions wanting cheap liposuction in Brazil. Another friend, after noting how thin Beth is, accuses her of not eating at all. Beth protests; she does eat, "but if you put it in, it stands to reason you can take it out." Her friends do not believe her, so she eventually teaches them. She shows how she puts her fingers down her throat, though she also suggests a toothbrush can work, and instructs them to make sure to turn on the water, to cover up the noise. One friend actually tries to purge, but cannot. Beth reassures her that it just takes practice.

These moments, where the young women share their story or confide in someone, illustrate both how necessary a support system is for these young women, many of whom have troubled family lives, but also emphasize eating disorders' prevalence. In the 1980s and 1990s, these types of interaction would take place typically at school or sports clubs, particularly at those where a thin female body is desirable and/or beneficial (it is not surprising, then, that many of these film discussed involve dance or gymnastics). By the late 1990s and 2000s, these communities developed online on a variety of pro-anorexia or pro-bulimia websites, deemed pro-ana or pro-mia respectively (Boero and Pascoe 34–36; Norris et al. 443–447). The need to share these experiences allows women to bond with other women. As Stephanie Houston Grey notes, there has been a development of "a culture of confession in which individuals find entry into the 'women's community' by discussing the pressures levied against them by the diet industry. The most vivid moments of oppression and subsequent awakening for many white, middle class women often center upon issues of weight and appearance." In these films then, this moment when women share their experiences and secrets, they are bonded together while emphasizing the shared pressures that are placed upon women in Western society.

## "You lose some weight? You look good."

Once the women start losing weight—and seeing success—they often receive praise or admiration, which is the validation they need to see that their eating disorder is working and causing them to lose weight. This can be shown in a number of different ways. In *For the Love of Nancy* (1994), it comes from a simple remark, made from a trusted brother to his sister as she getting ready to leave for college. Nancy is finishing packing up her room as her brother comes up to grab some boxes. He looks at her and asks if she has lost weight, after which he tells her how good she looks. For Nancy, this is all the affirmation that she needs. The recent extreme dieting and her general avoidance of eating is paying off, as this simple compliment confirms.

In the sports-themed Eating Disorder films, this affirmation comes in the form of improved performance. In gymnastics, that might mean being able to do more difficult and better gymnastic skills, as seen in *Little Girls in Pretty Boxes* (1997) and *Perfect Body* (1997). For films concerning ballet or dance, it means advancing in the troupe and earning more opportunities for solos, evident in *Sharing the Secret* (2000), *Dying to Dance* (2001), and *Starving in Suburbia* (2014). It is important for these initial successes to be measurable and to be noticed and that these instances be dramatized in the film, so that as an audience, we understand *why* these girls want to continue pushing their bodies in such a punishing manner.

## "The rumor is you aren't taking care of yourself."

After the high of being complimented on their weight loss, the movies inevitably shift their focus to the protagonists' decline. After all, these movies are not supposed to encourage eating disorders, but rather are meant to discourage the practice and promote awareness of the severity of the disease. In *Perfect Body*, Andie wants to be an Olympic gymnast. For better training, she had to leave the safety of her home gym for one that could offer her more opportunities. After learning how to purge from a fellow gymnast, Andie gets caught up in a cycle of intense anorexia and exercising, followed by binging and purging. The first warning sign comes when she injures her ankle. The situation grows worse at a competition, where Andie expresses that her stomach will not stop growling. She manages to complete her beam routine, but then she passes out. She convinces the doctors and her parents that it was a one-time occurrence; she just forgot to eat. Things continue to escalate, however, as Andie starts losing her hair, stops sleeping to work out instead, and generally has a terrible attitude. She is pushing away her friends and anyone who might want to help. In inspired casting, real-life Olympic gymnast Cathy Rigby plays an assistant coach at the gym where Andie trains, and she tries to talk some sense into her, asking her about her eating disorder:

> "I've seen a lot of girls do it. Especially when they get to your level of competition. I know, I did it too! You've got to be thin to win, you've got to go higher and faster. So you lose the weight and you do go higher and faster and you and think you're doing better. But the fact is you're not. 'Cause your body can't han-

dle it, and you're already losing strength. Eventually you are going to lose everything you have worked so hard for. What you are doing is dangerous, and it isn't necessary" [*Perfect Body*].

This was not just Cathy Rigby the actor talking, this was Cathy Rigby the former anorexic/bulimic talking (Rigby McCoy). Her real experience certainly gives weight to her words, and undoubtedly, producers and casting directors depended upon it.

The premise of a previous suffer trying to help others also appears in *Dying to Dance* (2011). Alyssa's ballet mistress eventually comes out as an anorexic and wants to work to help prevent others' suffering. This does not happen, unfortunately, as Alyssa's experience in ballet mirrors that of Andie's gymnastics career. While at first Alyssa loses weight and succeeds, she gradually gets weaker, starts losing her hair, and increasingly experiences cramps and muscle pain. Alyssa, however, goes farther than Andie, even trying to seek out cocaine to help provide her with energy. Her mental state deteriorates dramatically as well, calling herself a fat pig repeatedly and violently smashing a mirror, as if she can beat herself up physically that way. This culminates with Alyssa passing out while driving home, from which she luckily escapes unscathed. These symptoms that both girls experience are so regular and direct, it is as if the filmmakers follow a checklist. These negative effects of the disorders play an important role, working to expose the darker side of eating disorders and making sure that they will appear undesirable.

## "Wouldn't you die to be this skinny?"

Death plays a pivotal role in each of these films. It is logical, of course, because of the staggering statistics concerning anorexia. The mortality rate of women aged 15–24 with anorexia is twelve times higher than for women of the same age from the general population (Hudson et al. 348–58). Additionally, people who suffer from eating disorders have the highest mortality rate of any mental illness (Sullivan 939–946). It is not, then, out of reach that these made-for-television movies bring in such a heavy subject; indeed, it is the reality of the disease. At the same time, death often helps advance the plot, as it allows the lead character to confront the stark reality of anorexia and bulimia. *Kate's Secret* (1986) is a bit unusual in that the lead character who suffers from bulimia is not an adolescent. Instead, Kate is a married housewife with a thriving young daughter and what appear to be all the markers of a happy life. But Kate feels deeply pressured to be perfect, and her use of binging and purging gives her some sense of control in her life. After pushing her body too much and crashing her car because she loses consciousness, Kate is hospitalized. Her roommate is Patch, a young model who has been hospitalized repeatedly and knows the tricks of the trade. Kate's friend admires Patch's body when visiting so much that she makes the foreshadowing joke, "Wouldn't you die to be this skinny?" Through field trips, Patch is able to stockpile diuretics, and one night takes them all and has a heart attack. It is this event that pushes Kate to actually commit to her therapy and eventually embrace the process.

By contrast, *The Karen Carpenter Story* focuses on the anorexic who died, rather than a best friend or competitor. Carpenter was one of the first, most visible celebrities who suffered from an eating disorder, and her death in 1983 stunned many. In the 1989 movie based on her life and made with her brother Richard's support, Karen is shown being pressured from a wide variety of angles—her parents, her managers, music critics, and even herself. Karen does eventually get treatment, though she leaves the hospital despite the doctors' concern that she might not be ready. Eager to get back to the studio and restart her life, she has not regained enough strength and dies at the age of 32. This flips the narrative a bit, focusing on someone who succumbs to the disease. In this instance, the viewer plays a similar role to Kate in *Kate's Secret*, as we are both shocked and saddened by Karen's death.

In some films, there may not be a literal death, but there is something that functions in a similar way, which often ends up being the death of a career or a dream. In *Little Girls in Pretty Boxes* (1997), Katie is very similar to Andie in the *Perfect Body*. She moves to a new gym to pursue her Olympic dreams. Katie is doing everything she can to rise up the ranks and become the best gymnast in the world, including purging and practicing when hurt.[1] As she is pushing her body farther than she should, her plight is paralleled by her competitor and friend Dana, who has had numerous back problems that she has been masking with pain pills. At a competition, Dana misses a vault, landing painfully on her back and breaking her neck, effectively ending her career. While no one dies, the full impact of the disease and the harshness of the sport they are pursuing is made clear. Katie's parents recognize that their daughter is on the same path as Dana was, and they decide to pull her out of the gym. Katie's eating disorder is a symptom of a larger problem: their daughter risking her life in pursuit of her gymnastics career. While Katie's or Dana's purging may not figure as prominently in this film as in other movies, its role is significant. Dana's injury, an undoubtedly dramatic and traumatic event that was in larger part caused by her eating disorder, creates the same type of situation or feeling as a death in a film. It pushes the viewer to the edge and directly emphasizes the impact of the disorder.

## "It's my brain, it's eating me alive."

Eating Disorder films often include not just the treatment process, but also a recognition of how treatment often does not succeed. It is estimated that only one in ten people who have an eating disorder seek treatment, and even then, only 35 percent get help at a specialized facility for eating disorders. Further, in that study, only 8% of patients claimed to have completely recovered (Noordenbos et al. 25–39). *Hunger Point* (2003) deals with variations of recovery, as two sisters have to deal with serious food issues and eating disorders. Franny and her younger sister Shelley are constantly fighting with their bodies, their mother, and each other. Shelley has the reputation for being both the chosen child and the perfect one, graduating from an Ivy League school and on her way to law school. Shelley has also been thin, but at what turns out to be a very significant cost. Early in the movie, Shelley tells her family that she is seeking in-patient treatment for an eating disorder. Her mom tries to dissuade her, but Shelley knows this is what she needs. The hospital is tough—Shelley struggles immensely. Her roommate had tried to kill herself, and besides dealing with her eating disorders, Shelley has started cutting her arms. She tells Franny, "I'm just a big black hole getting sucked in on itself…. It's my brain, it's eating me alive."

Shelley does not seem to be getting better to Franny, but suddenly the visits start to go more smoothly. Eventually Shelley is released, but unfortunately, comes home to the same terrible family dynamic leading her to take a large quantity of pills and kill herself. In her own grief, Franny starts to pick up Shelley's bad habits and starts to show symptoms of an eating disorder herself. Eventually, Franny goes to a therapist. The climactic moment of the movie ends with Franny eating a piece of bread to distinguish her from the troubled Shelley. Franny's treatment worked, whereas Shelley's did not. The different kinds of treatment and variety of levels of success in *Hunger Point* illustrates the reality of treating eating disorders.

Similarly, *When Friendship Kills* (also known as *A Secret Between Friends: A Moment of Truth Movie*, 1996) includes two close-knit women who are struggling to come to terms with the size of their bodies. In this case, Lexi bonded with Jen as Jen taught her how to both restrict her eating and purge. Lexi never quite seems to attain the balance that Jen does, and eventually she passes out and her parents force her into treatment. After she gets out, the two girls are fighting about Lexi's outing of Jen's eating disorder. Jen runs off, only to be struck by a car. While the impact was not too severe, Jen's weak heart could not hold up to the trauma, and she dies from complications of anorexia. This event sets back Lexi's healing, even though her mom is determined to get her to eat again. This film similarly explores a variety of approaches to treatment and emphasizes that certain types of treatment may not work for everyone. Simultaneously, each of these films includes a glimmer of hope, a moment that lets the audience know the sufferer can recover.

## "Ana's not your friend, Hannah.
## She is the devil in your ear."

There is a need in Eating Disorder films to distinguish women from their disease, to show that they have strengths and characteristics beyond just an eating disorder. Thus, the lead character is frequently shown dancing or succeeding at school, and the disease is portrayed as outside of her and is often described as a demon or a devil. This is best epitomized by *Starving in Suburbia* (2014), a recent film that deals with the increasing online presence of anorexia and bulimia communities, in which the main character is involved. Hannah's interactions with these websites and message boards push her to extreme behavior, resulting in anorexia, purging, and over-exercising. When Hannah is at her lowest weight, she is especially manic, and the film heightens this feeling by using a fish-eye camera and showing her almost physically attacking her mom. When talking to her therapist, her mom expresses serious concerns, saying it is as if someone else has taken over her daughter, and she is afraid of her. Her therapist responds, "It's like a demon. This is a world about numbers. How small can I become? How little space can I take up? This disease is living death."

This is echoed in a later therapy session with Hannah herself, when she tells her, "Ana's not your friend, Hannah. She is the devil in your ear." Hannah retorts, "You just want me to be fat." The therapist replies, "You're not choosing between fat and skinny, honey. You are choosing between life and death. You think that you can play with this. You will lose." Hannah replies, "I'm not losing. I'm winning. Emptiness is pure. Starvation is the cure." For Hannah, her restriction of food and her relationship with a pro-ana friend online are her only priorities; she cannot engage in life in any other ways. It is only when she can confront these issues that she can be whole again. It takes the death of her brother from anorexia for her to realize the seriousness of her disorder and to engage with her therapy intensely. The film ends with Hannah dancing, empowered by taking back control of her life. Showing her dancing is also the way the film makes clear that she has regained the parts of her identity that she lost.

## Lifetime Versus Other Eating Disorder Films

Now that the typical "Lifetime" film on eating disorders has been established, it is worth examining these films in light of other attempts to depict eating disorders in films. While these made-for-television movies do tackle true stories like those of Ellen Hart Peña and Nancy Walsh, they do not approach them in a documentary manner. The stories still include a fair amount of fictionalization and are shaped to fit a dramatic mold. This differs greatly from two other films that were made in the same time frame by very different networks—HBO and Thames TV in the UK.

HBO's *Lifestories: Families in Crisis* series ran new episodes from 1992 to 1996 and is still aired in reruns occasionally. The Emmy award-winning show tackled tough issues like steroid abuse, drug use, illegal abortion, and homelessness, among other stories. In the episode "The Secret Life of Mary-Margaret" (originally aired August 1, 1992, season one, episode three), tells the story of Mary-Margaret Carter, a bulimic. Mary-Margaret's voiceover makes clear that the model and successful student was incredibly insecure, explaining, "I did everything I could to be the perfect person you always see in the pictures, but I never felt beautiful." Originally, Mary-Margret tries to restrict her calories, but she struggles, and when she hears about another girl throwing up her food, it occurs to her that might be a better option.

In one of its most memorable scenes, Mary-Margaret decides to purge in a jar in her room to prevent questions from her mother about why she was in the bathroom so long. She then stores the jars in her closet and takes them out with the trash when she is alone in the house. Her binging and purging escalate, and follow her to college, where she makes good friends with a fellow anorexic/bulimic who later dies, which pushes Mary-Margaret to get help. This film is disturbing and much more graphic than the previously discussed films. Additionally, the end of the film introduces us to the real Mary-Margaret Carter, who speaks to the audience directly, pleading with anyone who needs help to seek treatment. Further, this show is only thirty minutes, so there is less time to get into nuances of relationships and personality traits of anyone besides Mary-Margaret.

Similarly, *Catherine* (first aired in the UK on July 1, 1988, and known in the U.S. as *An Anorexic's Tale: The Brief Life of Catherine*) tells the true story of Catherine Dunbar, based on a book by her mother, Maureen Dunbar. Like the HBO series, this film is much more graphic and direct than anything seen on Lifetime. Catherine is shown throwing up and binging repeatedly. Despite repeated attempts, Catherine does not accept treatment. Forcibly hospitalized under mental health laws in the UK, Catherine resists with everything she has and escapes numerous times. Over the course of a few years, Catherine withers away before her parents' and the viewers' eyes. Even when hospitalized, she continues to lose weight, and she describes her feelings: "For the first time today, I realized that death is inevitable. I can actually feel my body giving in. I know in myself that time is running out. I can't open the door to life. I wish for all our sakes that God would take me." Eventually, she is taken home to die, and her family takes care of her. Her mom and sister give her a bath, lifting her out and displaying her full nude body to the viewer.

This movie doesn't sensationalize the story nor does the film romanticize eating disorders; there is no happy ending here.

It is useful to compare *Catherine* with the well-known *For the Love of Nancy* (1994), an ABC film that found a second life with repeated airings on Lifetime, as both are based on true stories. In this dramatization, we see the story of Nancy Walsh, a young woman with anorexia. Walsh's story rose to prominence when she refused to get treatment, causing her parents to seek guardianship of her. Because the U.S. does not have the same mental health laws as the UK, this was the parents' only avenue to help their daughter. Besides illustrating key differences in the health policies in the different countries, a general sanitization happens in *For the Love of Nancy*. Nancy is often talked about, many times without her contribution, almost as if she is a child. The cast of characters is greatly expanded: the viewer is introduced to Nancy's friends, family, extended family, and lawyers. In *Catherine*, the film focuses primarily on the immediate family itself. The film is so intense and so closely follows Catherine's disorder that it is often hard to watch. Furthermore, Catherine's death at the end of the film is upsetting and alarming. Nancy does not die; rather, her father convinces her that she does need help and she eventually gets treatment. The tone of the "Lifetime" film works hard to make a terrible tough subject manageable, where *Catherine* doesn't offer any escape from the reality of the situation.

## Absence of Lifetime Eating Disorder Films Between 2004 and 2013

After *Hunger Point* was released in 2003, Lifetime did not produce a new film on eating disorders until *Starving in Suburbia* in 2014. In the interim, however, a number of television documentaries and docu-series aired across Lifetime and similar cable channels. Preferring nonfiction to fiction, these shows paralleled the rise of reality programming and society's sustained interest in redemption television, where the lead participant achieves a goal, oftentimes against the odds.

The most visible program was undoubtedly A&E's *Intervention*. A&E, which acquired all of the Lifetime channels in 2009, gambled and won big with the new program. It had the highest ratings that the network had ever seen and won an Emmy for Outstanding Reality Program in 2009. It aired first in March in 2005 and ended in February 2013. Reruns still air frequently on A&E, Lifetime, and its partner channels. Over the thirteen seasons of the show, roughly 10 percent of the episodes (20 episodes of the 194 that aired during the show's original run) actually dealt with eating disorders. What is unique, however, is that an intervention is not typically used for treating this type of illness, and it is hard to be sure of its long-term success (Kosovski and Smith 855).

*Intervention* was, as mentioned, immensely popular, and a number of different reality shows followed suit and attempted to help people. A&E produced another show, *Heavy* (January–April 2011) which documented the weight loss of severely overweight people over the course of eight months. A similar show was made by MTV, *I Used to Be Fat*, which aired from December 2010 to December 2011. The Oprah Winfrey Network (OWN) documented eight people as they sought help at Shades of Hope, an eating disorder and addictions treatment center, in *Addicted to Food* (2011). Not to be left out, E! produced six episodes of *What's Eating You?*, which aired from October to November 2010. Each episode followed two people who were struggling to deal with their eating disorders. Many of these episodes sound similar to the stories represented in a Lifetime film—a dancer's career is in jeopardy due to anorexia ("Adrienne and Danni," Season 1, Episode 1) or a former model who struggles with family criticism ("Marc and Kristy," Season 1, Episode 2). The show, with its frank and intense content, never quite found its audience, and only six episodes aired.

Lifetime itself premiered a reality show about eating disorders, airing six episodes of *Starving Secrets with Tracey Gold* in December 2011 and January 2012. Tracey Gold, an actress best known for her role as Carol Seaver on the sitcom *Growing Pains*, had suffered substantially from eating disorders herself and had been very public with her struggles. In fact, she explained to Larry King in 2005 that she chose to star in the movie *For the Love of Nancy* because of her own issues and filmed that movie as she was going through recovery herself. Gold described *Starving Secrets* as an attempt to show the reality of eating disorders: "We get in there with real women to show that it's not a glamorous thing. It's an isolating, lonely, hard, raw disease. It's not skinny women on a red carpet; it's an all-consuming thing in life where everything is falling down around you" (qtd. in Nordyke). Despite concerns regarding the fitness of the participants and whether airing the show was moral, producers claimed a 60 percent recovery rate, in that six of the ten women followed fared well after the show aired (Wheeler Johnson). So while Lifetime may have taken a break from airing fictional films concerning eating disorders, their programming addresses similar topics, and in 2014, they returned to their popular fictional format with *Starving in Suburbia*.

## Conclusions

With three decades of Lifetime films on eating disorders aired (and aired repeatedly), it is possible to now examine what their cultural effect has been. Joan Jacobs Brumberg has articulated the damning effect that the media has had on women:

> In general, it seems that knowledge about the disease, garnered through popular culture sources, may be implicated in generating what Hilde Bruch (1982) called "me too anorectics" or mimetic behavior that erroneously links the process of starvation to glamour rather than pain. What we may be facing is a transformation peculiar to mass culture: the shift of a predominantly psychosomatic disorder into the category of a communicable disease ["Fasting Girls" 95].

By continuing to draw attention to the disorder while simultaneously promoting a thin ideal, the U.S. media likely helped to perpetuate the development of the disease in young women. Many have argued, perhaps rightly so, that these movies, which are intended to help and offer guidance and support to eating disorder sufferers, actually teach women how to further their own eating disorders—much like the communicable disease that Brumberg articulates.

In a few powerful instances, women have publicly claimed that these films instructed them on how best to be anorexic. In an article for *XOJane*, Jessica Olien describes how she saw *For the Love of Nancy* in health class as the kick off for an eating disorders section of her class. She reflects, "The point of the movie may have been that her eating disorder was killing her, but you try explaining imminent death to a 14-year-old.... Who wouldn't want an eating disorder the way it was presented in school? Tracey Gold had one for Chrissake, and she was a celebrity." Andi Zeisler echos that remark: "Ask a middle-class white girl of a certain age what she remembers about Steven Levenkron's 1978 case study *The Best Little Girl in the World* and chances are she'll tell you that her thoughts on reading the book weren't, 'Wow, sucks for her,' but 'Huh, maybe I should stop eating, too'" (51). Even actress Christina Ricci learned from these films, saying, "I did get all my tips from a Tracey Gold *Lifetime* movie on anorexia. It taught me what to do. There was also one on HBO, starring Calista Flockhart when she was really young. She was bulimic and anorexic. She'd vomit into Tupperware containers and keep them in her closet. It was so crazy to me that for some reason it was appealing" (Haynes 138). These women are not alone in their inspiration for eating disorders; in fact, the refrain is common, and it is generally understood that Lifetime movies, as well as images and film in the broader mass media, provide inspiration and instruction to nascent anorexics and bulimics (Levine and Murnen 31–35; Thompson and Heinberg 344–350; Berel and Irving 416–421, 427).

In an insightful article, Kelsey Osgood discusses her own struggles with anorexia and maintains that her entry into the disease is now quite typical: "Today, no teenage girl needs to be told what anorexia is—it's the constant subject of memoirs, young adult novels, Lifetime movies, and episodes of Dr.

Phil. Stories about Mary-Kate Olsen, Demi Moore, or the latest celebrity to be admitted to rehab for anorexia are a regular tabloid feature." The numbers seem to support her arguments; just as eating disorders rose 24 percent between 2000 and 2009, "Eating Disorder Awareness Weeks" were popular on campus in 2001. Osgood recalls reading memoirs of women who had suffered eating disorders and taking notes. Similarly, Margaret Wheeler Johnson describes watching Lifetime movies, including those discussed here, while she was at treatment for anorexia in 2001 (Wheeler Johnson). These films made anorexia interesting and desirable, and most importantly, accessible. Osgood astutely notes, "I believe that so many young women want to be anorexic because our society has communicated not the horrible consequences of eating disorders, but what might seem to be the benefits of them, namely, that they make you skinny and special."

And yet, by focusing on the stories of young women, these films are saying that these stories are worth telling—that these voices should be heard. Looking at the films over time, beginning with *The Best Little Girl in the World* and *Kate's Secret*, all the authority figures were men. The dad and/or husband made the decisions for the sufferer, and the doctors were always men. By the 2000s, moms were becoming the voice of reason, and doctors and nurses were increasingly women. Additionally, even the treatment of the women improved. Whereas the sufferer's condition and treatment was always discussed with others and rather than the patient, in later films, the women have taken active roles in their treatment, from requesting certain types of therapy to recognizing when things were not working and they needed help. In the thirty years that these films have been made, there has been a marked improvement in how women are treated.

These films provide a very important capsule of our time. They document the varying theories and treatments of anorexia. They show the way women are taking more and more control of their health care. But they also show the way that our narratives are structured, how we tell people about eating disorders, and what information we believed is needed to encourage people to seek out help. Lifetime is relying on a very careful balance of information and morality, hoping to create a story that is entertaining and watchable but also can actually help people. Whether they succeed or not is up to the viewer.

## CHRONOLOGICAL LIST OF LIFETIME AND MADE-FOR-TV MOVIES ON EATING DISORDERS

*The Best Little Girl in the World.* ABC. 11 May 1981. Television.
*Kate's Secret.* NBC. 17 Nov. 1986. Television.
*Catherine.* Thames Television. 1 July 1988. Television.
*The Karen Carpenter Story.* CBS. 1 Jan. 1989. Television.
"The Secret Life of Mary Margaret." *Lifestories: Families in Crisis.* HBO. 1 Aug. 1992. Television.

*For the Love of Nancy.* ABC. 2 Oct. 1994. Television.
*When Friendship Kills.* NBC. 19 Feb. 1996. Television.
*Dying to be Perfect: The Ellen Hart Pena Story.* ABC. 24 Nov. 1996. Television.
*Little Girls in Pretty Boxes.* Lifetime. 19. Jan. 1997. Television.
*Perfect Body.* NBC. 8 Sept. 1997. Television.
*Sharing the Secret.* CBS. 10 May 2000. Television.
*Dying to Dance.* Lifetime. 12 Aug. 2001. Television.
*Hunger Point.* Lifetime. 13 Jan. 2003. Television.
*Starving in Suburbia.* Lifetime. 26 Apr. 2014. Television.

## NOTE

1. It is worth acknowledging that Vanessa Atler, who did the gymnastics stunt work for Katie's character and was the United States National Champion in 1997, later went public with her own eating disorder struggles, which were documented in part on the syndicated NBC reality program *Starting Over* in 2005.

## WORKS CITED

Berel, Susan, and Lori M. Irving. "Media and Disturbed Eating: An Analysis of Media Influence and Implications for Prevention." *The Journal of Primary Prevention* 18.4 (1998): 415–430. Print.

Boero, Natalie, and C.J. Pascoe. "Pro-Anorexia Communities and Online Interaction: Bringing the Pro-Ana Body Online." *Body & Society* 18.2 (2012): 27–57. Print.

Bruch, Hilde. *The Golden Cage.* New York: Basic Books, 1978. Print.

Brumberg, Joan Jacobs. "'Fasting Girls': Reflections on Writing the History of Anorexia Nervosa." *Monographs of the Society for Research in Child Development* 50.4/5 (1985): 93–104. Print.

_____. *Fasting Girls: The History of Anorexia Nervosa*, Rev. ed. New York: Vintage, 2000. Print.

Fonda, Jane. *My Life So Far.* New York: Random House, 2006. Print.

Grey, Stephanie Houston. "A Perfect Loathing: The Feminist Expulsion of the Eating Disorder." *KB Journal* 7.2 (2011). Web. 17 July 2015.

Haynes, Esther. "Gettin' High with Christina Ricci." *Jane* May 2002: 138. Print.

Hudson, James I., et al. "The Prevalence and Correlates of Eating Disorders in the National Comorbidity Survey Replication." *Biological Psychiatry* 61.3 (2007): 348–58. Print.

"Interview with *Growing Pains* Star Tracey Gold." *Larry King Live.* CNN. 21 Feb. 2005. Web. Transcript. 17 July 2015.

Kosovski, Jason R., and Douglas C. Smith. "Everybody Hurts: Addiction, Drama, and the Family in the Reality Television Show *Intervention.*" *Substance Use & Misuse* 46 (2011): 852–858. Print.

Levenkron, Steven. "Structuring a Nurturant-Authoritative Psychotherapeutic Relationship with the Anorexic Patient." *Theory and Treatment of Anorexia Nervosa and Bulimia.* Ed. Steven Wiley Emmett. New York: Routledge, 2013. 234–245. Print.

Levine, Michael P., and Sarah K. Murnen. "'Everybody Knows That Mass Media Are/Are Not [pick one] a Cause of Eating Disorders': A Critical Review of Evidence for a Casual Link Between Media, Negative Body Image, and Disordered Eating in Females." *Journal of Social and Clinical Psychology* 28.1 (2009): 9–42. Print.

Martin, Courtney E. *Perfect Girls, Starving Daughters: The Frightening New Normalcy of Hating Your Body.* New York: Free Press, 2007. Print.

Noordenbos, Greta, et. al. "Characteristics and Treatment of Patients with Chronic Eating Disorders." *Eating Disorders: The Journal of Treatment & Prevention* 10.1 (2002): 15–39. Print.

Nordyke, Kimberly. "Tracey Gold on Hollywood's Weight Obsession, 'Nasty' Online Critics and Whether She Keeps in Touch with Leonardo DiCaprio." *The Hollywood Reporter* 2 Dec. 2011. Web. 17 July 2015.

Norris, Mark L. et al. "Ana and the Internet: A Review of Pro-Anorexia Websites." *International Journal of Eating Disorders* 39.6 (2006): 443–447. Print.

Oldis, Katherine O. "Young Adult Literature: Anorexia Nervosa: The More It Grows, the More It Starves." *The English Journal* 75.1 (1986): 84–88. Print.

Olien, Jessica. "Health Class Taught Me How to Have an Eating Disorder." *XOJane.* Say Media, Inc., 17 Oct. 2011. Web. 17 July 2015.

Osgood, Kelsey. "Anorexia Is Contagious, and I Wanted to Catch It." *Time* 15 Nov. 2013. Web. 17 July 2015.

Rigby McCoy, Cathy. "A Onetime Olympic Gymnast Overcomes the Bulimia That Threatened Her Life" *People* 22.7 (13 Aug. 1984). Web. 17 July 2015.

Seid, Roberta Pollack. *Never Too Thin: Why Women Are at War with Their Bodies.* New York: Prentice Hall, 1989. Print.

Sullivan, Patrick, et al. "Outcome of Anorexia Nervosa: A Case Control Study." *American Journal of Psychiatry* 155.7 (1998): 939–946. Print.

Thompson, J. Kevin, and Leslie J. Heinberg. "The Media's Influence on Body Image Disturbance and Eating Disorders: We've Reviled Them, Now Can We Rehabilitate Them?" *Journal of Social Issues* 55.2 (1999): 339–353. Print.

Vandereycken, Walter. "Emergence of Bulimia Nervosa as a Separate Diagnostic Entity." *International Journal of Eating Disorders* 16.2 (1994): 105–116. Print.

Wheeler Johnson, Margaret. "Tracey Gold's *Starving Secrets*: Could on Camera Recovery Work?" *Huff Post Women* 2 Dec. 2011. Web. 17 July 2015.

Zeisler, Andi. "Chewing the Scenery." *Bitch* 35 (April 2007): 51. Print.

# "Your Life. Your Time"

## Addressing a Fractured
## Audience through Docudrama

### STACI STUTSMAN

On May 2, 2012, the Lifetime cable network launched its most recent
rebranding campaign, its eleventh one in its twenty-eight- (now thirty-one)
year lifespan. In addition to a new, simplified red and white logo, they
unveiled their new tag line: "Your Life. Your Time." Nancy Dubuc, president
and general manager of Lifetime Networks, says of the rebranding, "Nothing
is more valuable to women than time" (qtd. in Bibel). According to *The Hollywood Reporter,* this rebranding effort was "designed to integrate the network's
new programming direction with the sensibilities of today's multitasking
woman" (Guthrie). The effort supposedly serves as the "next step in Lifetime's
bid to shed its image as the home of maudlin made-for-TV movies" (Guthrie).
This initiative includes an increase in screen time for reality programs and
dramas such as *Dance Moms* (2011–), *Project Runway* (Bravo 2004–08, Lifetime 2009–), and *Army Wives* (2007–2013). The network, though, still continues to produce and distribute made-for-TV movies for their weekend
schedule and the spin-off Lifetime Movie Network (LMN) channel and make
them available for viewers to stream on mylifetime.com and the Lifetime
mobile application.

Lifetime launched LMN in 1998 in order to "devote less of its daily sched-
ules to replaying older films, while not forfeiting the value of what had developed into an expansive film archive" (Lotz 41). The creation of LMN worked
in tandem with Lifetime's shifting understanding of its demographic. Lifetime
created the network in order to retain the interests of its current consumer
base while appealing to new ones. Lifetime, understood as a network for
women since its genesis in 1984, constantly revises and updates this brand in
order to remain desirable to female viewers aged 18–49 while not completely

losing the interests of a broader audience. Lifetime's identity becomes split through its constant negotiation between niche and broad appeal and its evolving understanding of what that specialized "female" audience desires. Carolyn Bronstein notes that Lifetime's "fractured identity as both a 'women's network' and a general entertainment service is an inevitable consequence of market demand" (231).

The identity of its audience is just as split as Lifetime's. This is because the viewer is not necessarily always female, and the female viewer cannot be singularly defined. Amanda Lotz rightly points out that not only are "women different from one another, but individual women have different needs and interests at different times" (62). The plural audience is not a monolith, and neither is the female viewer. In its most recent rebranding, Lifetime now aims different weekday nights at different audience segments in order to rein in a distracted viewership. Writing in 2012 after the rebranding, Sara Bibel claims, "Thursday is 'make it work time' and captures the urgency of *Project Runway.* Tuesday is 'mama drama time' as the *Dance Moms* watch their daughters take the stage and Sundays are 'love time' with Jennifer Love Hewitt of *The Client List.* On-air messages speak directly to viewers' experiences, laughter, and emotional connection—'me time,' 'girl time,' and 'drama time' ... it's all about 'your life' and 'your time'" (Bibel). The nature of television scheduling and flow, a system which resists containment and closure, allows Lifetime to speak multiply through their varied media offerings. This solution serves as an effort to respond to the multiple desires of an increasingly distracted audience who might look to other channels by offering a multitude of diverse content within one space. Lifetime assures viewers that, despite differing desires and needs, viewers can remain unified around a single channel.

Though executives did not specifically articulate the role of made-for-TV movies in this new rebranding strategy, I will explore how these movies, which still have a visible presence on the network, are conversant with the network's new awareness of and attempts to hail its divided audience. Specifically, I examine the shift in the arguments made by Lifetime's "True Story" docudramas immediately after the 2012 rebranding. I argue that, with their focus on the simultaneous doubling and fracturing of female figures, *Taken Back: Finding Haley* (2012) and *Abducted: The Carlina White Story* (2012) offer up visual media as a way to negotiate split identities; *Taken Back* makes a case for the importance of photographs and home movies in this process, while *Abducted* argues for television. *Abducted*'s focus on television articulates the importance of Lifetime in solidifying one's identity.

Lifetime's most recent slogan "Your Life. Your Time." stresses individuality and the wide-ranging desires of its audience. While its audience might have always been more varied than Lifetime acknowledged, this is the first rebranding that specifically works to address that multiplicity. Throughout its long history of subtle rebrandings, Lifetime continues to successfully hold the attention of an increasingly divided audience that might be wooed by the growing availability of channels and web content.[1] Lifetime has been able to hold this attention by offering a broader selection of programming within one space while still making room for their previous staples. According to a report in the summer of 2013, Lifetime has been thriving since its most recent rebranding. It reported a "+10% jump among Total Viewers and Adults 25–54, +9% increase in Women 25–54, +3% with Adults 18–49 and +1% in Women 18–49" for the 2012 second fiscal quarter (January 1, 2012, to March 31, 2012) (Eisner). While their original rebranding efforts claimed a desired move away from made-for-TV movies, those movies have remained a viable and valuable presence in the network brand as the report confirms that "the network was 2013's number one cable network for original movies among Total Viewers, Adults 25–54, Women 25–54, Adults 18–49, Women 18–49, Adults 18+ and Women 18+" (Eisner).

These made-for-TV movies exist in many forms but, regardless of categorization, tend to rely on melodrama and focus on victimized women who must overcome an extraordinary challenge (Lotz 41). These women often work "within the system to correct some injury" and find a generally personal solution to the social problem (Byars and Meehan 155). When packaged as true stories, these films offer a unique pleasure that is especially successful at attracting "large audiences of women, especially the 18–34-year-old females that advertisers prize highly" (Byars and Meehan 148). According to Derek Paget, true story dramas, also known as docudramas, are especially pleasurable because they incite an "imaginative response to the claim of the 'life-like'" and invite one to empathize "with the trauma of the Little Person in society" (201, 206). This proves especially true with the "feminised docudrama[s]" of Lifetime (Paget 203). These films claim their emotional and persuasive power due to their "proximity to the real" and their ordering of reality into melodramatic terms that invite viewer identification and empathy with the women who struggle against some social injustice. Further, because of their relatively formulaic melodramatic plots, true story dramas are also especially economically viable as they are relatively simple to produce and market to consumers (Lipkin et al. 18). Steven Lipkin, Derek Paget, and Jane Roscoe note that "network executives, producers, and writers who make 'movie of the week' docudramas all use the same terms—all seek the 'rootable, relatable, and promotable,' all acknowledge that docudrama offers cost-effective product that can be marketed directly to consumers" (24). The relatively low-risk nature of the docudrama has resulted in its permeating existence on Lifetime. Due to docudramas' success with female audiences and their persuasive power, it proves advantageous to look to how Lifetime speaks to its diverse viewership through its docudramas, especially as Lifetime often uses these films to focus on "issues" that are "central to Lifetime's identity," issues that Lifetime categorizes as women's issues (Lotz 53).

In order to promote social justice topics such as domestic abuse and breast cancer awareness, Lifetime films typically center on stories of individual success or individual trauma as women struggle against injustice. One common type of trauma represented in the Lifetime docudrama is that of the missing family member. Sometimes this manifests as a missing sibling, a missing infant, or a teenager who has been abducted while on spring break. These narratives are often used to reconfirm the importance of family and the home by depicting the trauma that results when one is not allowed to return to the domestic space. For example, *Bringing Ashley Home* (2011) tells the story of an adult searching for her missing sister, *Taken from Me: The Tiffany Rubin Story* (2011) narrates a mother's daring rescue of her son abducted by his biological father in South Korea, and *Justice for Natalee Holloway* (2011) provides an in-depth examination of Natalee's disappearance in Aruba. All three stress the importance of familial relationships and make an argument about the inadequacy of law enforcement institutions. There are slight variations in these narratives but, in general, they follow the formula typical to Lifetime made-for-TV movies: a strong female protagonist struggles against a social institution in order to bring a loved one back home. No real change occurs at the institutional level, but the films present personal solutions to social problems.

The first two docudramas about missing persons that were produced after the 2012 rebranding effort take up these same tropes but shift them in noticeable ways with an overt focus on the trauma associated with fragmented identity. The "issue" becomes less about the inadequacy of a public institution and more about the importance of addressing one's identity crisis, a concern in line with Lifetime's own awareness of their shifting identity. *Taken Back: Finding Haley* (11 August 2012) and *Abducted: The Carlina White Story* (6 October 2012) dramatize the real life stories of child abductions. *Taken Back* begins with Karen Turner (Moira Kelly) taking photographs of her daughter Haley (Alexandra Perry) at a carousel. As the carousel revolves, Haley disappears. In the aftermath of her disappearance, Karen loses her husband and her art photography job because she devotes all of her time to searching for Haley. Twelve years pass and the story picks back up as Karen, now a school photographer, travels to local school districts to take pictures of the students in search of one who looks like Haley. Karen begins stalking a pre-teen student named Emma McQueen (Kacey Rohl) because she believes that Emma is her lost daughter. The film follows Karen's manic pursuit of Emma (who does indeed turn out to be Haley) and ends in a final confrontation with Susan McQueen (Amanda Tapping), the woman who had abducted her.

*Abducted* commences as Joy White (Sherri Shepard) visits Ann Pettway

(Aunjanue Ellis) in jail and then cuts to 1987 as 16-year-old Joy (Heather Claire-Nortey) is being pushed in a hospital wheelchair, about to give birth to a child. The camera cuts to a screaming Ann, also about to give birth. The image continues to cut between the two as Joy successfully delivers a healthy baby girl named Carlina and Ann miscarries for the third time. The doctor tells Ann that a hormone imbalance prevents her from having children, and she lays taciturn in the hospital for days before finally being sent home. She dresses up as a nurse and returns to the hospital a couple of weeks later and steals Joy's baby, who is being treated at the hospital for a small fever. Time passes more quickly in *Abducted* than it does in *Taken Back*. Ann takes Carlina as her own, names her Nejdra and moves from New York to Connecticut. Joy and her boyfriend Carl (Eli Goree) search for Carlina, but to no avail and, like Karen and her husband, eventually break up due to the stress. Carlina/Nedjra (Keke Palmer) grows up with Ann and her aunt Cassandra (Afton Williamson), becomes pregnant at age sixteen, and discovers that her birth certificate has been forged when she attempts to enroll for government assistance. This discovery causes a rift between her and Ann. Nedjra (nicknamed Netty) searches for her mother but does not find her until years later, when her own child Maya (Alyssa Wellington) is six years old. The last two-thirds of the film deals with the fall-out of the discovery as Netty attempts to consolidate her two identities and lives and negotiate her complex relationship with Ann and her birth mother Joy.

Both stories draw on the authority offered by their relationship to the real. This authority is established by opening captions as well as their generic classification. *Taken Back* opens with a black screen with a white intertitle that asserts the story was "inspired by true events," and *Abducted* opens with a similar intertitle that reads "based on a true story." Mylifetime.com also classifies both within their "true story" dramatic subgenre. Both intertitles and classification work as paratexts that present the films to the viewer and guarantee their authenticity.

Through this authority, docudramas tend to offer up arguments about how to respond to their narratives. Lipkin et al. note that "[w]orks based on true stories ... do not simply represent their subjects and forms, but offer arguments about ways to perceive those subjects and forms" (23). Taken together, I assert that *Taken Back* and *Abducted* argue for the importance of consolidating one's ruptured identity. The films persuasively argue that visual media and reality television can provide the solution for this crisis. In doing so, they emphasize the network's own importance to audience's daily lives. The films argue that visual media and television can help center one's splintered identity and, in doing so, reassert the position of Lifetime. The films' focus on identity resonates with Lifetime's understanding of its audience's fractured identity and, through an allegorical reading, I emphasize the way the filmic content "encapsulate[s] the network's identity" (Lotz 63).

In *Taken Back,* Karen becomes a broken figure without her daughter and attempts to use photographs and home videos to regain a sense of her identity. At the film's open, the viewer witnesses a portion of the carousel scene through Karen's lens as she frames and focuses on Haley and a clicking sound indicates the photographic capture. The image briefly freezes and then resumes as Karen continues to watch Haley. These photographs take on enormous weight throughout the film as their purpose shifts. Karen uses them for the fliers she distributes all over town, frames and hangs them throughout the house in memory of their last happy day together, and uses them to jog Haley/Emma's memory toward the end of the film. For Karen, the photographs attest to the existence of a space of innocence to which she wishes to return, a trope typical to the melodramatic mode according to Linda Williams (28). In the months after Haley's abduction, Karen roams her house in a daze and pauses to look at the framed images of Haley's smiling face that adorn her walls. When her husband decides to leave her, Karen hardly looks up at him because she remains too absorbed in the photo album. Without her daughter, Karen does not know how to exist as a complete person. She is willing to give up her profession and marriage in order to find Haley and restore her place as "mother." When an art gallery curator attempts to get Karen to take part in a show, Karen refuses and says, "*This* is what I'm doing now," as she hangs up fliers with Haley's picture. Two years after the abduction, Karen has all but given up on finding Haley. She goes to Haley's bedroom, clutches the carousel photograph, and ingests a bottle of pills. A friend saves her, but when the scene ends and opens on a day ten years later, it is clear that Karen is unable to move on.

Karen's friend Megan (Nicole Oliver) discovers that Karen has stalked young girls on many occasions because she mistook them for Haley. While the film shows Karen attempting to use photographs and home videos to reconfirm her own fractured identity, it warns against the danger of equating resemblance with truth. In the film, the mistaking of identities produces disastrous results. Soon after Haley's abduction, Karen spots the back of a young child in a pink coat on a park swing. She slowly creeps closer and grabs the girl. The girl, who turns and reveals a face that is not Haley's, screams. The girl's mother yells at Karen, and Karen retreats, defeated. Susan, Haley's abductor, also finds herself in trouble for mistaking someone's identity. Susan catches Karen idling in her car outside of their house earlier in the week and follows her back to Megan's house. Later, when Karen steals Haley/Emma back, Susan goes to Megan's house. Unaware that it was Megan's house and not Karen's, Susan goes inside to confront her. Susan inaccurately identifies Megan as Karen and shoots her in the chest.

Similar types of identification errors happen in *Abducted*. When Ann goes to the hospital and steals Carlina, she is dressed as a nurse. Joy confuses Ann for a nurse, and this allows Ann to convince her to go home and leave Carlina unattended at the hospital. The security guard also misidentifies Ann as hospital personnel, so he does not question her as she discretely slips out of the hospital, baby in tow. As Carlina/Nejdra grows up, Ann insists that she looks just like her and has everyone call her "little Ann." Ann, through an insistence on resemblance, creates a false sense of security about Netty's parentage. Through these films, Lifetime demonstrates the dangerous nature of equating resemblance with identity. Just because the pink-coated girl looks like Haley does not mean that she is Haley. Though Ann resembles a nurse, she is not one. Lifetime might have thought that all women viewers appear similar and want the same type of programming but they do not, as Lifetime has tried to address in this rebranding effort.

The films further underscore the importance of understanding the diverse nature of female identity through their doubling of characters as physically represented in the split daughter figures Haley/Emma and Carlina/Nejdra and double mother figures Karen and Susan and Joy and Ann. In both films, the daughter's identity is split, and she must find a way to resolve this trauma. In *Taken Back,* the daughter is defined as Karen's biological child Haley and Susan's named child Emma. Similarly, the daughter in *Abducted* is identified as Joy's biological child Carlina and Ann's named child Nejdra. The films also show each of the mothers with a varying degree of disintegrating identity. As mentioned above, Karen is stuck in arrested development in search of Haley and has questionable psychiatric stability. Susan kidnapped Haley to cope for the loss of a first child and, by the end of the film, is shown as increasingly unstable. Ann is mentally unbalanced after three miscarriages and, due to her drug use, the film portrays her as retaining only a tenuous grip on reality.

When Haley/Emma discovers the truth about her identity in the final climatic scene, her fractured identity becomes apparent. In order to get Haley/Emma back to her house, Karen drugs her and puts her in her car trunk. When Haley/Emma wakes up she is understandably frantic and scared. She cowers on her old bed while Karen shows her memorabilia from her childhood, a stuffed bunny and an old dress. Karen, who is increasingly out of touch with reality, begins to play a toy xylophone and insists that Haley/Emma should try to remember the song. "I'm not your daughter," Haley/Emma yells in response. Despite her brutal kidnapping, though, Haley/Emma overcomes her fear oddly quickly. This recovery is due in large part to the persuasive power of photographic evidence and home videos.

Karen eventually leaves the bedroom and goes to the kitchen to look at her family photo album. Haley/Emma tentatively joins her and looks at the album with her and asks questions about the pictures. Karen then takes her to the living room to watch the birthday home video. Haley/Emma slowly enters the living room and watches the screen. Haley/Emma sits down and the viewer witnesses the screen through her point of view on the couch. The image cuts between a close-up of Haley/Emma's face and the home video as framed by the television and back again as it zooms in closer in an extreme close-up of her face as her bewildered eyes begin to cry. On-screen, Karen asks two-year-old Emma, "How much do I love you?" The camera cuts back to Haley/Emma who mouths the words along with on-screen child Haley, "More than you'll ever know." Haley/Emma breathes in deeply as recognition registers on her face. She and Karen sit on the couch, briefly reunited as a family unit, and Karen suggests that she try to call Susan.

The camera cuts to Susan as she answers the phone. The camera remains in a close-up of Susan as the now-disembodied voice asks over the phone, "Who is Haley Turner?" Susan drops the phone and the camera cuts to a close-up of Haley/Emma's hand ending the call. The lack of response serves as a second moment of confirmation, and Haley/Emma is shaken. The camera reveals her contorted face and glassy eyes. Karen says to her, "Those people you think are your mom and dad, took you from me, took you from your real parents." Haley/Emma cuts her off, "They are my family—stop!" In search of answers, Haley/Emma asserts, "I need to talk to them." Between these too statements, though, "my family" has been replaced with the more tentative pronoun "them," which signifies Haley/Emma's budding uncertainty about their identity and her own.

Haley/Emma sits at the table as Karen brings her a glass of water. She clutches her phone and says, "Everything you've told me, everything I've known, isn't real. This is wrong! This is crazy!" A knock on the door announces the supposed arrival of the case detective. Karen opens the door, though, and Susan bursts in, "Emma! Are you in here? It's your mother." Despite Susan's claim of motherhood, Karen insists, "You are not taking my daughter again!" The camera cuts between Karen and Susan as Karen asserts, "She's not your daughter!" and Susan insists, "She is my daughter!" Emma, off-screen in the kitchen, is physically removed from this scene and she, too, has become not Haley or Emma, but "she" and "daughter." Haley/Emma enters the frame and Karen addresses her, "Emma, don't listen to anything she says, it's a lie." The camera cuts to Haley/Emma's face as she looks about frantically and frightened. "Mom," she asks Susan, "what is going on?" Karen claims that Haley/Emma is her daughter and that her friend at the police department can prove it. Susan informs her that she shot that friend and Karen pins her against the wall angrily.

Susan pulls a gun and presses it to Karen's head. Haley/Emma yells, "Mom, no!" though it is not clear if she is informing Susan to not shoot Karen or is exclaiming on Karen's behalf. Karen instructs her, "Haley, call 911!" but, when Haley/Emma does not immediately move, Karen modifies her statement, "Emma, now!" Haley/Emma runs to the kitchen to retrieve her cell phone. "My mom has a gun," she tells the 911 operator. At this moment, though, the camera cuts ironically to Karen as *she* gains possession of the gun. Susan smashes Karen over the head and takes the gun back and addresses Haley/Emma, "Hang up the phone Emma. Now." The phone hangs at Haley/Emma's side and the viewer can discern a muffled operator asking, "Can you hear me, miss?"

Afraid of Susan, Haley/Emma runs and locks herself in a bathroom. Susan follows her to the bathroom, knocks on the door, and begs her to come out. "I am your mom," Susan tells through the door, "I've always been your mom." The music swells as Haley/Emma catches a glance of the carousel photograph pinned on the bathroom mirror. Her face and tearful eyes are shown in extreme close-up as the image cuts between Haley/Emma's face and the face of young Haley. After intercutting between the two a few times, Susan's voice dissolves and the image cuts to the scene of the carousel. The edges of the scene are slightly blurred which indicates its status as Haley/Emma's memory. She remembers being on the carousel as Susan removes her from the horse. She remembers Karen yelling frantically, "Haley! Haley!" This name continues to echo as the scene returns to the bathroom. The camera again frames Haley/Emma in close-up as her eyes widen, her breath quickens and she whispers, "You're not my mother" to Susan in a final moment of identity recognition. This quiet verbal recognition is placed in contrast to Susan's voice that is growing more manic. Susan is shown in an extreme low-angle shot as she leans against the bathroom door, "Emma," she says, "please open the door for Mommy. We can talk about this."

After Susan shoots the door open, Haley/Emma walks with her down the hallway. Susan puts her arm around her, "That's my girl." As she walks out Karen instructs her to get the gun from Susan and calls her Emma, "Emma, the gun!" Susan then refers to Haley/Emma as an "ungrateful little brat" and Karen tells Susan to "leave her alone." Haley/Emma again becomes abstracted into pronouns and signifiers. In an attempt to calm Susan down as she aims the gun at Karen, Haley/Emma takes her identity into her own hands. "Mom," she addresses her, "it's me, it's Emma. I'm your little girl. I know that. I'm your baby, I'm Emma." She convinces Susan to leave Karen and leave the house. At that moment, the police pull up and take Susan away. The film ends as Haley/Emma approaches Karen in an ambulance. Haley/Emma reaches out to hold Karen's hand. The camera cuts to a close-up as she wraps her fingers around Karen's, an implication of her willingness to accept her role as Karen's child. After the image fades out, typical docudrama closing captions appear on screen. Though they do not provide a concluding explanation of Haley/Emma and Karen's fate, they do showcase an image of the two actresses hugging and smiling in Karen's home, an implication of a real life resolution. The captions read: "Over 2,000 are reported missing in the U.S. per day. Most abductions occur within a quarter mile from the children's home." These closing captions serve as a warning for parents while the image of Haley/Emma and Karen hugging acts as a coda to their story and secures their identities as a mother and daughter who have been properly reunited now that Haley/Emma has returned home.

The negotiation of identity works slightly differently in *Abduction* because the majority of the film focuses around Carlina/Nejdra growing up as opposed to the broken mother's search for a lost child. With this slight shift in focus, the viewer has access to Carlina/Nejdra's identity negotiation and formation. Furthermore, because the identity revelation happens early in the film instead of in the final scene, the viewer is also privy to how Carlina/Nejdra adapts to her simultaneously fractured and doubled identity. After Ann steals Carlina/Nejdra, she takes her home and introduces her to her sister Cassandra. She rocks her and coos in a baby voice, "My name Nejdra Nance. My name Nejdra Nance." Cassandra, though, renames her again. She says to the baby, "You look like a Netty. I'm gonna call you Netty," and so begins Carlina/Nejdra's early identity formation.

The film presents a couple of brief scenes of Carlina/Nejdra's childhood: Ann gives her a doll for Christmas one year so that she can learn to do hair, she goes to her first day of school, she has a sweet sixteen party. Shortly after her sweet sixteen, though, Carlina/Nejdra announces that she is pregnant and has to go to the welfare office to sign up for assistance. While there, she is informed that her birth certificate is a forgery. She goes home and confronts Ann. She turns off Ann's television show and exclaims, "You called me little Ann because I looked just like you!" Ann insists that there has been a mistake but soon changes her story. She tells Carlina/Nejdra that a drug addict dropped her off on Ann's doorstep so that Ann could take care of her. Carlina/Nejdra does not believe her, though. "If I don't know who I am," asks Carlina/Nejdra stressing the importance of identity, "how am I supposed to tell my baby who she is?"

Time elapses and Cassandra moves to Atlanta for a job and Carlina/Nejdra has her baby. As Carlina/Nejdra lies in a hospital bed after giving birth to her daughter, her voiceover relays the content of a letter she has written to Oprah. "Dear Oprah, I'm writing to you because I can't think of anyone else who can help me. I recently found out that the woman who raised me is not my mother. I had a healthy baby girl and moved to Atlanta to be near my aunt. My baby makes me happy but inside I feel lost. Can you help me find my parents? I need to know the truth in a life filled with lies. Sincerely, Nejdra Nance." The voiceover serves as a sound bridge and an indication of passing time as it links the hospital scene to the next one in which her daughter Maya gets ready for her first day of school.

As they walk to school, Carlina/Nejdra has Maya rehearse details about herself to tell her teacher, which further emphasizes the importance of identity articulation. Carlina/Nejdra begins, "My name is…" and Maya finishes, "Maya Nance. I'm six years old." Carlina/Nejdra prompts again, "and I live in…" "Atlanta, Georgia," Maya finishes. "But I was born in?" asks Carlina/Nejdra. "Bridgeport, Connecticut." Maya then asks her mother if she was also born in Bridgeport, Connecticut to which she responds, "I don't know where I was born, baby, but I'm going to find out." Carlina/Nejdra ends up finding out by searching a website for missing children. She finds a photograph of Carlina White and notes to her aunt how much she looks like Maya when she was born. They contact the agency which performs a progressive aging sequence on the baby photograph. The sequence reveals the likelihood of a match and attests to the power of photographic proof of identity. Carlina/Nejdra and Maya fly to New York to meet her biological parents Joy and Carl (Roger R. Cross) and wait for the official DNA results. This visit begins Carlina/Nejdra's negotiation of her split identity.

While visiting New York, Carlina/Nejdra has a chance to spend time with her half-siblings, her parents, and her extended family. She realizes all of the ways she is similar to Joy. Joy, though, is upset whenever Carlina/Nejdra refers to Ann as "Mom" and erroneously assumes that Carlina/Nedjra plans to move to New York to be with them. Joy also tells Carlina/Nejdra, who enjoys her work as a hairdresser, that it is important that *her* daughter goes to college. It becomes too overwhelming for Carlina/Nejdra and so she goes back to Atlanta and is unwilling to take either Ann or Joy's phone calls. She does visit Cassandra when she gets back in Atlanta, though. Cassandra wants to talk to her about helping recently-arrested Ann. Carlina/Nejdra refuses to help. Cassandra admonishes, "You can and you will. She's family. Netty, you hear me?" As Cassandra speaks, the camera quickly cuts between her face and Carlina/Nejdra's as the rising music indicates the heightening tension and renders the conversation melodramatic. The camera cuts to a close-up of a straight-faced Carlina/Nejdra who corrects Cassandra, "Look, I'm going by Carlina now." The camera cuts back to Cassandra as she does a double take. "You're Netty to me." The two go back and forth:

CARLINA/NEJDRA: "My name is Carlina."
CASSANDRA: "Your name is Nejdra."
CARLINA/NEJDRA: "Not according to my birth certificate."

Carlina/Nejdra utters the last line and the music comes to an ominous crescendo as she stands up and walks out of the room.

After this, Carlina/Nejdra further withdraws. She watches Joy and Carl discuss her lack of communication on a fictional television show called *Real Chat.* She watches the show in the dark in her living room while Joy explains how much Carlina/Nejdra's lack of contact hurts her. She clicks the television off, picks up her phone and dials. She informs someone on the other line that she would like to change her number. Cassandra, unable to contact her, finally visits her at her apartment again. She walks into a dark room filled with dirty dishes. Carlina/Nejdra lies on the couch in the dark with disheveled clothes and hair. Cassandra informs her that she needs to get up and live her life to which she responds, "Whose life am I living? Joy's? Ann's? Yours? If I spend time with Joy I'm betraying you. If I spend time with you or talk about Ann, I'm betraying Joy." Cassandra tells her that she can call herself "Carlina or Nejdra," she doesn't care. "It doesn't matter to me what you call yourself," she says. "The point is, you have to get up and get on with your life." She insists that Carlina/Nejdra needs to figure out who she is and where to go from here. The scene cuts to Carlina/Nejdra knocking on Joy's door. Joy opens the door to reveal a newly hairstyled Carlina/Nejdra who has cut off over a foot of her hair. As Joy hugs her, the camera moves to shoot them from behind so the viewer can see the drastic nature of Carlina/Nejdra's new short hair that stands in for the new identity she has chosen.

Carlina/Nejdra and Joy come to an understanding about their new relationship and how to move forward, and the film wraps back where it started, with Joy's visit to the jail to see Ann. The two mothers confront each other and argue about who has the right to be considered Carlina/Nejdra's mother. Joy insists that Ann stole the formative stages of motherhood from her; the right to witness "Carlina's" first steps, prom, and the birth of a grandchild. Ann says, "I saw you all on TV; I thought about giving her back. Then *Netty* would look up at me ... everyday she became more and more mine.... I fed her, I clothed her, I taught her right from wrong!" (emphasis added). As she realizes her loosening grip on the child, though, Ann moves to discussing her through tentative signifiers, referring to her as "that little girl" as opposed to Netty, Nejdra, or "my daughter." Joy leaves without resolution to the dispute. The scene cuts to Ann as she confesses in front of the court. The court sentences Ann to twelve years in prison, yet the legal ruling of motherhood and fault cannot fully settle Carlina/Nejdra's identity crisis.

This crisis is finally settled in the following scene as it is now Carlina/Nejdra who speaks to an interviewer on *Real Chat.* Carlina/Nejdra sports another new haircut and addresses the interviewer and the viewer directly. The interviewer asks which name she prefers to be called. After blinking slowly and looking around, she responds, "I'm not Nejdra. That's the name that was forced on me. I'm not Carlina. That's the name that was taken from me. My name is Netty, that's the name that feels more like me, the name that feels most like home." As she begins speaking, melodramatic music begins.

It swells as she says the name "Netty" and the image switches to Carl looking at a picture of Carlina/Nejdra and Maya while the address continues as a voiceover. The viewer never returns to the actual interview, but the voiceover extends as Carlina/Nejdra hugs Maya and they get in a taxi. The voiceover drops away as the taxi drives off and arrives at the prison so that Maya can see her grandmother.

This brief address offers the answer to Netty's identity crisis. She has chosen an identity that incorporates many parts of her life, and the viewer witnesses her coming to this conclusion while on *Real Chat,* an interview that is left without a closing parenthesis. The authenticity of the representation of this choice is reinforced by the closing epilogue. The film ends and a black screen appears with a picture of the real Ann Pettway. The caption reads, "On July 30, 2012, Ann Pettway was sentenced to twelve years in prison for the kidnapping of Carlina White. Carlina did not attend the sentencing hearing." This frame dissolves and the next one showcases an image of the real Carlina/Nejdra and Joy White. The captions read, "Carlina maintains a strong relationship with her biological parents Joy White and Carl Tyson and her aunt, Cassandra Pettway. She still uses the name Netty Nance." The third frame addresses viewers directly, stating, "If you have reason to believe a child is missing or has been abducted, call the National Center for Missing and Exploited Children." Finally, the credits roll and the first credit reveals Nejdra Nance and Joy White as consulting producers, which further underscores the authenticity of this film and confirms their unity and identity as mother and daughter.

In the final few moments, the film asserts its authority as well as the power of television in negotiating identity. Television appeals to diegetic viewers throughout the film. Seeing Joy and Carl on television *almost* persuades Ann to give the child back. Carlina/Nejdra turns to Oprah in her moment of weakness. After being reunited with Carl and Joy, Carlina/Nejdra participates in many televised news conferences that help her come out at Carlina. Seeing Carl and Joy on *Real Chat* encourages Carlina/Nejdra to cut off communication, a move that was necessary in order for her to finally come around to making a decision. Finally, it was through *Real Chat* that Netty was able to affirm and articulate her identity publically. The creation of a Lifetime film about her journey further reinforces this articulation.

By ending this way, the film (and Lifetime) offers up a solution to identity crises: television. Both films attest to the fractured nature of individual identity, but *Abducted* assures viewers that television can assist in this process, an assurance that attempts to center the divided audience around Lifetime. Though *Taken Back* ends before Haley/Emma has a chance to go through this same progression, the film demonstrates the persuasive power of visual media in the form of photographs and home movies. It is through the power of visuals that Haley/Emma can begin to remember and accept Karen as her mother. Lifetime assures viewers that it is "Your Life" and "Your Time" and that time, says Lifetime, is best spent with your family in front of the television. Through *Abducted,* Lifetime assures viewers that television can solidify familial ties, as it did for Netty and Joy. With this move, Lifetime attempts to hail its fractured viewing audience through an insistence of its own validity and necessity. While it is impossible to assert the persuasive power of any one (or two) Lifetime films in isolation, it becomes clear that these films work in conversation with their other branding strategies in their address to a diverse and distracted audience. By calling these audiences back to Lifetime, the channel itself also tries to consolidate its own identity and, looking at their rating numbers, it appears as if they have been relatively successful.

## NOTE

1. See *Camera Obscura*'s 1994–1995 special issue on Lifetime's branding strategy.

## WORKS CITED

*Abducted: The Carlina White Story.* Dir. Vondie Curtis-Hall. Front Street Pictures and Lifetime Television, 2012. Film.

"Army Wives (2007–13)." *IMDb.* IMDb.com, Inc., n.d. Web. 25 Apr. 2014.

Bibel, Sara. "Lifetime Unveils New Iconic Logo and Tagline to Tap into Cultural Shift Among Women." *TV by the Numbers.* Tribune Digital Ventures, 2 May 2012. Web. 22 Mar. 2014.

*Bringing Ashley Home.* Dir. Nick Copus. Front Street Pictures and Lifetime Television, 2011. Film.

Bronstein, Carolyn. "Mission Accomplished? Profits and Programming at the Network for Women." *Lifetime: A Cable Network "For Women."* Spec. issue of *Camera Obscura: A Journal of Feminism, Culture, and Media Studies* 33–34 (1994–1995): 213–242. Print.

Byars, Jackie, and Eileen R. Meehan. "Once in a Lifetime: Constructing the 'Working Woman' through Cable Narrowcasting." *Television: The Critical View,* 6th ed. Ed. Horace Newcombe. New York: Oxford University Press, 2000. Print. 144–168.

*The Client List* (2012–). *IMDb.* IMDb.com, Inc., n.d. Web. 25 Apr. 2014.

D'Acci, Julie. "Women Characters and 'Real World' Femininity." *Television: The Critical View,* 6th ed. Ed. Horace Newcombe. New York: Oxford University Press, 2000. Print. 100–142.

*Dance Moms* (2011–). *IMDb.* IMDb.com, Inc., n.d. Web. 25 Apr. 2014.

Edgerton, Gary R., and Kyle Nicholas. "'I Want My Niche TV': Genre as a Networking Strategy in the Network Era." *Thinking Outside the Box: A Contemporary Television Genre Reader.* Ed. Edgerton and Rose. Lexington: University of Kentucky Press, 2008. Print. 247–268.

Edwards, Jim. "Lifetime's New Logo Is its 11th in 28 Years: See How They Evolve from 'Yuck' to 'Meh.'" *Business Insider.* Business Insider, Inc., 2 May 2012. Web. 2 Apr. 2014.

Eisner, Les. "Lifetime Locks in Double Digit Year-Over-Year Growth for Second Quarter 2013, Marking Best Second Quarter in Four Years Among Key Demographics." *A&E Networks.* A&E Television Networks, LLC, 2 July 2013. Web. 25 Apr. 2014.

Feuer, Jane. "Feminism on Lifetime: Yuppie TV for the Nineties." *Lifetime: A Cable Network "For Women."* Spec. issue of *Camera Obscura: A Journal of Feminism, Culture, and Media Studies* 33–34 (1994–1995): 133–146. Print.

Guthrie, Marissa. "Lifetime Unveils New Logo, Tagline 'Your Life. Your Time.'" *The Hollywood Reporter.* The Hollywood Reporter, 2 May 2012. Web. 22 Mar. 2014.

*Justice for Natalee Holloway.* Dir. Stephen Kay. Front Street Pictures and Lifetime Television, 2011. Film.

Lipkin, Steven N. *Docudrama Performs the Past: Arenas of Argument in Films Based on True Stories.* Newcastle: Cambridge Scholars, 2011. Print.

Lipkin, Steven N., Derek Paget, and Jane Roscoe. "Docudrama and Mock-Documentary: Defining Terms, Proposing Canons." *Docufictions: Essays on the Intersection of Documentary and Fictional Filmmaking.* Ed. Gary D. Rhodes and John Parris Springer. Jefferson, NC: McFarland, 2006. Print. 11–26.

Lotz, Amanda. *Redesigning Women: Television After the Network Era.* Urbana: University of Illinois Press, 2006. Print.

Mumford, Laura Stempel. "Stripping on the Girl Channel: Lifetime, *thirtysomething,* and Television Form." *Lifetime: A Cable Network "For Women."* Spec. issue of *Camera Obscura: A Journal of Feminism, Culture, and Media Studies* 11–12.33–34 (1994–1995): 213–242. Print.

Mylifetime.com. *Lifetime.* N.d. Web. 25 April 2014.

Paget, Derek. *No Other Way to Tell It: Dramadoc/Docudrama on Television.* Manchester: Manchester University Press, 1998. Print.

*Project Runway* (Bravo 2004–2008, Lifetime 2009–). *IMDb.* IMDb.com, Inc., n.d. Web. 25 April 2014.

Spigel, Lynn. "Women's Work." *Television: The Critical View,* 6th ed. Ed. Horace Newcombe. New York: Oxford University Press, 2000. Print. 73–100.

*Taken Back: Finding Haley.* Dir. Mark Jean. Reel World Management and Lifetime Television, 2012. Film.

*Taken from Me: The Tiffany Rubin Story.* Dir. Gary Harvey. Front Street Pictures and Lifetime Television, 2011. Film.

Williams, Linda. *Playing the Race Card: Melodramas of Black and White from Uncle Tom to O.J. Simpson.* Princeton: Princeton University Press, 2002. Print.

Wilson, Pamela. "Upscale Feminine Angst: Molly Dodd, the Lifetime Cable Network and Gender Marketing." *Lifetime: A Cable Network "For Women."* Spec. issue of *Camera Obscura: A Journal of Feminism, Culture, and Media Studies* 33–34 (1994–1995): 104–131. Print.

# Subversion of the Final Girl in Rape Revenge Narratives and the Normalization of Violence Against Women in *The Tenth Circle* and *The Assault*

JENNY PLATZ

During the 1970s, rape revenge films became increasingly popular as frank discussions of sexuality became less taboo, film censorship laws were no longer as strict, and the cultural consensus on the legitimacy of rape grew after the rise of second-wave feminism. Because the rape-focused films range in characters, settings, budgets, and cinematic style, theorists have difficulties in creating a fixed genre definition (Heller-Nicholas, intro.). Instead, the films are referred to as cycles (Read 23) or tropes that use rape as a central narrative component where a character, either the rape victim or someone connected to the victim, takes revenge against the assailant (Heller-Nicholas, preface). Although the majority of the films are from the point of view of the female protagonists, the experience of rape is often gendered as male because the films are created for male audiences (Clover 6).

The cycles or tropes of rape revenge narratives are also affected by current events and cultural views on rape and consent. The 1970s, the era when the most rape revenge films were released, are connected to the historic moment of second-wave feminism (Read 155–166). During the 1980s and 90s the rape revenge storylines also moved away from the space of exploitation cinema and into the space of mainstream films and television (Heller-Nicholas, ch. 4).

Since the 2000s, a cycle of rape revenge plots has been presented by the Lifetime Television Network. Beginning in 1990, Lifetime has produced original films with various topics regarding women's experiences (Hundley 176). However, until the 2000s, other networks produced most of the films airing on Lifetime concerning rape. In 2003, Lifetime produced *We Were the Mulvaneys*, based on the book by Joyce Carol Oates, a film that follows the breakdown and reunion of a family after one of the members is raped (Elias). Starting in 2003, Lifetime produced and aired other films regarding rape such as *A Date with Darkness: The Trial and Capture of Andrew Luster* (2003), *The Capture of the Green River Killer* (2008), *The Tenth Circle* (2008), *The Assault* (2014), and *Big Driver* (2015). The original films are in addition to all the other films about rape that air on the network but were originally produced by other channels. The more recent films connect to the current historic moment by exploring the timely debates on rape culture, developments regarding social media and consent, and the increasing protests for more victim rights. Although not all the films can be considered rape revenge films— some are only about the trauma of the assault—Lifetime's growing trend to produce rape-related arcs illustrates the network's contribution to the continuing cycle of cinema about sexual assault.

The cycle of rape stories found in Lifetime Television films not only examines contemporary concerns of rape, but also subverts many of the negative character traits found in earlier rape revenge films. By using Carol J. Clover's theories of the Final Girl, a term coined in her 1992 book *Men, Women, and Chain Saws*, to study the Lifetime films *The Tenth Circle* (2008) and *The Assault* (2014), it becomes apparent that Lifetime is one of the only spaces that creates powerful female characters who are raped, but who do not serve as surrogates for the male audiences. In most other rape revenge tales the female victims typically become figures men identify with in order to work through their own castration fears. The films, then, are not about a woman's experience of rape, but are about a man's experience of rape (Clover 140–162). Clover's book is key in film theory history because it was one of the first texts to examine the merits and cultural work at play in slasher and exploitation films. Although Clover's book explores the Final Girl specifically in slasher films, the concept of the Final Girl can be applied to rape revenge films because the Final Girl is metaphorically raped when she is penetrated and pursued by the killer's symbolic phallus of the knife. In brief, Clover's theory of the Final Girl claims the girls of slasher films only survive because they repress sexual and hedonistic urges and are masculinized through their appearances, names, intelligence, and possessions of a phallus through the use of knives. Because the girls are moral and exhibit male-gendered traits they survive, while their sexually active, feminized friends die. In their revenge the women transform into phallic killers and lose any traces of femininity (Clover 40–46).

The heroines in Lifetime films are at first presented as being Final Girls through their sexually unavailable bodies, non-sexualized clothes, and "good girl" behavior. But, unlike typical Final Girls, the girls of the Lifetime films are able to overcome their attackers while retaining their femininities. Moreover, the characters do not have to gain power by becoming symbols of the phallus like the Final Girls who only defeat the killers by possessing a phallus. Through the subversion of the Final Girl trope, the Lifetime films suggest that there is a cinematic space that showcases the empowerment of women against sexual attacks without gendering the women as men, thereby rewriting the trope's conventions.

The cycle of rape revenge narratives on Lifetime is also located within one of the only networks that exclusively targets female viewers. Since Lifetime Television's launch in 1984, the channel has been dedicated to airing programs that reflect the female experience and attract women viewers (Hundley 175). Unfortunately, Lifetime's programming is often filled with scripts of violence towards women, marking the channel as a place that instructs women that rape is a constant threat. Although the presentation of rape connects to the network's attempt to depict certain realities of the female experience, the films unintentionally encourage the female audience to be wary about relying on the police to help them in seeking justice and inform the viewers that they will be further victimized and hurt after the rape. Thus, Lifetime films support the idea the women will always face prejudices and hardships in reporting rape. Because the network's goal is to present truthful stories, the channel is implying that rape and the questioning of the validity of the crime are normative aspects of women's lives, and because women's bodies are in constant danger, all women are destined to be victims.

In examining the films *The Tenth Circle* and *The Assault*, this essay will explore how Lifetime successfully subverts the restrictions placed onto Final Girls, the girls who are allowed to survive in accounts regarding rape or metaphorical rape, by having the female protagonists retain their femininity in their paths to justice. Through subverting the conventions of the Final Girl, revenge and justice are then obtained through the power of the female body, instead of the power of a body that is symbolic of the male phallus. However, the reality presented by Lifetime is troubling because of the networks' abundance of narratives regarding violence against women, the role of the police in the films, and the disbelief women will encounter when reporting the assault. These factors present a reality where rape culture is inescapable.

## The Final Girl on Lifetime

In the beginning of *Men, Women, and Chain Saws: Gender in the Modern Horror Film*, Clover explains that she will only be analyzing American films from the 1970s and 1980s due to the films' connection to second-wave feminism (4–5). Although rape revenge films have existed throughout film history and date back to silent films such as *Birth of a Nation* (1915) and *Way Down East* (1920), the films became increasingly popular in the 1970s and 1980s. Women's goals in second-wave feminism were to gain equal pay with men, increase reproductive rights, end workplace discrimination, and dismantle patriarchal regulation of women's bodies (Krolokke and Scott Sorensen 8–10). The rape revenge narrative of the 1970s is a direct response to second-wave feminism due to the new rape laws and anti-rape culture created at the time (Projansky 7). In the early 1970s, the New York Radical Feminists held a Rape Speak-Out where women publically shared accounts of rape, awakening the public to sexual violence against women. The period was also full of sociological and psychological books written about rape, such as Susan Brownmiller's 1975 *Against Our Will: Men, Women and Rape* and Diana E. H. Russell's 1982 *Rape in Marriage*. The books were important cultural texts at the time due to their exploration of issues of the historical oppression of women and marital rape (Projansky 7). America's perception of rape also changed through the creation of anonymity statutes for women who report rape, the rise of rape crisis centers, and the cultural realization that acquaintance rape was a significant problem (8).

In *Men, Women, and Chain Saws*, Clover examines rape revenge films from the 1970s and 1980s as cultural texts that engage the emergence of female empowerment during second-wave feminism also in addition to America's repressed fears about the growing empowerment of women (Clover 11). The independence and female strength that arose through second-wave feminism is showcased in the rise of strong female protagonists in 1970s horror and exploitation films, the first time women played heroic roles that carried the narrative of the film and were given agency outside of domestic desires. Clover ties the creation of the female action star to second-wave feminism when she writes,

> The women's movement has given many things to popular culture, some more savory than others. One of its main donations to horror, I think, is the image of an angry woman—a woman so angry that she can be imagined as a credible perpetrator ... of the kind of violence on which, in the low-mythic universe, the status of full protagonist rests. It is worth remembering that the victim and hero functions are also fused in the so-called action film—but in the person of a male [17].

According to Clover, due to the language utilized by the women's movement, female characters in American films have been given the tools needed to voice women's victimization in society (4). The creation of stronger female characters then led to the female action star, a role usually reserved for men. In the action star role, the female characters often became symbols of maleness through their possession of male traits of agency and their powers to propel the narratives of the films. These traits are read as male because agency and the ability to move the plots of the films forward are the results of intelligence and strength, and not beauty, sexuality, or motherhood, the only cinematic powers female characters had before the 1970s. After second-wave feminism, Clover argues, women became full characters.

The rise of the strong female hero also reflects repressed fears regarding masculinity. Because the female characters traverse into male space, male characters become emasculated through heroines' independence and lack of need for male protection. Male characters change into secondary and weak characters instead of the protagonists of the films. Notably, the heroines in the horror genre also force male audiences to identify with female characters, a phenomenon that largely did not exist before the 1970s. In pre–1970s films, women always serve to be objects of the male gaze and male-centric narrative (Mulvey 19–21). Because the strong female character is often located within the horror genre of the 1970s and 1980s, the woman must also suffer in order to alleviate male audiences' castration fears by eliminating the threat of women, creating a sadistic pleasure for the viewers. Through the sadistic pleasure of enjoying and identifying with the female's torment, the male audience members are able to deal with their repressed castration anxieties that have been triggered by second-wave feminism. The women are empowered by defeating the killer and becoming the film's central protagonist, but the women are also tortured because of their strengths, allowing the genre to represent the cultural backlash against feminism and provide a place where men can work through their own issues regarding the women's movement (Clover 18).

Clover's second chapter, "Her Body, Himself," continues her argument that films serve as cultural signifiers of current conceptions of sexuality and gender. Clover examines various narrative conventions, but the traits most relevant to rape revenge films are the killer and Final Girl. The killer is almost always male and is sexually disturbed due to childhood traumas. The killer's impotence leads to his hatred of female sexuality, resulting in his murderous pursuit of women (Clover 26–35).

The person who is able to escape the killer's sexual rage is the Final Girl. Unlike the victims who are killed because they are sexually promiscuous, the Final Girl is a virgin or sexually unavailable, avoids other hedonistic pleasures like drinking and drugs, stays focused on school, and is calm and intelligent. She also dresses modestly and is not sexualized by her attire. The Final Girl is an embodiment of female purity and morality, unlike the victims who are represented as impure through their participation in sex. The Final Girl is also more cunning than her friends because of her observant powers. By being vigilant the Final Girl usually sees or is aware of the killer early in the film, making her prepared for his attacks. When he does attack, unlike the other victims, she is able to fight him off and even kill him (35–40). Thus the Final Girl is seen as more intelligent and resourceful than the film's other characters.

In the Lifetime original films *The Tenth Circle* and *The Assault,* the female characters who are raped share many similarities with the Final Girl. Although numerous rape revenge films repeatedly air on the Lifetime Network and mirror components of Clover's arguments, such as *When He's Not a Stranger* (1989), *Sin and Redemption* (1994), *She Fought Alone* (1995), *She Cried No* (1996), and *Silencing Mary* (1998), this essay will focus only on *The Tenth Circle* and *The Assault,* two more recent rape revenge films that were produced and distributed by the network. Although Lifetime recently released a new rape revenge film called *Big Driver* (2015), the female character is middle aged and therefore the film's treatment of rape is markedly different than the rape and revenge in the two other films, and therefore will not be considered in this paper

*The Tenth Circle,* directed by Peter Markle, stars Britt Robertson as Trixie and Kelly Preston and Ron Elward as her parents Laura and Daniel. The film, which is based on the 2006 novel of the same name written by Jodi Picoult, follows the family as they recover after Trixie is raped by her ex-boyfriend Jason, played by Jamie Johnston. Trixie only attends the party where she is raped in order to win Jason back by seducing him, but after he reveals he just wants to be friends with benefits while kissing her, she attempts to stop Jason from taking the kissing any farther. Jason ignores her cries and rapes her. She immediately reports the rape to the police and goes through the invasive procedure of a rape kit and informing the police of her former sexual relationship with Jason. Eventually Jason is arrested after Trixie tests positive for a date rape drug, but he is released shortly thereafter. Upon release he gets drunk and accidently falls off a bridge and drowns. Later it is revealed that Jason only fell off the bridge after losing his balance while having an argument with Laura, who randomly encounters him while looking for Trixie.

Through her schoolwork, clothes, and sexual experience, Trixie exhibits traits of the Final Girl exemplified by her innocence and goodness. According to the arguments of Clover, the Final Girl's goodness is measured by her sexual abstinence, academics, and modest attire. Trixie's moral disposition is established during her first scene where she is practicing a school presentation about her family illustrating that she is concerned about doing a good job on the assignment. As the scene cuts to her actual presentation the next day, Trixie's connection to her studies is revealed through her clothes and glasses. During her presentation, Trixie is wearing glasses, a symbol that is culturally associated with intelligence and studying. Although it has become a cliché, glasses are also often used in films as signifiers of female's morality and lack of vanity. Notably, Trixie never wears the glasses again in the film, further tying them to her schoolwork. In the scene, Trixie is also wearing a blue collared blazer, a symbol of professionalism through its connection to workplace attire. The blazer is in contrast to the more relaxed and revealing clothes of her peers who wear t-shirts and low-cut blouses. Her use of the blazer visually showcases Trixie's dedication to her studies, but also her status as a good girl.

The use of clothes to reveal Trixie's purity continues through the rest of the film as Trixie avoids sexual and form-fitting clothes. During her rape, she is wearing a black genderless hoodie, and after the rape she is often covered up by wearing a bulky winter coat or multiple layers. She is also always shown in dark colors, both before and after the rape, symbolizing her trauma over the assault but also making her blend into her surroundings. She does not want to have attention drawn to her body. The only moment where Trixie wears bright and sexualized attire is during the party. At the party she is wearing a pink halter-top and hip hugger jeans. Importantly, the clothes belong to her friend Zepher. In the scene before the party, Trixie's inculpability is revealed through Zepher doing her makeup, instructing her how to flirt with guys to make Jason jealous, and demanding that she not wear a bra with the outfit. Trixie's response to Zepher's advice is confusion and to question the amount of makeup her friend is putting on her face. She does not understand why not wearing a bra would help her win Jason back. The scene clearly establishes Trixie's virtue. Although she is not a virgin, she is shown to be naïve to methods of seduction.

Trixie's chastity is indicated during earlier moments from the film and events of the party. After Trixie learns Jason has a new girlfriend and their relationship is thus over, Zepher tells her that guys cannot be monogamous and prefer to be friends with benefits. Trixie responds by stating that she does not understand that concept, illustrating that although she is not a virgin, she is chaste to all others besides a committed Jason. During the party Trixie also reveals her refusal to be sexually active by not wanting to play strip poker. Although she plays the poker part of the game, she refuses to take off her shirt when she loses. Through the rape, Trixie's refusal to have casual sex is also evident. Moments before Trixie is forced to have sex she is consensually kissing Jason. She only changes her mind about having sex with Jason after he implies he will not be monogamous and will sleep with other girls. Trixie's desire to only sleep with a committed partner is implied in the scene because she does not believe in sharing her body unless the sex is about love instead of lust. Trixie's lack of fetishized clothes and refusal to have casual sex prevents her from becoming a sensual figure, linking her to the sexually unavailable Final Girl.

In *The Assault*, directed by Jason Winn, the main character Sam (Makenzie Vega) is also a Final Girl in many ways. Sam, a cheerleader, is raped by a group of football players before the events of the film. While still in shock, Sam attempts to commit suicide by setting herself on fire in the middle of a football game. After she is stopped by her ex-boyfriend, she reveals that she was raped. Prior to the film's opening, the football players involved in the rape also uploaded photos, videos, and quotes from the night on social media platforms. The rest of the film revolves around Sam's pursuit of legal justice for the crimes committed against her. Helping her determine the timeline of the night she was raped since she does not remember everything that happened due to alcohol, is her friend Frankie (Amy Bruckner). After a video of the rape is found, Sam is warned that her attackers may only receive light sentences. To gain justice, she then publicly plays the audio of her rape during a football game. The film ends with all the women in the bleachers standing up and applauding Sam's refusal to allow her rape to be ignored.

Sam possesses many Final Girl qualities. Like Trixie, Sam is not sexualized through her clothes, and although she is not a virgin, she is celibate. Because Frankie helps Sam investigate the night of the rape and releases the audio for her, and because it is suggested that she was raped herself, she is also a Final Girl. Sam's and Frankie's clothing is mostly asexual or non-sexualized rather than being feminine. The only time Sam's clothing is coded as feminine is when she wears her cheerleader uniform during the beginning of the film and flashbacks to the rape. While wearing the very feminine uniform, she is not sexualized because she is crying and covered in gasoline. The girls are representative of the sexual unavailability of the Final Girls.

During the rape Sam is shown in her bra and athletic shorts, but her underwear is used to show her vulnerability during the assault and not to make her body erotic. While wearing the underwear the camera angles never turn into the boys' erotic gaze by lingering on her body. Instead the camera remains unattached to the characters and lingers on Sam's pained and scared face to prevent any sexualization of her body. After the rape Sam no longer wears her cheerleading uniform but dresses instead in black hoodies, long sleeved shirts, big sweaters, and jackets. She only wears a bare t-shirt in the privacy of her home or Frankie's home. Frankie wears similar clothes: she always wears black, has Goth stylized makeup, and like Sam, she is always covered up, wearing multiple layers and hats. Because Sam and Frankie are constantly covering up their bodies, they are hiding their bodies from sexual gazes of the rape culture that controls their town.

Sam's and Frankie's refusal to become sexual objects is important because female characters in rape revenge films other than Final Girls often become eroticized after the rape occurs. In Jacinda Read's *The New Avengers: Feminism, Femininity and the Rape-Revenge Cycle* (2000) and Rikke Schubart's *Super Bitch and Action Babes: The Female Hero in Popular Cinema, 1970–2006* (2007), both authors comment on the extreme sexualization of the female characters after rape. Schubart's work claims that the women are objectified after their rape and are often played by actresses who are typecast in sexual roles. Schubart states, "Gender and sexual attraction are at the core of rape-revenge. Victims are always played by strikingly beautiful actors" (90), citing actresses such as Jennifer Lopez, Raquel Welch, Farrah Fawcett, and Margaux Hemingway. Because the actresses' star personas revolve around their beauty, they are cast so the film can sexualize their bodies. Read argues that the women often begin the film as non-sexualized characters, but after the rape occurs their sexualities are heightened through the women's clothes, the film's fetishizing cinematography, and the women's promises of sexual favors while luring their rapists to their deaths (35–51). It is important to note that according to Read, the characters are usually asexual or plain before the events of the rape, allowing the characters to still follow aspects of the virginal or virginal like Final Girl (36). Reading Schubart's and Read's arguments together regarding the sexualization of the women's bodies after rape, it becomes apparent that eroticizing the heroines' post-rape bodies can be staples of the trope. If the women can only become strong through rape and sexuality, then the women are not really becoming empowered at all, removing any authority that films may grant the characters.

Sam and Frankie are not sexualized after the rapes, suggesting that the sexualization of post-rape bodies does not have to be a convention of the rape revenge trope. Sam's lack of a sexualized body is supported by the film's cinematography. In Sam's initial scenes, she is shot in isolating close-ups of her body parts. Her feet, legs, torso, and face are all first shown in individual shots before her full body is displayed in a long shot. The effect of her visually fragmented body is not sexual, but instead effectively showcases her pain after the rape. Her cheerleading outfit is tight, but because she is crying and pouring gasoline on herself, the film is preventing her body from being sexualized. Unlike the women in the rape revenge films that Schubart and Read analyze, Sam does not have to become objectified by the film after becoming objectified by the film's characters.

Both Sam and Frankie are also not virgins but are sexually unavailable, connecting the characters to Clover's concept of the Final Girl once again. Sam reveals that she had sex before the rape, but because she was in a committed relationship, her lack of virginity does not mark her as a sexualized creature. Frankie is also implied to not be a virgin through the implications that a football player raped her, and thus she is not portrayed as a sexual transgressor. Through the rest of the film Frankie's is never in a frame with male students, visually informing the audience that she is not pursuing sexual desires. Although Sam drinks the night she was raped, she later reveals that she does not usually drink and therefore her alcoholic consumption that night was a rarity. She is not portrayed as a hedonistic character who behaves in immoral activities. Frankie is never associated with drugs or alcohol either, preventing her from being seen as a girl who breaks moral codes.

Frankie's intelligence also positions her as a Final Girl. Although she is never masculinized and always retains her femininity, she does possess traits usually reserved for men. She is a computer genius, capable of hacking social media systems, is skilled in detective work, observant, and is the one who insists Sam pursue justice after the attack. Frankie's skills with computers are first seen through her ability to trace the fake social media accounts that uploaded photos of Sam the night of the rape. Her tracing of the accounts results in the realization that more than one person raped Sam. Frankie is also able to determine the time the rape occurred and locate the identity of another social media account, which leads to the girl's discovery of where the rape took place. Finally, Frankie's computer expertise is apparent at the end of the film when she hacks the football field's speakers, projecting the audio of Sam's assault. Frankie's skills are important not only because they empower her through technology, a power usually reserved for men because it is not a sexual power, but because her hacking abilities lead to the narrative movement of the film. Without Frankie convincing Sam to not let the boys get away with the rape, helping her friend identify the rapists, discovering the identity of the boy who housed Sam's rape, and providing Sam with the capacity to tell her story of rape to her community, the assault would go unrecognized. Through her non-sexualized body and possession of male traits, Frankie appears to be a typical Final Girl of rape revenge films, who is always intelligent and resourceful.

## Lifetime's Rejection of the Limits of the Final Girls

Although Trixie, Sam, and Frankie exhibit Final Girl qualities such as goodness, sexually inactive bodies, and observant powers, the characters from the Lifetime films do not exhibit the problematic aspects of the concept. Instead, Trixie, Sam, and Frankie reject the restraints of the Final Girl that requires the characters to reject their femininity in order to be powerful enough to defeat their attackers and serve as surrogates to the male viewers. In "Her Body, Herself," Clover explains the consequences of femininity for Final Girls. Similar to the killer's inability to be fully masculine, the Final Girl is also never fully feminine. She often has a male name, and because she possesses typical male traits such as intelligence and physical strength, she becomes masculinized by film by using her symbolic phallus to violate the killer and castrate him (Clover 48–50).

Through the Final Girl's crossing of the boundaries of gender, her power is connected to her maleness instead of femaleness due to her possession of a phallus. The female protagonist then serves as a male surrogate who can use the experience of being the Final Girl and her penetration by the killer's knife to manage his own fear of castration (Clover 63). The Final Girls' experiences are not feminist texts then because the cross-gender identification process marks the narratives as male experiences. Clover makes it clear that the Final Girl is not an embodiment of feminism:

> The Final Girl is, on reflection, a congenial double for the adolescent male. She is feminine enough to act out in a gratifying way, a way unapproved for adult males, the terrors and masochistic pleasures of the underlying fantasy, but not so feminine as to disturb the structures of male competence and sexuality.... It may be through the female body that the body of the audience is sensationalized, but the sensation is an entirely male affair [51–52].

The Final Girl is only a device for male audiences to work through their own desires (Clover 53). Manhood then becomes the superior power in the film, and womanhood is inferior through the Final Girl's shedding of her femininity in order to survive.

Trixie, Sam, and Frankie are only Final Girls through their sexual unavailability and intelligence, preventing the characters from becoming standard Final Girls because they do not lose their femininities to become surrogates for male viewers. As explained earlier, Trixie, Sam, and Frankie rarely wear sexualized clothes. Instead they wear multiple layers or unisex hoodies. The use of non-sexualized clothes does not make the girls lose their femininities, however. Although Sam and Frankie have boys' names, nothing about them or Trixie are boyish. The girls' female gender is never questioned by the film, unlike other Final Girls who always turn into phallic symbols. The girls' possession of femininity empowers them over standard Final Girls because their strength in standing up to their rapists and seeking justice is not coded as an act of masculine powers. The girls are strong and are fully women.

One of the clearest ways the films reject the negative components of the rape revenge narrative is through Lifetime films' targeted audience. Because of the network's primarily female audiences, the films are marketed as attempts to speak to female experience rather than male experience. Lifetime's goal to create programming that speaks to and for a female audience is supported by the network's history. Since its launch, Lifetime has remained the leading network that attracts mainly female audiences, and until 2000, it was the only network to air content exclusively for women (Hundley 175). Since 2012, ratings and viewers have also grown significantly while still attracting mostly women (Eisner). The network has also strived to create programs that relates to women's real life seen through special programming that examines current issues such as health, child care, and balancing career and family (Tankel and Banks 266).

By creating a site for female audiences to engage in cinema about women's lives, the network not only provides a space where rape revenge plots can be told through female experience, it is also developing an electronic space. In "Lifetime Television and Women: Narrowcasting as Electronic Space," Jonathan David Tankel and Jane Banks introduce the concept of electronic space, where the viewer forms a relationship with the world exhibited through a TV, computer, or other electronic device (267–268). They argue that Lifetime creates an electronic space with the viewer that explores the female experience and allows women to directly interact with the channel through call-in programs, talk shows where viewers can buy tickets to be in the audience, and public service announcements (260). Since the publication of the article in 1997, the scope of the electronic space has grown even more by allowing viewer and network interaction through social media, the channel's website, and spaces other than the home through smart device technology. Tankel and Banks' argument about the electronic space of Lifetime further supports the networks' ability to craft programs that can tell stories of women's lives and emotions, instead of stories of men's lives and emotions because the channel is directly interacting with women.

Based on Lifetime's history, it is clear that the female characters in their films are not serving as surrogates for men to manage issues of masculinity. The films, then, do not have the problem of representing a prominent female issue of the threat of rape, for a male audience. Through the films' intentions to create female protagonists for female viewers, outlined by the network's history, the heroines are not limited by the misogynistic restraints of the Final Girl. The stories are about women's experiences only and are not just masquerading as tales about women. The girls then do not fulfill Clover's classification of the Final Girl but retool her concept into actual feminist attacks against sexual violence.

## Lifetime's Normalization of Violence Against Women

Although Lifetime's rape revenge films *The Tenth Circle* and *The Assault* present accounts of post-rape empowerment without gendering the girls as male, a key component of the Final Girl, the storylines are still problematic. By studying the post-rape experiences with the law and community in the two films, it becomes clear that the Lifetime channel is attempting to tell truthful stories, but is doing so by presenting women as constant victims. As explained earlier, Lifetime has strived to cultivate programming to attract female viewers and tell their experiences. The use of *The Tenth Circle* can be connected to Lifetime's attempt to broadcast material with timely issues through its connection to the book it was based on. Jodi Picoult's work is known for weaving current controversial issues such as stem cell research and medical ethics into the structures of her novels. The sensational topics are usually central parts of the books' narratives and end in twists where the reader is left to decide the moral implications of the issue for themselves (Montello 20–21). By turning one of Picoult's novels into a film, Lifetime automatically linked itself to the author's drive to include controversial and current topics in her work.

The network's desire to tackle current issues faced by women is notably apparent through *The Assault* and recent discussion about prevailing rape culture in America. *The Assault* was released in September 2014, a year after the events of the Steubenville, Ohio, rape case occurred. The film's plot closely follows the events of the case. Similar to Sam's rape, the victim involved in Steubenville was raped by football players while she was intoxicated and passed out. The girl was unaware of her assault until she saw pictures of her attack on social media. A video of the assault was also posted on YouTube (Strasser). Lifetime confirmed that the film emerged out of the news coverage of the case (Hess). The film, and Lifetime's mission statement and history, can then be read as an attempt to capture issues of the current female experience regarding consent, privacy, and rape culture.

By covering various issues that affect women's lives, Lifetime is attempting to present truthful life stories. Lifetime's rape revenge films can then be interpreted as plots that are presenting an issue that effects women's everyday lives. Rape of course is a problem that affects countless women in America; approximately one out of every six women has been raped or sexually assaulted ("Who Are the Victims?"). However, through the abundance of the rape revenge trope and the channel's attempt to show a relatable story, Lifetime is normalizing sexual assault. By looking at the sheer number of films regarding rape that air on the network, sexual assault is presented as a threat all women face in their daily lives. According to Lifetime, all women are labeled as potential victims: even if a woman has not been victimized yet, the channel implies that because she is a woman, she is automatically in danger of being violated in some way. The film's suggestion that women are always in danger of rape is supported by the statistics: 17.7 million American women have been victims of rape or attempted rape ("Who Are the Victims?"). But by normalizing female victimization, even though it is true that women are raped and assaulted in alarming numbers, Lifetime is failing to create cinema that deters the world from exploiting women, instead accepting rape as a reality that is part of American culture. According to research on the media's objectification of women and coverage of sexual assaults, the prevalence of rape myths in the media does encourage society to accept violence against women as common experiences. By surveying men and women who were exposed to pornography, films, and music that contain scenes or lyrics of assault, the study discovered the men were then more likely to accept rape myths (Hildebrand and Najdowski 1069–1070). Although the survey found men were primarily affected by rape culture rather than women, the typical audience of Lifetime, the films still participate in rape culture by normalizing violence against women even if men are not the audience encouraged to assume women will always be victims.

Rape culture is the perseverance of falsehoods about when and why rape happens, as well as the legitimization of sexual assault. In rape culture, assaults are rationalized based on beliefs such as the victims brought the situation on themselves, the women were dressed too revealing, the women were responsible for fighting off their attacker, women cannot be raped if they knew their assailant, women are sexual objects who always desire sex, and various other troubling and incorrect assumptions (Hildebrand and Najdowski 1060–1067). In general, rape culture can be described as a society that encourages violence against women by male aggressors. The culture emerged out of patriarchal culture where women are placed in submissive roles and men are placed in positions of power (Hildebrand and Najdowski 1062–1063). Institutions such as the police, religious groups, and even rape crisis centers support rape myths (1064).

The unfortunate truth that institutions of power often do not believe rape victims is exhibited in the Lifetime films when the girls who report the rape encounter hostile and useless police and are bullied and shamed by their communities. In *The Tenth Circle*, the detective investigating Trixie's rape initially expresses doubt of the crime when talking to her father: "I know this is hard, but I have seen these things before, you know, a lot of girls think they're ready to have sex, and they change their minds after the fact" (*The Tenth Circle*). Although the detective immediately claims to believe Trixie after her father asks if he is calling his daughter a liar, his statement reveals that he does doubt her and any girl who reports rape. The doubt of the legitimacy of the rape also occurs through the other reactions of the characters. Zepher initially does not believe that rape happened because Trixie willingly had sex with Jason before. It is also unclear if Jason will be prosecuted for the rape. He is arrested in the film but is quickly released, and nothing is stated about the trial process beginning. The film then implies that Jason may have gone free if he had not died. This potential turn of event is supported by various data from real life. According to a study published in 2012, only five percent of cases involving sexual assault end in the defendant's conviction (Hildebrand and Najdowski 1060). Statistics from RAINN, the Rape, Abuse, and Incest National Network, provide even grimmer data on rape and state that of 100 people who are raped, only 32 victims will report sexual assaults, 7 of the alleged rapists will be arrested, and 2 of the suspects will spend a night in jail ("Reporting Rates"). Cases where the victim knew her attacker and did not receive physical injuries are reported even less (Hildebrand and Najdowski 1060). The troubling statistics on rape mirror the problems Trixie and Sam face regarding creditability and the likelihood of conviction, but because the films do not offer a solution to the problems, the films suggest the statistics will always remain the same.

Although the Detective Jodi Miller always believes Sam's story, she is shown as extremely incompetent. Frankie and Sam are the ones who discover the identities of the other rapists, the time and place the rape occurred, and the social media sites that posted the videos and photos. Miller is also revealed to be ignorant of technology and has to be told what social media is. In addition, she accepts tainted evidence by taking clothing Sam was wearing during the rape from Sam's father. Because she did not find the evidence herself, the clothing would never be admissible in court. When visual proof of the rape is actually found, Miller warns Sam that the boys still may not be prosecuted. The police's incompetence, their distrust of the girls, and the lack of legal justice imply that women who report rape will have similar experiences. Studies have shown that police officers often do blame victims for attacks or believe the rape did not actually happen (Wentz and Archbold 25). Officers surveyed have also responded that since becoming policemen or policewomen they have changed their attitudes and no longer always believe rape victims (Wentz and Archbold 35–36). Police officers' definition of rape was also problematic in that they defined "real" rape as assaults made by men unknown to the victim that end in not only the woman's rape, but also other physical injuries to a woman's body (Wentz and Archbold 26–27). Even though it is true that women's credibility may be doubted when reporting the crime, because the films only present accounts involving police hostility or incompetence, the films are suggesting that women can always expect the justice system to fail or not believe them.

The girls are also harassed after reporting the rapes. When Trixie returns to school, she is called a slut and finds condoms in her locker. Sam is also harassed by her school and community; at school, kids text her a cartoon of a cheerleader that calls her a bitch and shows her pom poms on fire. Additionally, pictures and videos of her assault are posted online, her friends ignore her, the football players say she was asking for it and wear shirts that support the first boy accused of rape, and people remark that Sam should have known better than to drink so much. In reality, there are numerous media reports that reveal rape victims and families of rape victims are often harassed after reporting the crime to the police. In 2013, a young girl from Missouri was raped after attending a party and then left unconscious on her parents' lawn, a fact eerily similar to Sam's rape in *The Assault*. After reporting the crime to police, the family was also threatened online and at work (McDonough). In a separate rape case that occurred in Oklahoma, the victims were also harassed by their school, just like Trixie, Sam, and Frankie. A 2014 report by *Jezebel*, which was published after the victims from Missouri contacted the website directly with their story, revealed that after reporting the rape, the three victims were forced to leave school after the bullying became too much. The school administrators were also not helpful when the girls' parents called in seeking help with the harassment. One mother was told it would be easier for her daughter to stay home instead of disciplining the other students who were hurting her daughter (Merlan).

The only way Trixie, Sam, and Frankie are able to end their harassment and achieve justice against their rapists is through the films' convenient and fantastical endings. Through Jason's death, Trixie is able to avoid the hardships of a trial and the risk that Jason will be declared not guilty. The film allows Trixie and her family to have their revenge, but the revenge only occurs through chance and not the actions of the protagonist. Because justice against Jason only happens due to random events, the film is suggesting that in rape cases, in real life and in the film, reparations may only be fulfilled through happenstance. In *The Assault*, Trixie and Frankie are only able to publically shame their attackers and achieve resolution through the film's fantastic ending. In real life, it is very unlikely that the girls would be able to seize police evidence by taking the tape, orchestrate a complex plan to play the audio at the game, and suddenly earn the support of a town that previously did not believe the girls' claims of rape. Moreover, at the end of the film, Sam and Frankie appear to be totally recovered from the rapes and are no longer angry or traumatized about what happen. The ending can be interpreted as a fairy-tale conclusion, only possible in a fictional world. Because the films' resolutions of the rapes are fantasy, female viewers are again instructed that real life justice against sexual assault is not possible.

Lack of legal justice, harassment, and the questioning of the validity of rape occur in life, but by always presenting the report of rape as a traumatic experience, the films are inadvertently discouraging girls from reporting the rape. If no one will believe the rape occurred and the legal system will be useless, then why would viewers want to put themselves through the painful process of prosecuting rape? The films may present depictions of rape and show the reality of prosecuting rape, but they imply that only more trauma will come by reporting the crime and the hardships will be for nothing since the rapists will likely go free. Thus the presentation of rape does not create any change in society, because sexual violence against women is portrayed as an unavoidable aspect of women's lives that legal justice cannot fight. When justice does occur in the films it is through the power of fantasy or chance, again suggesting that in real life, without the aid of plot twists, justice will likely never occur. In "The Potential Impact of Rape Culture on Juror Decision Making: Implications for Wrongful Acquittals in Sexual Assault Trials," Meagen M. Hildebrand and Cynthia J. Najdowski reveal that false assumptions that lead to rape culture do not evolve over time unless programs and systems dedicated to overthrowing the myths are woven into people's lives (1065). The Lifetime films do the first step in ending rape culture by creating characters and cinematography that defy assumptions about rape victims, but through the other characters and scripts, the films inadvertently fall into rape culture again by doing nothing to change ideas about the prosecution of rape and myths about sexual assault.

## Conclusion

In the Lifetime films *The Tenth Circle* and *The Assault*, the female characters Trixie, Sam, and Frankie reject the problematic conventions of the rape revenge trope. The girls initially fulfill character conventions of Clover's Final Girl. Trixie, Sam, and Frankie are shown as sexually unavailable characters who possess intelligence. As the films continue, however, the girls reject the restrictive elements of Clover's characters. The girls are not sexualized through their revenge, they do not have to give up their femininities in order to gain strength, and their narratives are about women's experiences instead of male experiences of castration anxieties through a male gendered protagonist. Trixie, Sam, and Frankie then rewrite what it means to be a Final Girl, creating actual feminist stories about post rape justice instead of stories designed to entertain men.

However, the girls' empowerment is located in films that also present legal justice as an impossibility and suggest reporting the rape will be as traumatic as the assault. Because Lifetime's intentions are to present real life and air an abundance of rape revenge narratives, rape is presented as a normative aspect of women's lives. Instead of presenting only the trauma of rape and the cultural problems of believing women's claims of rape, Lifetime must create scripts that suggest there is hope for women after the violation. Although *The Assault* implies that Sam's community will now support and believe her story of rape, community support does not lead to legal justice or stop the problem of sexual violence against women. Moreover, Sam's support at the end of the film does not make sense because the town was earlier fiercely against her claims and even harassed her. Sam's mental anguish is also suddenly solved, indicating that the film's resolution of the rape is fantastical. By retooling the trope of rape revenge to demonstrate that legal justice can happen without unrealistic plot twists, that negative consequences of reporting rape can be mitigated, and that women do not have to expect to be victimized by society, Lifetime films can encourage culture to handle rape in the same way and potentially inspire women to reject being labeled as victims.

## Works Cited

*The Assault*. Dir. Jason Winn. Perf. Makenzie Vega and Amy Bruckner. Lifetime Television, 2014. DVD.

Clover, Carol J. *Men, Women, and Chain Saws: Gender in the Modern Horror Film*. Princeton: Princeton University Press, 1992. Print.

Eisner, Les. "Lifetime Locks in Double Digit Year-Over-Year Growth for Second Quarter 2013, Marking Best Second Quarter in Four Years Among Key Demographics." *A&E Networks*. A&E Networks Corporate, 2 July 2013. Web. 10 Aug. 2015.

Elias, Justine. "Original Movies Evolve." *Television Week* 23.15 (2004): 20–22. *Academic Search Complete*. Web. 10 Aug. 2015.

Heller-Nicholas, Alexandra. *A Critical Study: Rape Revenge Films*. Jefferson: McFarland, 2011. Kindle file.

Hess, Amanda. "Steubenville Gets the Lifetime Treatment (And a Cheerleader Erupts into Flames)." *Slate*. The Slate Group, 19 Sept. 2014. Web. 10 Aug. 2015.

Hildebrand, Meagen M., and Cynthia J Najdowski. "The Potential Impact of Rape Culture on Juror Decision Making: Implications for Wrongful Acquittals in Sexual Assault Trials." *Albany Law Review* 79.3 (2015): 1059–1086. *Academic Search Complete*. Web. 10 Aug. 2015.

Hundley, Heather. "The Evolution of Gendercasting: The Lifetime Television Network—'Television for Women.'" *Journal of Popular Film and Television* 29.4 (2002): 174–181. Web. 1 Aug. 2015.

Krolokke, Charlotte, and Anne Scott Sorensen. *Gender Communication Theories and Analyses: From Silences to Performances*. London: Sage, 2006. Print.

McDonough, Katie. "Missouri Town Harassed Victim of Alleged Rape and Her Family Until They Fled." *Salon*. Salon Media Group, Inc., 14 Oct. 2013. Web. 10 Aug 2015.

Merlan, Anna. "Why Were Three Teenage Rape Victims Bullied Out of School in Oklahoma?" *Jezebel*. Gawker Media, 21 Nov. 2014. Web. 11 Aug. 2015.

Montello, Martha. "Middlebrow Medical Ethics." *The Hastings Center Report* 40.4 (2010): 20–22. *JSTOR*. Web. 10 Aug. 2015.

Mulvey, Laura. *Visual and Other Pleasures*, 2d ed. New York: Palgrave Macmillan, 1989. Print.

Projansky, Sarah. *Watching Rape: Film and Television in Postfeminist Culture*. New York: New York University Press, 2001. Print.

Read, Jacinda. *The New Avengers: Feminism, Femininity and the Rape-Revenge Cycle*. Manchester: Manchester University Press, 2000. Print.

"Reporting Rape." *RAINN*. RAINN, n.d.. Web. 9 Aug. 2015.

Schubart, Rikke. *Super Bitches and Action Babes: The Female Hero in Popular Cinema, 1970–2006*. Jefferson: McFarland, 2007. Print.

Strasser, Annie-Rose. "Everything You Need to Know About the Steubenville Rape Trial." *THINKPROGRESS*. Center for American Progress Action Fund, 13 Mar. 2013. Web. 10 Aug. 2015.

Tankel, Jonathan David, and Jane Banks. "Lifetime Television and Women: Narrow-casting as Electronic Space." *Voices in the Street: Explorations in Gender, Media, and Public Space.* Ed. Susan J. Drucker and Gary Gumpert. Cresskill, NJ: Hampton Press, 1994. 255–270. Print.

*The Tenth Circle.* Dir. Peter Markle. Perf. Britt Robertson, Kelly Preston, and Ron Eldard. Lifetime Television, 2008. DVD.

Wentz, Ericka, and Carol A. Archbold. "Police Perceptions of Sexual Assault Victims: Exploring the Intra-Female Gender Hostility Thesis." *Police Quarterly* 15.1 (2012): 25–44. *Academic Search Complete.* Web. 11 Aug. 2015.

"Who Are the Victims?" *RAINN.* RAINN, n.d.. Web. 9 Aug. 2015.

# Conclusion—Lifetime at Thirty

## *Leading the Way for Women and Television*

### Emily L. Newman

"Some people are born great, others become great, and the rest watch cat movies, guess which one you are." In *Grumpy Cat's Worst Christmas Ever*, Grumpy Cat playfully admonishes her audience, acknowledging the ridiculousness of a film centered on a churlish cat. Lifetime premiered the film on November 29, 2014, which featured the viral sensation Grumpy Cat (real name Tardar Sauce). The film represented a shift in programming, as the network was beginning to shift their focus to a new demographic: the millennials. The film may have garnered disappointing ratings, drawing only 1.8 million viewers as compared to its rival Hallmark Channel's movie premiere *Christmas Under Wraps*, which reached 5.8 million people (Rife), but the ratings are simply not the only marker of success for the film. But for Grumpy Cat and her family, the numbers are insignificant. As James Hibbard aptly mentioned in a review on the film, "Somewhere Grumpy Cat is probably using a litter box lined with crumpled $100 bills and couldn't care less." Although the movie may not have lived up to the expected ratings, it was the most-tweeted program on TV that night, something that marks a significant investment of a younger audience. In addition, Libby Hill argued in her review that it likely wouldn't matter about the viewership of the film as the movie relied so heavily on product placement, which the movie itself mocked. She explains:

> The ads, of course, are of vital importance because that's how the network makes money, something the film makes continuous reference to. Also mentioned repeatedly are hopes for a sequel (twice) and mentions (with visual representations, no less) of all the Grumpy Cat merchandise available for sale (thrice)....
> The people who made *Grumpy Cat's Worst Christmas Ever* don't give a shit about

quality. They phoned it in, told us they were phoning it in, and cackled all the way to the bank.

As Hill articulated, many people did *not* like this movie. Samantha Highfill called it the worst Christmas movie ever, saying, "Grumpy Cat would hate her movie. Like *hate*-hate it." At *Gawker*, LaToya Ferguson elaborated, "Hopefully one day Tardar Sauce the Grumpy Cat will gather up her strength to rebel against all those who allowed this movie to be made. Until then, she will continue to be a cog in the meme machine and an unwitting weapon in the war on Christmas."

There were a few supporters, though, and many of them took to Twitter to share. It was clear, however, from all the conversation surrounding the film, that the film was getting attention. It was an unusual endeavor, certainly one that might have seemed strange for the network known for melodramatic romances and over-the-top films centered on women as victims. But that is the Lifetime of years past. Lifetime in its thirtieth year is about creating content that engages and spurs conversation in reviews, on talk shows, on Twitter, and on Internet forums. Lifetime's community is no longer just women, as its new slogan "Your life. Your time" illustrates by using a gender-neutral pronoun. Additionally, and as *Grumpy Cat's Worst Christmas Ever* demonstrates, Lifetime is now targeting the millennial generation intensely. Throughout the film, Grumpy Cat repeatedly tells the viewer to take advantage of the break (commercials) and tweet the film, using the hashtags #worstchristmasever and #whyamiwatchingthis.

As the hashtags epitomize, Lifetime created a film that even questioned its own existence as well as what it means to be a Lifetime film. The film begins with the character of Grumpy Cat providing the opening monologue:

> Hello. Hi. How are you? Welcome to *Grumpy Cat's Worst Christmas Ever*! The movie! You don't have to watch it. But I know you are going to. So, if you do, you might be treated to high speed car chases … huge explosions … a hero in a leotard and cape who saves the world…. Anyway, I only mention those things to get your hopes up. That way I can enjoy your disappointment when you realize this movie is just a sappy melodrama mostly about me, Grumpy Cat. You're welcome.

This meta-exploration of Grumpy Cat and Internet memes in the twenty first century provided an opportunity for the network to have a little fun at its own expense. Openly and repeatedly, Grumpy Cat wishes for a sequel, at one point even requesting the filming of *Grumpy Cat's Worst Vacation Ever*, which she would prefer be filmed in Maui. When the owner of the pet store where Grumpy Cat currently lives is trying to figure out ways to make money, he first suggests that they take Grumpy Cat and make her an Internet meme, "and it is sure to go viral. Her face will launch a thousand products—everything from t-shirts to coffee mugs, after that TV appearances, and, oh, I don't know," and pausing, he turns directly to the camera and speaks to the viewer, "maybe, a Lifetime movie." Later, in one telling moment toward the end of the film, they even poke fun at the types of films the network is known for. As the young heroine is reunited with her mother after defeating three robbers and saving the pet store from ruin, her mom runs up to greet her, and quickly asks, "Those guys didn't *do* anything to you, did they?" Before she can even answer, Grumpy Cat tells the viewer, "That's a *different* kind of Lifetime movie, if you know what I mean."

Yet, as the introduction and the previous essays have illustrated, Lifetime can no longer just be described as the network for women. The channel is complicated and complex, and seeks to serve a large, diverse audience with a variety of programming. The Lifetime brand, however, has increasingly become a part of popular culture. The network has repeatedly set out to capitalize on the idea of their brand itself, nowhere perhaps more obviously than the short-lived TV series *My Life as a Lifetime Movie* (2012). By looking at the slate of programming Lifetime has aired in 2015, as it transitions into its 31st year, we can see how the network is choosing to move towards a broader audience and address popular trends. Lifetime continues to surprise, greenlighting the edgy series *UnREAL* (2015) and airing *A Deadly Adoption* (2015), the maybe-parody movie starring Will Ferrell and Kristen Wiig. Finally, in keeping with their willingness to embrace technology, in August of 2015 Lifetime released their new app, Lifetime Movie Club. Lifetime enters its fourth decade as one of the leading cable networks, consistently producing original movies that win both awards and ratings, while creating programming that inspires conversation across Internet and television platforms. While often dismissed as being only for a limited audience or for making sub-quality programming, it is not just important, but necessary to consider Lifetime as the risk-taking, path-breaking juggernaut that it is.

In an attempt to capitalize on the power of their brand, *My Life as Lifetime Movie* aired real women's stories in seven episodes in 2012. Rob Sharenow, then Lifetime's executive vice president of programming, saw the show as an opportunity to try to capture a younger audience, explaining that "Lifetime is evolving and one of the steps in our evolution is to be able to look at ourselves and have a little fun with our own brand. We definitely saw it as an opportunity to announce to the world, 'Hey we're acknowledging the brand and taking it in a new direction'—contemporizing it" (Ritchie). The show was brought to the network by Liz Gateley, who produced the show with her partner Tony DiSanto and their firm DiGa. Inspired by a conversation with a girlfriend, Gateley recounts, "She found out that her husband had this double life going on and she knew I used to work at Lifetime so she said, 'Liz! My life is a Lifetime movie!'" (Ritchie). Once Lifetime approved the show, Gateley worked on developing it with the same intentions as she had worked on her other youthful reality-based programming for MTV: *Laguna Beach* (2004–2006), *The Hills* (2006–2010), *16 and Pregnant* (2009–present), and *Teen Mom* (2009–present). Each show focuses on two women's stories, which are often consistent with ones featured in lifetime films: extreme tales of sexual misconduct and affairs, obsession, double lives, life-changing decisions, and scandal. In an empowering move, the woman at the heart of the story speaks directly to the viewer, giving her agency and control of her narrative. Her monologues are supplemented with contributions of relevant parties (spouse, children, friends, cops, etc.). Re-enactments are used to dramatize the story, similar to what one might see on news magazines like *Dateline* and *20/20*, albeit to a different kind of audience.

Gateley wanted the show to focus on the women's home life because she felt that the core of Lifetime's films involved women in peril who were trying to protect "the nest." In that vein, she required that the stories on the show must involve the women's domestic life, but she also maintained that *My Life as a Lifetime Movie* should offer hopeful resolution to their stories (Ritchie). The stories told are often remarkable in their unbelievabililty. In the first episode, we are introduced to Ana Margarita, who fell in love with Juan Pablo, a Cuban refugee who swam to the United States. He became part of Brothers to the Rescue, an organization of pilots that helped people trying to flee Cuba. One day he left his family to go on a trip, and a few days later two Brothers to the Rescue planes were shot down. Ana Margarita was convinced he died. Instead, he was actually a Cuban spy sent by Fidel Castro to infiltrate the organization. While Ana may still be looking for love, after this whole incident she sued the Cuban government and won a $20 million settlement. *My Life as a Lifetime Movie* not only allowed real women to tell their own stories, it also allowed the network to articulate their conception of the Lifetime brand, which they presented as intimately connected to the female experience which could include victimhood and trauma, but always ended in hope.

Since the show did not necessarily draw great reviews or ratings, or any attention at all for that matter, the show was not picked up for a second season, though it did air in reruns and on Lifetime Movie Network (LMN), and the episodes are available for purchase via Amazon Instant Video. Arguably, the show ushered in a new more self-aware phase for network. In February of 2015 (less than three years after *My Life as a Lifetime Movie*), Richard Sharenow moved from his role as general manager of the channel to a larger role for the A&E Networks, and Liz Gateley became head of programming in April, leaving DiGa. For Gateley, it marked a return home; she not only had developed *My Life as Lifetime Movie*, but began her career at the network developing scripted and reality series (Ross). In the hiring of Gateley, Lifetime solidified the importance of reality programming to the network, but it also makes clear that they are actively seeking out the new, younger audiences that Gateley has made a career of targeting.

Gateley, however, has not abandoned Lifetime's overarching goal, and maintains a commitment to the network's relationship with women. Heather Hundley has perceptively argued that Lifetime's strategy of gendercasting, targeting their program to a narrow audience (in this case female), was imperative to their success and strength in the 1990s (175). Echoing the importance of gendercasting, Amanda Lotz adds that the network "play[ed] a crucial role in understanding changes in institutional perceptions about female audiences and how and why dramatic programs with central female characters began expanding at such a tremendous rate in the late 1990s" (39). Gateley is just the latest in a long line of important Lifetime executives who seek to articulate what is at once so appealing and unique about the Lifetime brand, but also represents the unwillingness to settle for the status quo.

While targeting the generic "woman" may have been the start of its brand, Lifetime has developed and specified its intended audience. In its first few years, the mid–1980s, Lifetime positioned its audience as "high spending women" who were "selective" in their programming choices. Defining their female audience as significant consumers helped establish Lifetime's ability to secure advertising and eliminate their established debt (Byars and Meehan 24). The early years were marked by an emphasis on "lifestyle" and "health-and-fitness" programming, which expanded quickly into talk programming (Hundley 175–176; Tankel and Banks 260). In 1992, Alex Wagner, then director of public affairs at the network, described their target audience: "Every woman is different—has different interests and tastes. Psychographies include all these different women: women who stay at home, women who work, women who are mothers, women who are single, women who are married.... It is for all of these women that Lifetime programs" (Tankel and Banks 262). Wagner here really embodies how Lifetime was describing its audience: simply put, the everywoman.

In 1998, Lifetime described their typical viewer more specifically as "female, college-educated, around forty-seven years old" (Lotz 51–52). Not much had changed in 2003, as a marketing executive described the viewer as "a woman in her early forties, she is probably a working mom. Psychographically, she is a busy, multitasking woman, very interested in a lot of different things: information about health, parenting, social issues, violence against women and how to break the cycles, so she's a multifaceted person" (Lotz 52). From 2001 to 2003, Lifetime was the most-watched cable network in primetime, and it was clear that the network was connecting to its intended audience. To solidify their brand recognition, LMN debuted in 1998 and Lifetime Real Women (LRW) in 2001. Lifetime recognized how important their original movies were to their audiences, and Lotz has argued that creation of LMN was meant to provide 24/7 access to their movie catalogue (including their original films, miniseries, theatrical films, and a smaller number of movies from second-run distributers). This also helped the network not alienate their fan base as they expanded their syndicated and original programming (Lotz 41).

In 2006, Betty Cohen, the new Lifetime CEO at the time, built on the earlier definition of the everywoman:

> "One of the things the research has shown is that, for the women who do love us, the connection to Lifetime the brand is a powerfully emotional one. They're mostly powering through their day and check their emotions somewhere else. They've got to get the kids to school. They've got to deal with the boss at work without blowing up. All these things.... We need to speak to the array of emotions that women need and want that gets shoved aside in their busy lives" [qtd. in Lieberman].

These comments were made at the time Cohen was helping Lifetime phase out the slogan "Television for Women," which they felt was too limiting of a designation. Cohen believed that they should not have to tell people who their audience was, rather, "you just have to be it" (Lieberman).

In 2012, Lifetime debuted their new slogan "Your Life. Your Time." Part of rebranding meant to breathe life back into the network after 2011 saw ratings decline; Lifetime's then-general manager Nancy Dubuc saw it as an expansion of their audience. She particularly liked the openness of the new slogan, saying, "The reaction among the women was really quite profound. It spoke to everyone. But it meant something different to every woman at the table, which to me was the perfect answer" (qtd. in Guthrie). Echoing the push to reach a broader base, in 2014, Richard Sharenow addressed what he envisions as the network's future: "My goal ... is to have our channel reflect kind of the true breadth of the American population better, and I think that means inviting a lot of different people into the tent" (qtd. in Neely). In particular, Sharenow was interested in expanding their programming to people of color. This included developing the series *Preachers' Daughters* (2013–present), *Devious Maids* (2013–present), *Bring It!* (2014–present), and *BAPs* (2014) and movies including an all-black remake of *Steel Magnolias* (2012), a biography of African-American Olympic gold medal gymnast Gabby Douglas (2014), and *Betty and Coretta* (2013), based on the lives of Coretta Scott King, wife of Dr. Martin Luther King, Jr., and Betty Shabazz, wife of Malcolm X. The expected audience has changed greatly since the network started; the network still embraces gendercasting but has expanded to include different classes and races of viewers. What often went unsaid in previous discussions of their brand was that Lifetime's generic woman was in actuality a white woman. By 2012, however, the network was realizing those limitations, and was actively rethinking their programming substantially to include people of color.

As they were increasing their audience base and developing new programming, there was a rise in the criticism of the quality of the programming on the network. Writing for *The Guardian* in 2014, Brian Moylan elaborated, "There's no concern for the quality of these movies as long as the marketing department can find a way to make sure they get a million blog posts written about them in order to trick viewers into tuning in. All they care about is that there are eyeballs on the screen—the 'click,' in internet parlance—not the experience people have once they get there." He allows that the network might put out a few quality programs and films each year, but he finds that programs he dubs "clickbait" are dominant. While the focus of his wrath is *The Unauthorized Saved by the Bell Story* (2014) and the *Flowers in the Attic* set of films (2014–2015), his harshness mirrors that of what critics had to say about *Grumpy Cat's Worst Christmas Ever*.

Moylan and others, however, are rather harsh, and in their willingness to take down the network, they brush aside the critical successes and risks that Lifetime has taken. Broad Focus, Lifetime's initiative, was established to provide opportunities to women wishing to enter the film industry who might otherwise not have had the support or ability to make their dreams a reality. This initiative comes directly on the heels of the creation of two important films: *Five* (2011) and *Call Me Crazy: A Five Film* (2013). Each of these movies is actually a combination of five shorter movies directed by and starring leading actresses of the day, including Jennifer Aniston, Demi Moore, Patricia Clarkson, Jeanne Tripplehorn, Annie Potts, Laura Dern, Bonnie Hunt, Ashley Judd, Jennifer Hudson, Melissa Leo, and Octavia Spencer, among others. Beyond their actions, the network has achieved recognition. In addition to taking action and increasing opportunities for women in filmmaking as well as expanding the Lifetime brand, the network is now earning more award nominations and awards than it ever has before. In 2013, the network received twelve Emmy award nominations, which peaked at seventeen in 2014, before dropping to ten in 2015.

Building on this acclaim, Lifetime premiered the TV series *UnREAL*, a scripted show centered on the behind the scenes of a reality dating program, on June 1, 2015. Before its debut, the show had generated significant buzz based on its content, and the excitement was perpetuated by Lifetime's delivery of the first four episodes for free across different platforms at the time of its premiere (on-demand viewing via cable providers, on the Lifetime website, through their downloadable app, and on streaming services like Google Play and iTunes). The show brought with it a significant pedigree in its production staff, including Marti Noxon of *Buffy the Vampire Slayer* (1997–2003) and more recently *Girlfriend's Guide to Divorce* (2014–present), and Sarah Gertrude Shapiro, who spent six seasons working on *The Bachelor*. Basing the show on her experiences, Shapiro wanted to create an edgy, dark series that truthfully addressed the problematic nature of the reality dating show. She was hesitant about airing the show on Lifetime at first, explaining, "My dream would have been to pitch to HBO or Netflix. I spent a lot of time asking other people in the industry if I should take the deal, because Lifetime scared me" (qtd. in Syme). Lifetime pushed both Noxon and Shapiro before solidifying the deal, having them detail the plot of the entire series in depth. Noxon elaborated, "As we were describing everything I kept waiting for them to go, 'what?' Nothing. Then we got to something else and nothing. We got all the way to the end and there was this pregnant pause and [one of the executives] leaned back and said, 'I love it!' That was a good moment" (qtd. in Easton).

Lifetime's willingness to tackle the bold content allowed Shapiro and Noxon to embrace the deal. *UnREAL* follows unstable reality show producer Rachel (Shiri Appleby), who is trying to rehabilitate her career after a breakdown shooting the previous season of *Everlasting*, a stand-in for *The Bachelor* that is based on the same premise of one man trying to find love among a cast of competing women. Rachel is manipulated and controlled by Quinn (Constance Zimmer), the show's demanding executive producer, who is in her own battle for creative control over *Everlasting* and its potential spinoffs. *UnREAL* exposes the machinations that take place behind the scenes of reality television, while also touching on and critiquing the ubiquitous stereotypes that support the industry. Anne Easton summarily describes the program: "The reality of *UnREAL* is that it's a scripted show about an unscripted series, a situation that seems utterly implausible of being done in a believable manner, but yet, clearly it is given the success of this series."

To understand *UnREAL*, we must understand ABC's *The Bachelor* franchise. 2015 saw the airing of the nineteenth season of *The Bachelor*, the eleventh season of *The Bachelorette*, and the second season of *Bachelor in Paradise*. Built on the premise of finding love, *The Bachelor* finds the leading man meeting and interacting with 25 women, gradually eliminating the contestants down to one, with the idea during the last (and most dramatic) rose ceremony of the season, the bachelor will propose marriage to the one remaining woman. Or, as scholar Susan J. Douglas perspicaciously put it, "After a serial sampling of this array of female pulchritude in typical everyday locales like hot tubs and stretch limos, the Bachelor rejects them one by one until he has chosen the one he likes the very best. They are supposed to get married. (They don't)" (202). Douglas is clearly being dramatic, but is also on point as the show has increasingly played up over-the-top and histrionic scenarios for ratings.

Further, the twists and turns of this elaborate dating show have progressively moved farther away from real life. Jennifer L. Pozner reads this show as an example of a twisted fairytale, as she expounds, "prospective princesses sit on their aimless, tiny behinds, fend off fellow ladies in waiting, and hope to be whisked away by a network-approved knight in shining Armani" (35). This overreliance on creating happy, fantastical narratives is for Pozner just a masquerade, hiding the "chauvinistic and anachronistic ideas about women and men, about love and sex, about marriage and money" (46). After all, the show is dependent upon its caricatures of women: the bitch, the slut, the smart one, the saint, and so forth. Douglas expands upon this idea:

> *The Bachelor* has, in its various seasons, offered highly normative female "types" into which most women allegedly fall, and ropes viewers into damning certain behaviors while applauding others…. Shows like *The Bachelor* urge girls to place themselves on a postfeminist scale of femininity to determine how far they have to go to please men without losing all shreds of their own identity and dignity. In the process young women calibrate, for better and for worse, what kind of female traits are most likely to ensure success in a male dominated world [212–213].

It is not a surprise, then, that *UnREAL* not just mimics these stereotypes, it exaggerates them and codifies them. A repeated motto on the show, "sluts get cut," refers to the fact each season there are often a few female contestants who are willing to be go farther in their relationship with the bachelor than is socially acceptable for the situation, maybe makes out with him, possibly even has sex with him. Often, shortly thereafter, these women are eliminated from the show. To create easily comprehendible narratives, producers pigeon-hole the women into definable characters that allow for quick sound bites and convenient storytelling (scripted or not).

In fact, each of the producer's roles on *Everlasting* is to shepherd groups of female contestants with the hope that one of their girls is the one chosen by the bachelor at the end of the show. Quinn initiates a contest, including numerous incentives not just for steering the chosen woman into the bachelor's arms, but also for fights breaking out, cops being called, ambulances being sent to the house, and other dramatic situations. At the start of the first episode ("Return"), we are introduced to Rachel's group in the limousine on the way to meet Adam, the bachelor. Immediately, Rachel is distinguished from the group. All of the contestants are dressed formally, while she wears very little make-up with her hair pulled back and earpiece tucked in. Most significantly, though, she wears a tattered t-shirt proclaiming, "This is what a feminist looks like," which stands in contrast to the more traditionally feminine garb sported by the contestants. The women are complaining about how long they have been in the limo and how they need to go to the bathroom, but Quinn is telling Rachel to get them ready, so she tries to psych the contestants up, showing them a picture of the bachelor. From the beginning, it is made very clear that Rachel prioritizes her job. Thus, in our introduction to Rachel, who presumably functions as a fictionalized stand-in for Shapiro herself, we see her beliefs at odds with her job.

Despite her declared "feminism," Rachel works for a show that is often marked as decidedly un-feminist, and on top of that, Rachel is *good* at her job. Each episode makes clear her facility and skill at manipulating the contestants to get what she wants. Arguably and significantly, Rachel emerges as an anti-heroine (Paskin, Robinson), a rare trope for female characters, whose predecessors could be seen as Jackie Peyton on *Nurse Jackie* (Showtime, 2009–2015) and Patty Hewes on *Damages* (FX, 2007–2012). The anti-hero is often defined as someone who the audience wants to root for, but is deeply flawed and exhibits villainous behavior at times. The past twenty years have seen a massive influx of anti-heroes on television. But is not just that these men were everywhere on TV, but rather, that these characters were immensely popular and fronted award-winning and critically acclaimed shows. Characters like Tony Soprano (*The Sopranos*, 1999–2007), Vic Mackey (*The Shield*, 2002–2008), Dexter Morgan (*Dexter*, 2006–2013), Don Draper (*Mad Men*, 2007–2015), and Walter White (*Breaking Bad*, 2008–2013) are just a few examples of recent anti-heroes that have dominated the airwaves recently.

These men have been labeled "unhappy, morally compromised, complicated, deeply human," (Martin 4) but these descriptions could easily be applied to Rachel on *UnREAL*. In fact, Shapiro directly referred to these anti-heroes as inspiration, saying: "We talk about *Breaking Bad* a lot in the writers' room. That's definitely something we aspire to—that kind of antihero, but for women. Tonally, we always calibrate back to, these people get to be like Don Draper, they get to be Walter White, they get to be Tony Soprano. And we threw out the word 'likability' really early on. We just don't care" (qtd. in Buxton). Rachel's looks are deceptive. Played by the stunning Appleby, but dressed down to appear as relatable, it is easy for viewers to see her as the good girl, the one who will have the moral compass amidst the chaos. On top of this, Rachel appears to be an empath. She can relate to characters instantly and deeply, seemingly and quickly becoming anyone's close friend. But as critic Willa Paskin notes, "Rachel always seems to want to do the right thing—to *not* sell out, expose, manipulate, and embarrass the women on *Everlasting* for good television—but not quite enough to, in fact, do the right thing." By placing this anti-heroine in a unique setting (a reality show), Paskin argues that the creators of *UnREAL* differentiate Rachel from previous anti-heroes and anti-heroines.

Additionally, Rachel (and the show by extension) is just as bold and brazen as her male anti-hero predecessors. The fifth episode ("Truth") opens with Rachel masturbating with a vibrator while watching porn on her phone in the back of a cargo truck. After a brief period, Rachel stops and looks dissatisfyingly at the camera, unable to climax. She pulls a t-shirt on, and it happens to be her "This is what a feminist looks like" shirt, which the viewer has not seen since the pilot. This is not a sexy scene in any way; rather, it is boring, mundane, and "normal." While male masturbation is fairly common on television, female masturbation appears much less frequently, and even then, it is often made into a spectacle. Shapiro describes the situation: "You've seen [male masturbation] a lot, and it's always a joke and there's a shorthand for it. But a healthy, adult woman who isn't having sex probably is jerking off—but no one talks about it" (qtd. in Gray). Marti Noxon elaborates, "I think it makes men uncomfortable. I think there's something really scary about the idea that [sex is] not always romantic for us, and that it's not always about needing a man there to take care of our needs. I think it's scary for guys to see that, and be confronted with this in-your-face idea of 'yeah, we've got it'" (qtd. in Gray). "Truth" shows Rachel having a very human experience. At the beginning of the episode she may be unable to orgasm, but by the end of the episode, after reconnecting with a former lover and now watching a video of the two of them instead of porn, she is able to achieve the much-needed release. In summarizing how important this scene is to contemporary television, Clem Bastow explains, "Rachel's sexual activity is portrayed as ordinary, and even a bit boring, which feels refreshing, and a little bit revolutionary."

Rachel is not the only female character on *UnREAL* with a strong sexual drive and a willingness to have her needs met. The executive producer of *Everlasting*, Quinn is dealing with her own relationship issues, as she is having an affair with married show creator Chet. While each woman has complicated romantic relationship(s) on the show, the two women's work and friendship is repeatedly made a central theme throughout the first season. Shapiro has referred to Quinn and Rachel as the central relationship and love story in the show, and the two figures are constantly bouncing back and forth between being friends and enemies (Kelley). Shapiro and Noxon wanted this focus on female relationships, as Shapiro explains: "We are very proud that we clobbered the Bechdel Test. Our female characters rarely talk about men with each other, and are very much in control of their own lives. And one of the great things about being on Lifetime, even though tonally and stylistic the show seems a little new for them, is that we didn't even need to have the conversation about having two female leads" (qtd. in Coffin).[1] In order to create these strong friendships, Shapiro and Noxon have ended up creating fully three-dimensional women whose lives are not dependent upon their relationships with men.

This focus on friendship and the closeness of women has consistently been a pivotal focal point for Lifetime's programming. This can easily be seen in the choice of syndicated programming that has aired in the past: *Designing Women* (reruns aired 1993–2006), *Kate & Allie* (1994–1999), *The Golden Girls* (1997–2009), *Laverne and Shirley* (2001–2004), *Hope & Faith* (2006–2009), *Desperate Housewives* (2006–2012), and *Grey's Anatomy* (2007–present).

While the content and depiction of *UnREAL* might be edgy and extreme, the prioritization of female friendship is nothing new, and yet, Rachel and Quinn's bond resonates much like those who came before. In the season finale ("Future"), Rachel has either manipulated everyone so much that they hate her or has pushed them away intentionally, leaving Quinn as her only ally. At the end of the episode, she finds out that Quinn pushed Rachel's love interest away from her, setting off a chain of events that destroyed relationships and exploded the finale of *Everlasting*. Rachel confronts Quinn, and even as she is clearly angry at her, Rachel confides her fear that her ex-boyfriend is going to retaliate against her. Quinn stands up for Rachel, telling her that he better not. Rachel tears up and realizes that Quinn is her only support system. After a thoughtful pause, Rachel tells Quinn she loves her, to which Quinn replies, "I love you too … weirdo." As viewers await the second season, it remains clear that the two women will continue to be the heart of the series.

While the pull of the two central characters remains strong, the show also unabashedly critiques reality television. It may be a fact universally acknowledged that reality shows are fake, exemplified by many of them have multiple writers on staff, but they are often still viewed as real. This contradiction is present throughout different series, as Susan Murray and Laurie Ouellette expand:

> Reality TV promises its audiences revelatory insight into the lives of others as it withholds and subverts full access to it. What results is an unstable text that encourages viewers to test out their own notions of the real, the ordinary, and the intimate against the representation before them. Far from being the mind-numbing, deceitful, and simplistic genre that some critics claim it to be, reality TV supplies a multilayered viewing experience that hinges on culturally and politically complex notions of what is real, and what is not [6].

*UnREAL* is constantly showing the viewer the fakeness of *Everlasting*. In one scene, the bachelor and one of the contestants are going on a horse ride. The viewer sees them talking on the horses in place for a few moments before stunt doubles are brought in to actually ride the horses. Moreover, many of the evening gathering scenes parallel a 2009 *New York Times* expose on reality programming. Edward Wyatt describes the scene of ABC's *The Bachelor*, which mirrors parts of the first episode "Return" to a tee: "The contestants waited in vans for several hours while the crew set up for a 12-hour 'arrival' party where, two contestants said, there was little food but bottomless glasses of wine. When producers judged the proceedings too boring, they sent out a production assistant with a tray of shots." Shapiro acknowledges that these experiences are based on fact, and Noxon articulates, "The women are hot-boxed. They are put in a house with no media, no music, no books, no magazines, nothing. Just each other and booze. So they literally develop a Stockholm syndrome, where the only way you get out is through the bachelor. By the end a lot of these women think they really are falling in love" (qtd. in Syme). By giving us a glimpse beyond the cameras and letting the viewer into the inner workings of dating reality shows, *UnREAL* feels like the rules have been broken and the viewers are witnessing something not intended to be seen, unlike the over-the-top murder mystery film, *Killer Reality* (2013), which uses the setting as a novelty, as site of complicated relationships and backstabbing that leads to numerous deaths. In this conventional Lifetime film, the melodrama is prioritized over the reality show backdrop.

Robert Sharenow has heralded *UnREAL*, calling it a "turning point" for the network (qtd. in Syme). In both its critical success and daring topic, the show has helped make the network incredibly culturally relevant. It is logical, then, that Lifetime would want to build on this buzz, evident particularly in their approach to responding to trends and fads of the moment. Following on the notoriety that accompanied the airing of *Grumpy Cat's Worst Christmas Ever*, Lifetime plans to air *Jim Henson's Turkey Hollow* in the 2015 holiday season. With the revival of the Muppet Movie franchise in 2011 (*The Muppets*) and the launch of a new ABC TV show of the same name in the fall of 2015, Lifetime has engaged the trend by working with the powerful and imaginative Jim Henson Company on a new original movie. Chris "Ludacris" Bridges narrates the film, which also stars Mary Steenburgen. The film follows a family who end up stuck in a small town, looking for a Howling Hoodoo, an elusive turkey. The script was based on a story by Jim Henson, Jerry Juhl, and Kirk Thatcher (who also directed). At a moment when Muppets are more culturally relevant than ever before (perhaps best evidenced by the hubbub surrounding Kermit and Miss Piggy breaking up just prior to the start of the 2015 TV series), it is logical for Lifetime to jump on the bandwagon and work with the Jim Henson Company (Moyer).

Further, the network continues to build on its own successes, by giving audiences more of what they like. *Dance Moms* (2011–present) continues to be a juggernaut, dominating one night of programming a week. Centered on the Abby Lee Dance Company (of Pittsburg and Los Angeles), the show features charismatic leader Abby Lee Miller, a small group of supremely talented pre-teen dancers, and their outspoken mothers. Besides the large quantity of episodes produced (in the first eight months of 2015 alone, 32 new episodes of the show aired), Lifetime aired repeats of the previous weeks' episodes with extended dance scenes called "Choreographer's Cut." Additionally, numerous reunion episodes and specials were filmed, along with reruns of the show with new commentary by the dancers and their mothers called "Throwback Tuesday." But the network has also seen success with its parallel show *Bring It!*, which focuses on Coach Dianna "Miss D" Williams and her Miss D's Dancing Dolls dance team, based in Jackson, Mississippi and specializing in hip-hop majorette competitions. *Bring It!* first aired in 2014, and has aired a second season in 2015. A spin-off, *Step It Up*, began in 2015, following one of the Dolls' main rivals, Traci Young-Byron's Young Contemporary Dance Theatre (YCDT). Lifetime has demonstrated a significant investment in these reality programs by creating numerous spin-offs and specials and investing two distinct nights of programming to reality programs about parents and their dancing children.

In addition, Lifetime has continued to devote Saturday nights to first-run original films. In the summer of 2015, the network accompanied the movie premieres with short comedic bits before and after the commercial breaks called "Mixologist and a Movie." Starring the comedian Erin Foley, the short clips are often exaggerated recaps of what has just taken place with commentary on the sheer ridiculousness of the plot. It should not come as a surprise, then, that these witty observations only accompany the more humorous and over-the-top Lifetime films, staying away from the docudramas and films based on true stories. Besides the comedic monologues, Foley often creates an alcoholic cocktail that relates to the film in a humorous way. On *Fatal Flip* (2015), Foley opines, "Is anyone else concerned that no one is searching for the realtor? Coworkers? Friends? Based on her outfit, her cat? Anyone? This is one of her properties, right? Also, what about the contractor's quick burst of anger? He goes from zero to DEATH." Lifetime uses Foley to promote the films, and in a similar way that Grumpy Cat critiqued the Lifetime brand, Foley points out the absurdity of the films that she is watching. But, and this is important, Foley is not mocking the Lifetime viewer. Instead, she engages the viewer in such a way, it is clear that the viewer and Foley are on the same page, in on the joke and laughing at the ridiculousness of the films together.

One of its most talked about original films in 2014 was the aforementioned *The Unauthorized Saved by the Bell Story*, and if Foley had been providing commentary then, she would have certainly have had a lot to say. While the film did not succeed in the ratings, it generated enough buzz and enough new network viewers that in 2015, Lifetime produced three similar films: *The Unauthorized Full House Story*, *The Unauthorized Beverly Hills 90210 Story*, and *The Unauthorized Melrose Place Story*. Tanya Lopez, senior vice president for original movies, explains the films' appeal: "This falls into the popular bucket by bringing in the audience that is engaged in the pop-culture zeitgeist. That is a bigger play for us to get a younger audience" (qtd. in Shattuck). These films speak to the desire for nostalgia and recognize Lifetime's awareness of current demands for old favorites, as seen in the revivals of *Full House* (*Fuller House*, debuting on Netflix in 2016), as well as recent attempts to reboot *Coach* (NBC), *Twin Peaks* (Showtime), and *The X-Files* (Fox). The unauthorized films about *Full House* and *Saved by the Bell* feel innocent, not addressing the rumored cattiness or controversy that followed the shows.

Screenwriter Ron McGee tried to push for more of these plotlines, but met resistance, as the network really wanted to be true to their primary sources of episodes, anecdotes in magazines and interviews, the casting process, and the on-set experiences. He elaborates, "There was never any talk about getting down and dirty with it. In fact, there were times when I would try to lean toward the drama, and Lifetime execs were like: 'Can we really validate that? Are we sure that's true, or is that just a rumor someone was airing?'" (qtd. in Shattuck). Over a year after *The Unauthorized Saved by the Bell Story* aired, *The Unauthorized Full House Story* followed suit, both airing to a less-than-desirable 1.6 million viewers (Kissell, "Lifetime's 'Unauthorized Full House Movie'"). At the same time, the movies are winning the night in terms of ratings and skewing young, which is beneficial to the network and certainly to its advertisers.

Further drawing on cultural memories, LMN is airing a special on O.J. Simpson in the fall of 2015, marking the twentieth anniversary of his acquittal in the criminal trial of the murder of Nicole Brown Simpson and Ron Goldman. The special, *The Secret Tapes of the O.J. Case: The Untold Story*, focuses on O.J. Simpson himself, illuminating details about his personality the criminal trial, as well as featuring both secret recordings taped prior to the infamous Bronco chase and interviews with Robert Kardashian and Kris Kardashian Jenner. Made by filmmaker Lawrence Schiller, who himself was close to Robert Kardashian, this film is meant to pair with one that is airing on A&E, *O.J. Speaks: The Hidden Tapes*. This documentary focuses more on the civic trial, showing long lost deposition tapes and new interviews with legal team members. The anniversary of the trial has undoubtedly sparked interest in his case, seeing not just these specials but features on *20/20* as well as being the basis of the first season of Ryan Murphy's scripted show *American Crime Story*, to appear in February 2016. Like the *Unauthorized* series of films, this O.J. Simpson special represents a way to connect with the audience in a particularly timely manner.

Once again, Lifetime is also trying to enter the late night talk show market. Following in the footsteps of 2014's *Undone with @AmandadeCadenet*, which only aired eight episodes, Lifetime is hoping for more success with its new show *Fashionably Late with Rachel Zoe*. Both shows have attempted to cash in on *Project Runway*'s popularity by airing directly after the program and hoping to sustain their audience numbers. Amanda de Cadenet, who had previously aired an unconventional documentary-cum-talk-show called *The Conversation* on Lifetime in 2012, never could quite seem to work out what *Undone* should be, struggling at first to engage the episode of *Project Runway* that aired just prior while shifting to more of a talk show format in later episodes. In a market that sees zero women hosting late night talk shows, despite recent retirements by David Letterman, Jon Stewart, and Craig Ferguson, there have been numerous rallying cries for networks to hire a female host—one that Lifetime has now tried more than once to answer (Kamp). Zoe defines her show's premise simply in her first episode, which aired September 24, 2015, saying, "The show where I tell you about this week's amazing, questionable, and the *so* not okay moments in fashion, style, and popular culture." Surrounding herself with Derek Blasberg (*Vanity Fair's* Man on the Street) and her husband Rodger Berman, Zoe brings a guest on the show to talk about trendy topics, as well as thematic bits like "Chic in Review" and "What Were You Thinking?" While the success of Rachel Zoe is underdetermined at the time of this writing, she offers a bit of hope for women in a tough market, aspiring to success that only been seen by Chelsea Handler (*Chelsea Lately* aired on E! from 2007 to 2014).

Nothing epitomizes Lifetime's interest in generating buzz more than the original made-for-television movie *A Deadly Adoption*. The film was originally meant to be a surprise, to be aired without marketing and attention. The network wanted to sneak it on the air and allow everyone to be surprised to see mega-stars Will Ferrell and Kristen Wiig starring in a sincere Lifetime thriller (Snierson). Unfortunately, news of the film leaked in April of 2015, and Ferrell released the following statement to the press, "We are deeply disappointed that our planned top-secret project was made public. Kristen and I have decided it is in the best interest for everyone to forego the project entirely, and we thank Lifetime and all the people who were ready to help us make this film" (qtd. in Kreps).[2] The film was executive produced by Ferrell and his comedic collaborator Adam McKay and written by Andrew Steele, who had co-created and written the spoof *The Spoils of Babylon* for IFC. Despite Ferrell and Wiig's apparent willingness to pull the film, Lifetime eventually announced they would premiere the film on June 20th, 2015, which was meant to coincide with the twenty-fifth anniversary of Lifetime making original movies.

Drawing 2.1 million viewers, *A Deadly Adoption* was not the massive success that the network might have been hoping, and it certainly was not the surprise phenomenon it was intended to be. But it was the night's most-watched cable program and attracted a young audience with one million adults between the ages of 25–54. Over the six broadcasts that first weekend, however, more than six million people tuned in, and just under one million unique users read about 35,000 tweets about the film (Kissell, "Will Ferrell's"). Reviews and tweets were mixed, no one seemed quite sure how to understand the film. Was it a parody? Was *A Deadly Adoption* a sincere Lifetime melodrama? Further complicating matters, the filmmakers and stars refused to easily quantify the film's intentions.

The narrative of the movie itself feels like it fits naturally on Lifetime, even at times recalling their made-for-television movies like *The Last Trimester* (2007) and *The Surrogate* (2013). *A Deadly Adoption* starts as so many Lifetime movies do, with a traumatic event. Sarah (Kristen Wiig) is on a dock, pregnant with her second child, and beckoning Robert, her husband (Will Ferrell), to come and take the boat out with her. But the dock is rotten and collapses before he gets there, causing Sarah to fall and hit her head and lose her baby. Everything about the scene is over-dramatized—the slow motion collapse, the extended close-ups on the faces of Robert and Sarah, and the instant switch of moods from incredibly happy to terribly upset. As the credits begin, sweeping shots of a luscious green landscape and a body of water dominate the frame. Nothing specific is shown; rather, the landscape is intended to read as generic, allowing this story to feel like it could happen anywhere, not just the aptly-named Storm Lake.

The movie revolves around our central couple wishing to adopt a child, leading them to take in a young pregnant woman, Bridgette (Jessica Lowndes), in hopes of adopting her unborn child. Forming a bond with their young diabetic daughter Sully, Bridgette makes her home in their house and quickly makes it clear that she has her sights set on Robert. As the film progresses, his behavior grows increasingly erratic; he is desperately worried about Sully and is constantly trying to protect her from everything, at one time frantically screaming, "You know the dangers of diabetic ketoacidosis!" After digging through Bridgette's things, Robert realized that he knew Bridgette as Joni, with whom he had a drunken one-night stand on one of his book tours. He realizes the potential dangers of having Bridgette/Joni in his house and leaving her alone with his daughter too late, discovering that Bridgette/Joni has kidnapped Sully. After a panicked search and several close calls, Bridgette/Joni returns to the family home to find Robert but runs into Sarah. After a fight, Bridgette/Joni sets an unconscious Sarah up to look like she committed suicide by leaving her in her running car with the garage door shut. Robert returns home only to find Bridgette/Joni and realize that she is not pregnant at all, but had a miscarriage with Robert's baby before moving into their home. Her impassioned speech feels familiar, one that has been in countless Lifetime films between a jilted, obsessed lover and her target: "We are free. Free to be happy. We have everything. We can start our lives together. This is what we always wanted." Robert, of course, maintains his loyalty to Sarah, only to be shot by Bridgette/Joni. Upset that she has shot the person she loves, she flees, and Robert is able to rescue Sarah. Unfortunately, the only way he can save Sully is by conquering his fear and taking a boat across the lake to cut off Bridgette/Joni's escape route. Unsurprisingly, he is able to halt their escape. Just before Bridgette/Joni can retaliate, Sarah shows up to save them by shooting her. The movie should be over, but first, the viewer is treated to Robert, Sarah, and Sully dancing ridiculously in the kitchen. They exude happiness, to an exaggerated effect, and the dancing goes on just a little bit too long; the scene is so forced that everything just feels off.

On the one hand, the film *is* a Lifetime movie of the melodramatic nature. The plot, with its over-the-top reveals and absurd dialogue, seems at home on the Lifetime network. Romance novelist Teri Wilson lists all the points that add up to the film naturally fitting into Lifetime's catalog: the slow motion tragedy at the start, the fact that it was inspired by a true story (at least according to the credits, but which seems to have just been a stunt as the film is fictionalized), the fake pregnancy, the "insane logic," the bad boyfriend, the false identity, Sully's kidnapping, the hero rescuing the damsel-in-distress, the ending resembling *Fatal Attraction*, and the celebratory dance scene. As she ends her article, though, the ambiguity of the film is made apparent: "As soon as Will Ferrell busted out his twist moves, I knew with absolute certainly that the movie was indeed a parody. Probably. Maybe." Like Wilson, most reviewers who enjoyed *A Deadly Adoption* did seem to imply they were in on the joke, or, at the very least, allowed for the possibility that it was an exploration of the genre (Sheffield, Thompson, Genzlinger).

Those who skewered the film generally seemed to believe that it fell flat, not living up to the definition of a parody. Critic Keith Uhlich explains his point clearly, which is worth quoting in depth:

> The best parodies are acts of loving possession that dig deep, even as they keep the laughs steadily coming. There's no sense that Ferrell, Wiig, Steele or director Rachel Goldenberg have any genuine feeling for the low art they're spoofing. Compare their cursory contemptuousness with Mel Brooks' *Young Frankenstein*; the Zucker-Abrahams-Zucker *Airplane!*; *SCTV*'s Ingmar Bergman lampoon, *Whispers of the Wolf*; or Charles Busch's women's melodrama satire, *Die, Mommie, Die!*—farces that both skewered *and* paid honor to their sources instead of wallowing in easy derision. And if the ultimate point here is that Lifetime movies are, by their nature, superfluous garbage … well, that's a pretty weak-tea basis for this project's existence. May its pop cultural shelf life be correspondingly short-lived.

Parodies are historically defined as a "a work written in mocking imitation of the style of another work, that style being exaggerated or applied to an incongruous subject" ("Parody"). Parodies often distort or reinterpret their subject, altering it so that it is clear it is not just repeating what has been done before and providing new meaning or insight (Palmer 92–87, Danesi 226). While these definitions differ substantially from how Uhlich is using the term parody, his central point that *A Deadly Adoption* is not a parody does hold. Rather, the film reads as a faithful recreation of a Lifetime film, and if it is exaggerated in anyway, it is only to emphasize the Lifetime-esque qualities of the film itself.

While Uhlich does not see any "genuine feeling" for the film that they are supposed to be spoofing, many, including myself, disagree. Will Ferrell's complicated faces, ones that are so often demonstrated in the numerous close-ups in the film, often seem to expand and recall ones seen frequently in Lifetime movies. In the mimicking of popular plotlines and the use of lines like "I'm your new mommy!" and "Don't call me crazy!," Lifetime is honoring its loyal audience, as these short bits of dialogue feel plucked from earlier films. Prior to the film's airing, no screeners were released and no interviews were allowed to be given. Since the film aired, and in response to the confusion about why the film was made, Kristen Wiig has said simply that she wanted to make a Lifetime movie (Ryan). She explained to *Vulture*, "It wasn't a parody at all. I think people assumed it was [a comedy] because Will and I were in it, but it wasn't. Well, I guess you can call it a mislabeling. I thought it was great, I was very happy with it and we had a lot of fun making it, but the goal was never to make a parody" (qtd. in Marchese). Jessica Lowndes echos Wiig's comments: "[Ferrell] wanted it to be as serious as possible so it felt like any other Lifetime movie—this one just happened to star Will Ferrell and Kristen Wiig." In fact, Lowndes even acknowledged that the confused response by the press was exactly what was intended, explaining, "That response is exactly what we wanted it to be. This was not meant to be a comedy, [but] I definitely knew what we were [making]" (qtd. in Wieselman).

While it may resemble a parody, or something like it, *A Deadly Adoption* can perhaps be more aptly described as a love letter to Lifetime films. At its purest, the story, the acting, and even the plot holes were consistent with films that air on LMN and Lifetime. In line with that, and to continue to engage their fan base, Lifetime created an app called Lifetime Movie Club in the summer of 2015. Playing on the popularity of book clubs with women, this app encourages women to log in and watch movies, with the ability to take part of the Lifetime catalog with them at any time. The app replies on a subscription-based service, which at the time of writing costs $3.99 a month, but allows for streaming with no commercial interruption. Allowing access to at least 30 different Lifetime films, the app both adds and removes films every Friday. As more and more viewers, particularly younger audience members, are moving away from subscription cable and paying directly for services they desire (HBO Now, Showtime Anytime, Netflix, Hulu Plus, etc.), this app clearly allows Lifetime a place to attract viewers who might not have access to the channel in its typical cable lineup. Where Lifetime Movie Club fails, however, is that there is no space for interaction between fans of the network. There are playlists and a wide variety of films to choose from, but no message boards or chat rooms exist. In stifling their fans' ability to interact, Lifetime is moving away from the forums and places for community that they have previously established online at their website.

At the same time, even without the potential for communication with other fans, the development of the app exemplifies Lifetime's willingness to be competitive with their peers. Andrew Wallenstein argues that in the creation of Lifetime Movie Club, Lifetime is attempting to figure out their place in the changing industry and how they can establish "a direct-to-consumer relationship that yields the kind of user data that give a sense of what consumers really want. Lifetime Movie Club may not exist in a year or two, but it represents a beachhead from where the company can eventually pivot into something that may be a more compelling consumer proposition." In figuring out a way to get older Lifetime movies to their audience, independent of subscription television, Lifetime is trying to expand its brand even further. While the app may disappear, just as the online mash-up program did, the app can be seen as exemplifying a network that takes chances and continues to think outside of the box. Not content with the status quo, Lifetime approaches each year as a place for exploration, a time to air new challenging films and programs, to tackle bold initiatives, to create new types of interactive viewing options, all while still holding onto their core fan base and continuing to produce what made them famous.

## NOTES

1. The Bechdel Test was created by Alison Bechdel in her comic strip entitled "The Rule" from the series *Dykes to Watch Out For* in 1985, in which two women discuss whether there are any movies worth watching playing in the theaters. The test requires the film or television show to meet the three following criteria: (1) the program must feature two women; (2) the women must have conversations with each other; and (3) the conversation must be about something besides men.

2. Kreps claims that the leaking of the film was possibly by a jilted former agent or employee of Creative Arts Agency in revenge for Ferrell and his agent Jason Heyman leaving the agency and moving to United Talent Agency on March 31, 2015.

## WORKS CITED

Bastow, Clem. "It's a Good Thing We're Finally Showing Female Masturbation on TV." *Daily Life*. Daily Life, 15 July 2015. Web. 19 Sept. 2015.

Buxton, Ryan. "*UnREAL* Creator on Creating a Brigade of Female Walter Whites." *HuffPost Life*. The Huffington Post, 29 July 2015. Web. 19 Sept. 2015.

Byars, Jackie, and Eileen R. Meehan. "Once in a Lifetime: Constructing the 'Working Woman' through Cable Narrowcasting." *Lifetime: A Cable Network "For Women."* Spec. issue of *Camera Obscura: A Journal of Feminism, Culture, and Media Studies* 33–34 (1994–1995): 13–41. Print.

Coffin, Lesley. "The Mary Sue Interview: *UnREAL*'s Creator Sarah Gertrude Shapiro on Feminism, Gender, & Reality TV." *The Mary Sue*. The Mary Sue, 23 June 2015. Web. 19 Sept. 2015.

Danesi, Marcel. "Parody." *Dictionary of Media and Communications*. Armonk, NY: M.E. Sharpe, 2008. Web. 20 Sept. 2015.

Douglas, Susan J. *Enlightened Sexism: The Seductive Message That Feminism's Work Is Done*. New York: Times Books, 2010. Print.

Ferguson, LaToya. "Aubrey Plaza's *Grumpy Cat* Movie So Much Worse Than It Wants to Be." *Morning After*. Gawker, 1 Dec. 2014. Web. 18 Sept. 2015.

Genzlinger, Neil. "Review: *A Deadly Adoption* Stars Kristen Wiig and Will Ferrell." *New York Times*. New York Times, 21 June 2015. Web. 20 Sept. 2015.

Gray, Emma. "The Power of Seeing Women Masturbate on TV." *HuffPost Women*. The Huffington Post, 6 July 2015. Web. 19 Sept. 2015.

Guthrie, Marisa. "Lifetime Unveils New Logo, Tagline 'Your Life. Your Time.' (Exclusive)." *The Hollywood Reporter*. The Hollywood Reporter, 2 May 2012. Web. 18 Sept. 2015.

Hibbard, James. "Grumpy Cat Movie Ratings Sub-Purr." *Entertainment Weekly*. Entertainment Weekly, 3 Dec. 2014. Web. 18 Sept. 2015.

Highfill, Samantha. "*Grumpy Cat's Worst Christmas Ever* Is the Worst Christmas Movie Ever." *Entertainment Weekly*. Entertainment Weekly, 29 Nov. 2014. Web. 18 Sept. 2015.

Hill, Libby. "How to Consume *Grumpy Cat's Worst Christmas Ever*." *A.V. Club*. A.V. Club, 3 Dec. 2014. Web. 18 Sept. 2015.

Hundley, Heather. "The Evolution of Gendercasting: The Lifetime Television Network—'Television for Women.'" *Journal of Popular Film and Television* 29.4 (2002): 174–181.

Kamp, David. "Why Late Night Television Is Better than Ever." *VF Hollywood*. Vanity Fair, Oct. 2015. Web. 19 Sept. 2015.

Kelley, Seth. "*UnREAL* Creators Talk Season 2's Focus on Quinn and Rachel, Possible Spinoff." *Variety*. Variety, 31 July 2015. Web. 19 Sept. 2015.

Kissell, Rick. "Lifetime's *Unauthorized Full House Movie* Just Average in Ratings." *Variety*. Variety, 25 Aug. 2015. Web. 19 Sept. 2015.

_____. "Will Ferrell's Lifetime Movie *Deadly Adoption* Draws 2.1 Million on Saturday." *Variety*. Variety, 23 June 2015. Web. 18 Sept. 2015.

Kreps, Daniel. "Will Ferrell, Kristen Wiig 'Forego' Secret Lifetime Movie *A Deadly Adoption*." *Rolling Stone*. Rolling Stone, 4 Apr. 2015. Web. 20 Sept. 2015.

Lieberman, David. "Lifetime Not Just a TV Network in CEO's Eyes." *Careers Today*. USA Today, 6 Mar. 2006. Web. 20 Sept. 2015.

Lotz, Amanda D. *Redesigning Women: Television After the Network Era*. Chicago: University of Illinois Press, 2006. Print.

Marchese, David. "Kristen Wiig Has Been Ignoring the *Ghostbusters* Hubbub; Plus, Watch Her 'Lost' Sex Scene from *The Spoils Before Dying*." *Vulture*. Vulture, 7 July 2015. Web. 20 Sept. 2015.

Martin, Brett. *Difficult Men: Behind the Scenes of a Creative Revolution: From The Sopranos and The Wire to Mad Men and Breaking Bad*. New York: Penguin, 2014. Print.

Moyer, Justin Wm. "Kermit the Frog and Miss Piggy Break Up Just in Time for New 'Muppets' Series." *Washington Post*. The Washington Post, 5 Aug. 2015. Web. 24 Sept. 2015.

Moylan, Brian. "How Lifetime Turned Clickbait into Original Programming." *The Guardian*. The Guardian, 2 Sept. 2014. Web. 18 Sept. 2015.

Murray, Susan, and Laurie Ouellette, eds. *Reality TV: Remaking Television Culture*. New York: New York University Press, 2004. Print.

Neely, Priska. "Hoping to Reach a Wider Audience, Lifetime Breaks Out Familiar Formula." *Code Switch*. NPR, 26 July 2014. Web. 20 Sept. 2015.

Palmer, Jerry. "Parody and Decorum: Permission to Mock." *Beyond a Joke: The Limits of Humour*. Ed. Sharon Lockyer and Michael Pickering. London: Palgrave Macmillan, 2005. 79–97. Print.

"Parody." *Concise Oxford Companion to English Literature*. Ed. Dinah Birch and Katy Hooper. Oxford: Oxford University Press, 2015. Web. 20 Sept. 2015.

Paskin, Willa. "Reality Check." *Slate*. Slate, 29 June 2015. Web. 19 Sept. 2015.

Pozner, Jennifer L. *Reality Bites Back: The Troubling Truth about Guilty Pleasure TV*. Berkeley: Seal Press, 2010. Print.

Rife, Katie. "*Grumpy Cat's Worst Christmas Ever* Got Terrible Ratings, But Lots of Tweets." *A.V. Club*. A.V. Club, 3 Dec. 2014. Web. 18 Sept. 2015.

Ritchie, Kevin. "The Real Story Behind *My Life Is a Lifetime Movie*." *Realscreen*. Realscreen, 17 Oct. 2012. Web. 18 Sept. 2015.

Robinson, Joanna. "How a Lifetime Show Gave Us TV's First Pure Female Antihero." *VF Hollywood*. Vanity Fair, 3 Aug. 2015. Web. 19 Sept. 2015.

Ross, L.A. "Liz Gateley Joins Lifetime as EVP and Head of Programming." *The Wrap*. The Wrap, 8 Apr. 2015. Web. 18 Sept. 2015.

Ryan, Patrick. "Kristen Wiig says *Deadly Adoption* Wasn't a Lifetime Movie Parody." *Entertain This!* USA Today, 3 July 2015. Web. 20 Sept. 2015.

Shattuck, Kathryn. "Lifetime Commits to *Unauthorized* Movie Franchise." *New York Times*. New York Times, 17 Aug. 2015. Web. 19 Sept. 2015.

Sheffield, Rob. "10 Most Brilliantly Lifetime-Gasmic Moments in *A Deadly Adoption*." *Rolling Stone*. Rolling Stone, 22 June 2015. Web. 20 Sept. 2015.

Syme, Rachel. "Lifetime's *UnREAL* Recycles a Producer's Dark Experiences." *New York Times*. New York Times, 2 July 2015. Web. 19 Sept. 2015.

Tankel, Jonathan David, and Jane Banks. "Lifetime Television and Women: Narrowcasting as Electronic Space." *Voices in the Street: Explorations in Gender, Media, and Public Space*. Ed. Susan J. Drucker and Gary Gumpert. Cresskill, NJ: Hampton Press, 1994. 255–270. Print.

Thompson, Arienne. "Lifetime's *A Deadly Adoption* Was NOT (Completely) a Joke and We Kind of Love It." *Entertain This!* USA Today, 20 June 2015. Web. 20 Sept. 2015.

Uhlich, Keith. "*A Deadly Adoption*: TV Review." *The Hollywood Reporter*. The Hollywood Reporter, 20 June 2015. Web. 20 Sept. 2015.

Wallenstein, Andrew. "Time for a Reality Check Among TV's Streaming Services." *Variety*. Variety, 3 July 2015. Web. 20 Sept. 2015.

Wieselman, Jarett. "How Will Ferrell & Kristen Wiig Became Lifetime Movie Stars." *BuzzFeed News*. Buzzfeed, 22 June 2015. Web. 20 Sept. 2015.

Wilson, Teri. "11 Ways *A Deadly Adoption* Was the Quintessential Lifetime Movie." *Hello Giggles*. Hello Giggles, 21 June 2015. Web. 20 Sept. 2015.

Wyatt, Edward. "TV Contestants: Tired, Tipsy and Pushed to the Brink." *New York Times*. New York Times, 1 Aug. 2009. Web. 19 Sept. 2015.

# Bibliography

Allen, Robert C., and Annette Hill. *The Television Studies Reader*. New York: Routledge, 2003. Print.

Banet-Weiser, Sarah, Cynthia Chris, and Anthony Freitas, ed. *Cable Visions: Television Beyond Broadcasting*. New York: New York University Press, 2007. Print.

Benedict, Helen. *Virgin or Vamp: How the Press Covers Sex Crimes*. New York: Oxford University Press, 1992. Print.

Bronstein, Carolyn. "Mission Accomplished? Profits and Programming at the Network for Women." *Lifetime: A Cable Network "For Women."* Spec. issue of *Camera Obscura: A Journal of Feminism, Culture, and Media Studies* 33–34 (1994–1995): 213–242. Print.

Brunsdon, Charlotte, Julie D'Acci, and Lynn Spiegel, eds. *Feminist Television Criticism: A Reader*. Oxford: Oxford University Press, 1997. Print.

Byars, Jackie, and Eileen R. Meehan. "Once in a Lifetime: Constructing the 'Working Woman' through Cable Narrowcasting." *Lifetime: A Cable Network "For Women."* Spec. issue of *Camera Obscura: A Journal of Feminism, Culture, and Media Studies* 33–34 (1994–1995): 13–41. Print.

Cuklanz, Lisa M. *Rape on Prime Time: Television, Masculinity, and Sexual Violence*. Philadelphia: University of Pennsylvania Press, 2000. Print.

D'Acci, Julie. *Defining Women: Television and the Case of Cagney and Lacey*. Chapel Hill: University of North Carolina Press, 1994. Print.

_____. "Introduction." *Lifetime: A Cable Network "For Women."* Spec. issue of *Camera Obscura: A Journal of Feminism, Culture, and Media Studies* 33–34 (1994–1995): 7–12. Print.

Douglas, Susan J. *Enlightened Sexism: The Seductive Message That Feminism's Work Is Done*. New York: Times Books, 2010. Print.

_____. *Where the Girls Are: Growing Up Female with the Mass Media*. New York: Three Rivers Press, 1994. Print.

Douglas Vavrus, Mary. "Lifetime's *Army Wives*, or I Married the Media-Military-Industrial Complex." *Women's Studies in Communication* 36 (2013): 92–112. Print.

Dow, Bonnie J. *Prime Time Feminism: Television, Media Culture, and the Women's Movement Since 1970*. Philadelphia: University of Pennsylvania Press, 1996. Print.

Feuer, Jane. "Feminism on Lifetime: Yuppie TV for the Nineties." *Lifetime: A Cable Network "For Women."* Spec. issue of *Camera Obscura: A Journal of Feminism, Culture, and Media Studies* 33–34 (1994–1995): 133–146. Print.

Gauntlett, David. *Media, Gender and Identity: An Introduction.* New York: Routledge, 2008. Print.

Genz, Stéphanie, and Benjamin A. Brabon. *Postfeminism: Cultural Texts and Theories.* Edinburgh: Edinburgh University Press, 2009. Print.

Gill, Rosalind. *Gender and the Media.* Cambridge, UK: Polity, 2007. Print.

Gregory, Mollie. *Women Who Run the Show: How a Brilliant and Creative New Generation of Women Stormed Hollywood.* New York: St. Martin's Press, 2002. Print.

Hall, Stuart, ed. *Representation: Cultural Representations and Signifying Practices.* London: Sage, 1997. Print.

Harris-Perry, Melissa. *Sister Citizen: Shame, Stereotypes, and Black Women in America.* New Haven: Yale University Press, 2011. Print.

Hundley, Heather. "The Evolution of Gendercasting: The Lifetime Television Network—'Television for Women.'" *Journal of Popular Film and Television* 29.4 (2002): 174–181. Print.

Jenkins, Henry. *Textual Poachers: Television Fans & Participatory Culture.* New York: Routledge, 1992. Print.

Jewell, Sue K. *From Mammy to Miss. America and Beyond: Cultural Images and the Shaping of U.S. Social Policy.* New York: Routledge, 1993. Print.

Johnson, Eithne. "Lifetime's Feminine Psychographic Space and the 'Mystery Loves Company' Series." *Lifetime: A Cable Network "For Women."* Spec. issue of *Camera Obscura: A Journal of Feminism, Culture, and Media Studies* 33–34 (1994–1995): 43–76. Print.

Johnson, Merri Lisa, ed. *Third Wave Feminism and Television: Jane Puts It in a Box.* London: I.B. Tauris, 2007. Print.

Kearney, Mary Celeste, ed. *The Gender and Media Reader.* New York: Routledge, 2011. Print.

Kenny, Lorraine Delia. *Daughters of Suburbia: Growing Up White, Middle Class and Female.* New Brunswick: Rutgers University Press, 2000. Print.

Levy, Ariel. *Female Chauvinist Pigs: Women and the Rise of Raunch Culture.* New York: Free Press, 2005. Print.

Lipkin, Steven N. *Docudrama Performs the Past; Arenas of Argument in Films Based on True Stories.* Newcastle: Cambridge Scholars, 2011. Print.

Lotz, Amanda. *Beyond Prime Time: Television Programming in the Post-Network Era.* New York: Routledge, 2009. Print.

_____. *Redesigning Women: Television After the Network Era.* Urbana: University of Illinois Press, 2006. Print.

_____. *The Television Will Be Revolutionized,* 2d ed. New York: New York University Press, 2014. Print.

_____. "Textual (Im)Possibilities in the U.S. Post-Network Era: Negotiating Production and Promotion Processes on Lifetime's *Any Day Now.*" *Critical Studies in Media Communication* 21.1 (Mar. 2004): 22–43. JSTOR. Web. 15 Mar. 2015.

Meehan, Eileen R., and Jackie Byars. "Telefeminism: How Lifetime Got Its Groove, 1984–1997." *The Television Studies Reader.* Ed. Robert C. Allen and Annette Hill. London: Routledge, 2004. 92–104. Print.

Milestone, Katie, and Anneke Meyer. *Gender and Popular Culture.* Cambridge, UK: Polity, 2012. Print.

Mittell, Jason. *Complex TV: The Poetics of Contemporary Television Storytelling.* New York: New York University Press, 2015. Print.

Morreall, John. *Comic Relief: A Comprehensive Philosophy of Humor.* Malden, MA: Wiley-Blackwell, 2009. Print.

Mullen, Megan Gwynne. *The Rise of Cable Programming in the United States: Revolution or Evolution?* Austin: University of Texas Press, 2003. Print.

Murray, Susan, and Laurie Ouellette, eds. *Reality TV: Remaking Television Culture.* New York: New York University Press, 2004. Print.

Newcomb, Horace, ed. *Television: The Critical View,* 6th ed. Oxford: Oxford University Press, 2000. Print.

Paget, Derek. *No Other Way to Tell It: Dramadoc/Docudrama on Television.* Manchester: Manchester University Press, 1998. Print.

Pozner, Jennifer L. *Reality Bites Back: The Troubling Truth about Guilty Pleasure TV.* Berkeley: Seal Press, 2010. Print.

Press, Andrea L. *Women Watching Television: Gender, Class, and Generation in the American Television Experience.* Philadelphia: University of Pennsylvania Press, 1991. Print.

Projansky, Sarah. *Watching Rape: Film and Television in Postfeminist Culture.* New York: New York University Press, 2001. Print.

Read, Jacinda. *The New Avengers: Feminism, Femininity and the Rape-Revenge Cycle.* Manchester: Manchester University Press, 2000. Print.

Rowe, Kathleen. *The Unruly Woman: Gender and the Genres of Laughter.* Austin: University of Texas Press, 1995. Print.

Sepinwall, Alan. *The Revolution Was Televised: The Cops, Crooks, Slingers, and Slayers Who Changed TV Drama Forever.* New York: Touchstone, 2012. Print.

Spiegel, Lynn. *Make Room for TV: Television and the Family Ideal in Postwar America.* Chicago: University of Chicago Press, 1992. Print.

Squires, Catherine R. *The Post-Racial Mystique: Media & Race in the Twenty-First Century.* New York: New York University Press, 2014. Print.

Stahl, Roger. *Militainment, Inc.: War, Media, and Popular Culture.* New York: Routledge, 2010. Print.

Stempel Mumford, Laura. "Stripping on the Girl Channel: Lifetime, *thirtysomething,* and Television Form." *Lifetime: A Cable Network "For Women."* Spec. issue of *Camera Obscura: A Journal of Feminism, Culture, and Media Studies* 33–34 (1994–1995): 167–192. Print.

Streeter, Thomas, and Wendy Wahl. "Audience Theory and Feminism: Property, Gender, and the Tele-visual Audience." *Lifetime: A Cable Network "For Women."* Spec. issue of *Camera Obscura: A Journal of Feminism, Culture, and Media Studies* 33–34 (1994–1995): 243–261. Print.

Tankel, Jonathan David, and Jane Banks. "Lifetime Television and Women: Narrowcasting as Electronic Space." *Voices in the Street: Explorations in Gender, Media, and Public Space.* Ed. Susan J. Drucker and Gary Gumpert. Cresskill, NJ: Hampton Press, 1997. 255–270. Print.

Tasker, Yvonne, and Diane Negra, eds. *Interrogating Postfeminsim: Gender and the Politics of Popular Culture.* Durham: Duke University Press, 2007. Print.

Torres, Sasha. "War and Remembrance: Televisual Narrative, National Memory, and *China Beach.*" *Lifetime: A Cable Network "For Women."* Spec. issue of *Camera Obscura: A Journal of Feminism, Culture, and Media Studies* 33–34 (1994–1995): 147–166. Print.

White, Susan. "*Veronica Clare* and the New *Film Noir* Heroine." *Lifetime: A Cable Network "For Women."* Spec. issue of *Camera Obscura: A Journal of Feminism, Culture, and Media Studies* 33–34 (1994–1995): 77–102. Print.

Williams, Linda. *Playing the Race Card: Melodramas of Black and White from Uncle Tom to O.J. Simpson.* Princeton: Princeton University Press, 2002. Print.

Wilson, Pamela. "Upscale Feminine Angst: *Molly Dodd,* the Lifetime Cable Network and Gender Marketing." *Lifetime: A Cable Network "For Women."* Spec. issue of *Camera Obscura: A Journal of Feminism, Culture, and Media Studies* 103–132 (1994–1995): 103–130. Print.

Wlodarz, Joe. "Smokin' Tokens: *thirtysomething* and TV's Queer Dilemma." *Lifetime: A Cable Network "For Women."* Spec. issue of *Camera Obscura: A Journal of Feminism, Culture, and Media Studies* 33–34 (1994–1995): 193–212. Print.

Yahr, Emily. "From Guilty Pleasure to Emmy Awards: The Delightfully Weird History of Lifetime Movies." *Washington Post.* Washingtonpost.com, 15 Jan. 2015. Web. 13 Sept. 2015.

Zeisler, Andi. *Feminism and Pop Culture.* Berkeley: Seal Press, 2008. Print.

# About the Contributors

Susannah **Bartlow** works with runaway and homeless youth in Milwaukee and is a writer, community worker and educator. During her fourteen-year career in academia, she founded the Dickinson College Women's Center (2008) and the Marquette University Gender and Sexuality Resource Center (2012, now defunct).

Shelby L. **Crosby** is an associate professor at the University of Memphis. Her research spans mid-nineteenth-century to early twentieth-century African American literature, representations of womanhood (particularly black womanhood) and critical race theory.

Mary **Douglas Vavrus** is an associate professor in the Communication Studies department at the University of Minnesota, where she conducts research in and teaches media studies. Her research focuses on media militarism and gender justice, including that represented by *Army Wives*, documentary film and television and news media more generally.

Lindsay **Giggey** is a PhD candidate in Cinema and Media Studies at the University of California, Los Angeles. Her dissertation focuses on the relationship between contemporary reality television and celebrity as sites for network and individual branding.

Emily L. **Newman** is an assistant professor of art history at Texas A&M University, Commerce. Her research concerns intersections of modern and contemporary art history, popular culture, and the body.

Lisa K. **Perdigao** is chair of the humanities program and a professor of English at the Florida Institute of Technology. Her research and teaching interests are in the areas of American literature, YA literature, television and film.

Jenny **Platz** is a PhD candidate in English at the University of Rhode Island. Her research has concentrated on the role of women in 1970s exploitation films, players' emotions in video games, the representation of the female eating disorder body in film and literature and coming of age narratives in television and literature.

Staci **Stutsman** is a PhD candidate in the English department at Syracuse University. Her dissertation uses a methodology of performance studies to deconstruct stereotypical notions of feminine virtue and to theorize the unruly woman of film and television melodrama. She served as a HASTAC scholar from 2013 to 2015 and co-edited the HASTAC Pedagogy Project.

Emily **Witsell** is a research librarian and coordinator of reference and instruction at Wofford College. Her research has explored cultural construction of illness and her book *Literary Research and American Postmodernism* is forthcoming from Scarecrow Press.

# Index